ALL MY
RIVERS
ARE GONE

---

*A Journey of Discovery
Through Glen Canyon*

ALSO BY KATIE LEE

Sandstone Seduction: Rivers and Lovers, Canyons and Friends

Katie Lee

ALL MY
RIVERS
ARE GONE

A Journey of Discovery
Through Glen Canyon

Introduction by **Terry Tempest Williams**

BOWER
HOUSE

DENVER

Special thanks to Northern Arizona University whose Special Collections and Archives houses the Katie Lee Collection, which Lee donated to SCA over the course of many years.

www.BowerHouseBooks.com

Cover design by Margaret McCullough
Cover painting by Serena Supplee
Front Matter map by James Lee Roth
Photographs provided by the author

Printed in Canada

Library of Congress Control Number: 2021934970

Paperback ISBN: 978-1-917895-15-6
Ebook ISBN: 978-1-917895-16-3

10 9 8 7 6 5 4 3 2 1

To ...
The Once And Future Glen Canyon
With Its Free Flowing Colorado River

For ...
Frank, Tad and Dick ... who knew it
&
For all of you who want it back

Contents

Introduction

by Terry Tempest Williams

KATIE LEE HAS GIVEN us an elegiac song of Glen Canyon. Bless her. Bless her for holding on to this story for almost four decades. Bless her for not forgetting. Bless her for remembering. Bless her for loving the river. Bless her for her anger when the river was dammed. Bless her for choosing to release her memories of "The Place No One Knew" now as we begin to imagine in very real terms the day when the Glen Canyon Dam will be dismantled.

What Katie Lee knows she knows in her body—through her hands that rowed the oars, through her feet that walked the canyons, through her heart that still carries the heat of those days in Glen Canyon. In so many ways, this is a woman who embodies the power and tenacious beauty of the Colorado Plateau. Her spitfire intelligence and redrock resolve provides us with an individual conscience that we would do well to adopt.

Katie Lee is a joyful raconteur, a woman with grit, grace, and humor. She is not afraid to laugh and tease, cajole, and flirt, cuss, rant, howl, sing and cry. Katie Lee is the desert's lover, her voice is a torch in the wilderness.

When I finally met Katie she exceeded my expectations. Her presence was electric. She was wearing a tiger-print (or was it leopard) sarong with a black leotard. Her clear eyes flashed mischief and her tanned skin bore the cachet of a woman who has spent more time outside than in. Within minutes, her ribald humor turned to a deep tenderness. Her eyes teared, "Did you ever know the canyon?"

Katie Lee caught me off guard.

"Did you ever see Glen Canyon?" she asked again.

I paused.

"Yes, but not like you. I saw it through the eyes of a child, an adolescent who saw going to Lake Powell as a chance to waterski in the desert—until it started to rise."

In that moment, my own memories of Glen Canyon began to surface. The year was 1965. The dam was completed two years earlier with the "dead water rising" on January 21, 1963. The slow drowning of Glen Canyon had already begun so I never knew it as a canyon with a free-flowing river down its center. I knew it as an expanding Lake Powell that seemed to swallow up sidecanyons almost as we watched. Every day, the water would rise. We would have to keep moving our camps further back from the water's edge. What I remember as a child sitting on the fiberglass roof of our motorboat were the towering redrock walls, the slit of blue sky, the cavernous alcoves that we would seek for shade, the power of our echoes as we would play with sound as it ricocheted off stone. I recall the fern grottos where we would walk in the morning heat for spring water and fill our bottles for day hikes, the pictographs that inevitably would be staring down at us. We realized early on, we were not the first ones here. And every subsequent year, the places we were coming to love, were no longer there. Drowned. I learned on a visceral level, beauty is not something to be taken for granted.

I didn't know the particulars, certainly not the politics. I was a child being taken on vacation by my parents. I overheard conversations. My father and his buddy, Gordon James, knew Glen Canyon, they had explored it through the years. They would tell us stories. They took us to Cathedral in the Desert and Davis Gulch. They told us to remember these places because they would be gone the next time we came to Lake Powell. They told the truth. I remember even then, harboring a sadness for the slickrock that seemed to have no rights.

In 1970 our family returned to Lake Powell, as we always did on Memorial Day, with neighbors. The water was high and still rising. We had been on the lake for several days. One afternoon, my father asked me if I wanted to waterski to the next camp. It would be a long ski and did I think I could do it. I said, "of course," and jumped into the water as my mother handed me a slalom ski over the side of the boat. I put my right foot into the rubber slip and my left foot into the back one and steadied myself with my arms. When the ski rope was thrown, I grabbed on to the handles and waited for the slack to run out as the boat straightened itself.

"Hit it!" I yelled.

My father put the throttle at full board. I was up in a flash skiing on water that appeared as glass. Pure exhilaration. I skied behind the boat, crossed the wake, picked up speed alongside the boat, then pulled back behind the boat again, coasting. It was a gorgeous day. We had been motoring along around fifteen minutes when all of the sudden I heard a terrible thump and then saw the boat jump up off the water and turn on its side, then bounce back center. The boat stopped. I slowly slipped back into the water as I watched our boat sink.

My mother and three brothers climbed on to the roof of the boat as my father tried to bale out the incoming water with a bucket. I began pulling myself in with the rope. Within a few minutes, our friends came back to find us; we all got inside as they hitched our sinking boat to theirs and then sped to the nearest marina which was several hours away. Our boat kept upright as long as speed was maintained, but once we got into the Wahweep Marina and had to slow down to five miles per hour, our boat sank for good.

Our boat had hit a newly drowned redrock spire.

That night in a motel in Page, Arizona, I wondered how many motor boats, engines, stoves, coolers, cups, shoes, even bodies, must be at the bottom of Glen Canyon. It all felt so wrong—the truth of this magical place underwater.

I have never been back.

I think about Katie Lee and the last song she sang in Music Temple on October 15, 1962, her last trip on "The Glen." It was a spiritual she had learned called, "They Crucified My Lord." She changed the words:

They crucified my River
    And he never said a mumblin' word—
They pierced him in the side
    But he never said a mumblin' word ... not a mumblin' word—

And the blood came trink-lin' down,
    Still, he never said a mumblin' word. ...
He just hung his head, and he died
    But he never said a mumblin' word. ...

Now wasn't that a pity and a shame—
    The way they done my River?
        Not a word ... not a word ... not a word.

The next morning, when I sat on the beach alone staring out over Lake Powell, while my parents were making arrangements for us to get home, something shifted in me. I didn't want to talk to anyone. I just wanted to listen. Who knows—maybe somewhere on the wind, Katie Lee's song was still being carried throughout the canyons.

Her voice has finally reached us in its most vibrant form. *All My Rivers* may in the end be written from the future. If Glen Canyon is to breathe once again, which I believe it will, we can thank Katie Lee for reminding us what once lived, what was then destroyed, and can now be resurrected.

A great passion, such as does really
  and truly devour your heart and soul,
    you cannot feel for individual beings.
      Perhaps you cannot feel it for anything
        that is capable of loving you in return.

—Isak Dinesen
Seven Gothic Tales

The river knows everything; one can
learn everything from it ...
They both listened silently to the water,
which to them was not just water, but the
voice of life, the voice of Being, of
perpetual Becoming.
... I reviewed my life and it was also a river.

—Hermann Hesse
Siddhartha

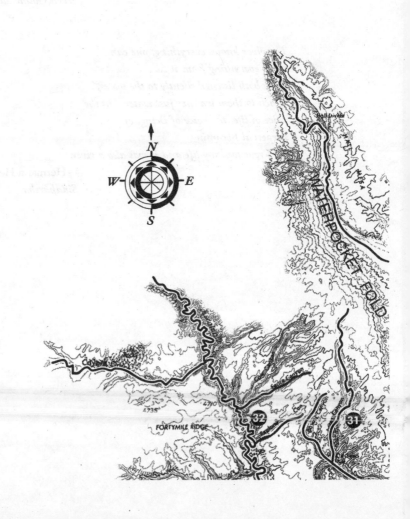

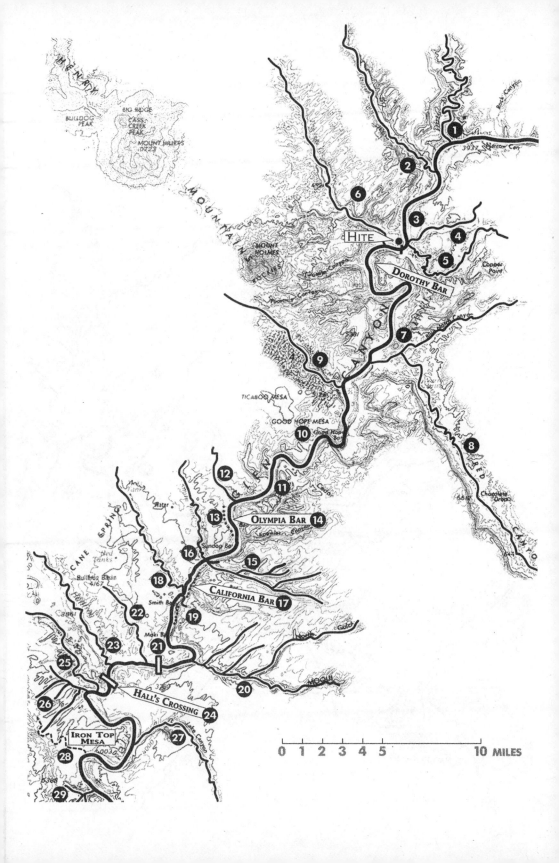

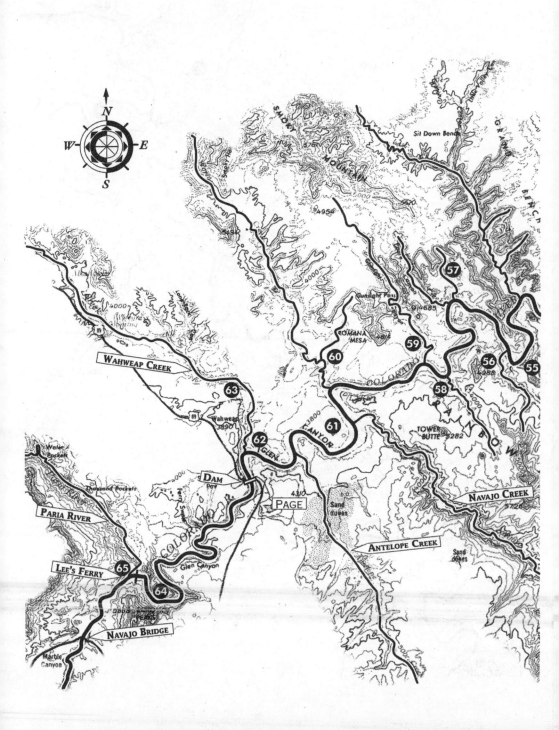

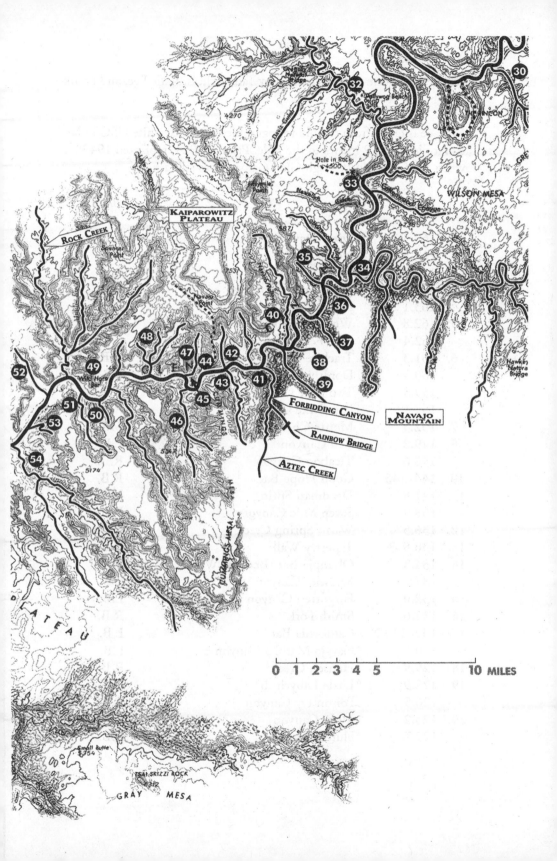

River Miles

Astericks indicate canyons named by Tad Nichols, Katie Lee, and Frank Wright, 1954–1957.

Mileage is taken from the old topographical black & white USGS Plan & Profile Maps, 2 inches to the mile. Printed 1924, reprinted 1943 ... when the Colorado through Glen Canyon was still a river.

	Mile	Name	Bank
1.	169.4	Dirty Devil River	R.B.
2.	167.5	North Wash	R.B.
3.	164.5	Slim's Cabin	L.B.
	164.0	Old Dandy Crossing	L.R.
4.	163.1	Farley Canyon	L.B.
5.	162.8	White Canyon	L.B.
	162.4	Hite Ferry Crossing	L.R.
6.	161.3	Trachite Creek	R.B.
	160.3	Dorothy Bar	L.B.
	159.3	Two Mile Canyon	R.B.
	154.1	Four Mile Canyon	R.B.
7.	152.5	Monte Christo Island	M.R.
8.	149.8	Red Canyon	L.B.
9.	148.6	Ticaboo Canyon	R.B.
10.	144–145	Good Hope Bar	R.B.
11.	141.8	*Deadman Spring	L.B.
	138.9	Seven Mile Canyon	R.B.
12.	136.5	Warm Spring Creek	R.B.
13.	136.5–3	Tapestry Wall	R.B.
14.	134.8	Olympia Bar (Bennett Wheel)	L.B.
	134.4	Knowles Canyon	L.B.
15.	132.0	Forgotten Canyon	L.B.
16.	132.0	Smith Fork	R.B.
17.	132–130.2	California Bar	L.B.
	130.1	*Navajo Marbles Canyon	L.B.
18.	129.9	Hansen Creek	R.B.
19.	128.9	*Little Labyrinth	L.B.
	126.5	Poison Ivy Canyon	L.B.
20.	125.2	Moki Canyon	L.B.
	122.7	*Fluted Canyon	R.B.

Mile		Name	Bank
21.	121.9	Hoskaninni (Stanton) Dredge	M.R.
22.	121.9	Stanton Canyon	R.B.
23.	120.5	Bullfrog Riffle	M.R.
24.	120.0	Hall's Crossing (upper)	L.B.
	119.3	Hall's Crossing (lower)	R.B.
25.	118.3	Hall's Creek	R.B.
26.	118.0	Lost Eden	R.B.
	116.9	*Two Deer Spring	R.B.
	114.0	Jacob's Pot	R.B.
	113.5	Moki Cave	R.B.
27.	113.2	Lake Canyon	L.B.
28.	110.6	Schock Trail	R.B.
	110.0	Schock Bar	R.B.
	108.0	Gretchen Bar	L.B.
29.	107.8	Annie's Canyon	R.B.
	104.9	Slickhorn (Death Valley) Canyon	L.B.
	103.3	*Fizzle Canyon	R.B.
30.	101.6	Iceburg (Wilson) Canyon	L.B.
	100.0	The Rincon (upper)	L.B.
	99.1	The Rincon (lower)	L.B.
31.	95.6	Navajo Creek (Bowns) Canyon	R.B.
	89.1	Natural Bridge	R.B.
32.	88.5	Escalante River	R.B.
	86.2	*Ribbon Canyon	L.B.
33.	84.3	Hole in the Rock	R.B.
	81.9	Llewellyn Gulch	R.B.
34.	78.0	San Juan River	L.B.
	77.0	Cottonwood Gulch (*Horse Canyon)	R.B.
35.	76.1	Hidden Passage	R.B.
36.	75.8	Music Temple	L.B.
37.	73.6	Mystery Canyon	L.B.
38.	71.5	Oak Creek	L.B.
39.	71.3	*Wishbone Canyon	L.B.
40.	70.8	Twilight Canyon	R.B.
	69.8–70.3	*Firelight Island	L.B.
41.	68.6	Forbidding Canyon (Aztec Creek)	L.B.
	67.8	*Cascade Canyon	R.B.
	66.9	*Quaking Bog Amphitheater	R.B.
	66.7	*Spring Pool Canyon	R.B.

	Mile	Name	Bank
42.	66.5	*Driftwood Canyon	R.B.
43.	66.2	*Cathedral Canyon	L.B.
44.	65.7	Klondike Trail	R.B.
	65.1–7	Klondike Bar	R.B.
45.	64.4	*Balanced Rocks Bar	R.B.
46.	64.2	*Little Arch Canyon (Fern Glen)	L.B.
	64.1	*Storm Cave	L.B.
47.	64.0	*Balanced Rocks Canyon	R.B.
	63.5	False Entrance (*Pick Ax) Canyon	L.B.
	61.6	*Notch Canyon	L.B.
48.	61.0	*Dangling Rope Canyon	R.B.
	59.7	*Cornerstone Canyon	R.B.
	58.7	Wetherill (Catfish) Canyon	L.B.
	58.2	*Nobody's Bizness	R.B.
49.	58–56.5	Wildhorse Bar	R.B.
50.	57.7	*Grotto Canyon	L.B.
51.	56.9	*Dungeon	L.B.
	55.5	Rock Creek	R.B.
52.	54.3	*Cattails Canyon (Pussywillow)	R.B.
53.	52.1	*Dove Canyon	L.B.
	51.4	*Happy Canyon (Mud Swamp)	L.B.
54.	50.9	West Canyon Creek	L.B.
	49.5	Navajo Bar	L.B.
	49.4	Last Chance Creek	R.B.
55.	45.6	*Spring Trail Canyon	L.B.
56.	44.3	Face Canyon	L.B.
57.	40.5	Kane Creek	R.B.
	39.5	Padre Creek	R.B.
	39.4-0	Crossing of the Fathers	R.L.
58.	34.4	Labyrinth Canyon	L.B.
59.	33.2	Cottonwood Creek (Gunsight)	R.B.
60.	27.9	Warm Creek	R.B.
	25.5	Navajo Creek	L.B.
61.	25.0	Loper's Cave	R.B.
	19.7	*Pink Titty (Antelope) Canyon	L.B.
62.	17.5	Outlaw Cave (Galloway)	R.B.
63.	16.7	Wahweap Canyon	R.B.
	15.0	Goddam Site	$$$$$
64.	10.8–11.0	Ferry Swale	R.B.
65.	00.0	Lee's Ferry	R.B.

Prologue

EVERY MORNING I STAND with my hands pressed flat against the wall, one on each side of the photograph, my nose only inches away from the glass. At first all I see is a vibrant, green blur, but when I press from the wall, pull one leg up behind me and focus, the blur takes the shape of a giant old cottonwood tree, a shimmering pool (which is also gulping the green of the tree), and behind it the massive streaked pink-and-buff walls of a narrow, twisting canyon.

By the second or third press, I'm no longer doing exercises in my room. The photograph takes me in; I'm walking in the stream. Cool water tickles my ankles. Bare feet hug the sand, caressing it with toes curling into that pure, clean, untouched place, trying to root there beside the grand, green cottonwood.

Forever.

Sunlight beams down on my back, not hot, but alive against my skin. When I bend over to look into the shallow pool, the sun glares up at me. Iridescent light-butterflies ripple by my face. I move into the curve of the sandstone wall under the overhang where the stream is shaded and watch it meander into stiff glittering stalks of grass, lighter even than the tree's greenery, alive and dancing with the motion of the water. Other grasses are waving beneath the surface with sensuous grace in rhythm to the flow. I stoop to feel their hairlike softness with my hands—they spread, buckle, twist, and move away! Alive! I move my hand under one and hold it up to the sun on one finger, almost ten inches long it curls up at both ends. I can't tell head from tail as it wiggles for the water first from one end then the other.

I'll be damned—little grass snakes!

Stooped beneath the overhang, I hear an intermittent sound overlying the stream's trickle. Sucked up on the morning breeze from probably a quarter mile away, the garble of the river at the mouth of Forgotten Canyon mutters amid the rocks. It calls, it fades. The trickle answers.

I've probably done only five or six presses against the wall while this scene with all its sensations moves behind eyes still fastened on my photograph. Some mornings I wander upstream around the bend to the first deep pool, which makes me swim if I want to go on to the ruins. My Mexican hat, bathing shorts, and top are left on the bank; on my head, tennies, socks, and camera swim to the other side. I need the shoes, I *want* the camera, but the clothes have always been superfluous here. I speed up a bit now, because I know when Tad and Frank have finished taking pictures or walking up the short fork, they won't want to wait around while I explore beyond their reach. Like bloody hell! Damn sissies can come up here if they want to—they can swim—it's not *that* cold. Anyway, the ruin is in the sun.

Hand over hand I climb the little chipped-out notches—Moki steps—to the house. Whoever she was, her fingerprints from a thousand years ago are still in the clay of the mortared walls that rise to the slant of a rose-colored overhang. Yes, she; women plastered and chinked while men toted the rock to this high, safe place for their cliff dwelling. So say the educated guessers. Roof beams are still in place, pictographs and petroglyphs detail the smooth stone beside the house. A *metate*, her grinding stone, mortared in place, rests beside the entrance. Centuries have passed here in Forgotten Canyon since an Anasazi family built this strong, beautiful house we now call a ruin. Along with no one knows how many hundreds or thousands, they left—disappeared—leaving no clues as to where they went, or why a river paradise no longer served their needs. What brings and holds me to this place is that very mystery. My imagination spins with sights and sounds of what was or might have been here, and as I run my hands over the *metate* or place my fingers in the indentations she left, or trace the visions they drew along the wall, I know we are connected by invisible threads through time and space, sharing the spirit of this canyon. I feel their presence, though now all is quiet, clean, sandblasted, and wind-smoothed, wild-smelling of batshit, ratshit, and catshit.

A shadow crosses the dark upper corner of the photograph wherein I've strayed. I stand back to find a superimposed reflection of my face staring back at me from the canyon. Stretches must be over. I'm back in my bedroom, up against the wall.

There are mornings when the vibrant green blur does not clear, when I cannot move in under the cottonwood, the overhang, or wade the stream. The blur stays, the tears well and spill. Such mornings portend a very bad day, a day when I'll be oversensitive to everything and everyone. My anger will resurface, tension in my neck and shoulders will badger me into a short-temperedness no one around me deserves, least of all myself. Because only this photograph—this photograph and my indelible sense memory—remain.

Everything else is dead. Buried. Drowned.

Two Opposing Realities

PART ONE

Two Opposing Realities

~

ONE

A Grain of Sand

THE ROOM IS DARK except for a light-cone pouring onto the screen, and quiet but for the whir of the sixteen-millimeter projector.

We're sitting on the floor of my mother's living room in Tucson, Arizona, watching my friend Tad Nichols' movie of the first Mexican Hat Expeditions powerboat run on the Colorado River through Grand Canyon. It's March of 1953. I don't know about the others, but I'm hyped to the quick. I've just given a two-hour folk music concert at the Temple of Music and Art and haven't even started to unwind, deflate, cool down. The party is in honor of my first "back home" performance after five years in Hollywood, and Tad has promised to show his movie before I split for Tinseltown tomorrow.

I cannot believe what I'm seeing!

These scenes have to be fake, like the movie sets I've been working on, but they're *not* fake! The twenty-one-foot Chriscraft Cabin Cruiser, a kit boat with a sixty-five-horse diesel engine, is being tossed ten feet above the spray of this boiling, chocolate rapid to come slamming down into a whirlpool on the downstream side with only its nose making circles above the waves. The people on the back deck have to be drowned! Next scene: They're jumping up and down, laughing, screaming (I can tell, even though there's no sound), hugging the boatman, hugging each other, and wringing out their clothes. Well, I can understand the hugging. They want to make sure they aren't dead!

I remember sitting there stunned, through the excited babble of my guests, knowing only one thing for sure—that I *had* to get there somehow, see and feel that place. But how? Lotta money for a struggling actress-folksinger-guitarist—$500 for the upper half (Lee's Ferry to Phantom Ranch) $500 for the lower half (Phantom to Pierce's Ferry). The man running the projector was Jim Rigg, boatman and part-owner of Mexican Hat Expeditions. Though I didn't know it at the time, he would come up with a solution to get me on the river that hadn't occurred to anyone else and be able, with his innate charm, to convince the rest of the crew that it was loaded with potential.

Often someone will ask how I got to the river. I usually smile because they never ask the important question: How did the river get to me?

~

Sunday night, June 14, 1953—a basement apartment off of Barham Boulevard in Hollywood. It's after eleven o'clock, I've just gotten to sleep, and the phone is ringing.

Who the hell is calling at this hour? "He'o ..."

"Kay, are you awake?"

"Not really ... wha'ya want? Whoizit?"

"It's Tad. Do you want to go on the Grand Canyon run?"

"Tad? The Gra ... what?" Awake now, I lament, "Tadito, are you outta your mind? You know I don't have that kinda money!"

"Not to worry. There's been a cancellation at the last minute. You can come for just the price of your food—fifty bucks. But you've got to be in Flagstaff by noon tomorrow, and Jim says the deal is you bring your guitar and sing for the passengers."

Sing for ... will it be the powerboat run?

Their second run in history. His voice is smiling.

I leave the valley at two A.M. and am in Flagstaff by noon Monday.

~

What surprises me when I read my journal of that first Grand Canyon run was my inability to express thoughts about what I saw and felt. Aside from not being able to find words for that awesome experience, there was a deeper reason: I was in shock, literally, like being in a car wreck and coming out unscathed. Nothing of that magnitude had happened to me before. To be on the razor's edge—to know you can die, to see how insignificant you are in relation to time, space, nature, beauty, history, our planet—is to be firmly put in your place. A grain of sand. That's all you are. So I wrote it down at the end of each day with all the individuality of *one grain of sand,* unaware that the course of my whole life had been altered, that nothing from here on would be as before.

There were eight of us in two Chriscrafts—two boatmen, Jim and Bob Rigg, six passengers (four men, two women). The run was six days; the flow 66,000 cubic feet per second (cfs), the volume of water flowing past a given point. And the grain of sand wrote ...

Journal Note: June 16, 1953

The sound of that first one is really something. I am prepared for anything, and nothing, because you can't know until you've had the experience just how wild your adrenaline rushes can be ... Jim starts singing every time he sloshes into white water ... as far as he knows, I'm the third woman to run all the rapids in the Grand Canyon—for sure we can't line these monsters. [Keeping lines from shore on both bow and stern—half floating, half lifting them over and around rocks.] This boy is one helluva boatman, been through this canyon more times than any other person, living or dead—this is his eighth trip. Tad tells me that two years ago Jim and Bob each took a Cataract boat from Lee's Ferry to Separation Canyon, 340 miles, for a record speed run of thirty-eight hours, running every rapid, arriving long after dark of the second day! With that in mind I'm not too worried, just a little scared ... High on a ledge in the Redwall is a whole skeleton lying beside a fire pit, one leg bone charred. The story Jim tells is that they are the bones of an old prospector who tried to find his way out of the canyon, broke his leg, and died in his sleep beside the fire ... The beauty I'm seeing in this new world makes me want to be a poet, or rather wish that I could create something—anything—that might last even an echo as long as these magnificent works of the "Old Lady." Down here we see how the earth is put together, then torn apart through millennia—humans aren't even a millimeter in this strata ... Oh-h-h, it's true, its true, the Little Colorado is BLUE, not in flood ... I've hoped and wished for this exquisite sight all the way. Water flows from travertine springs several miles up canyon, and when the silt-laden Little Colorado river runs dry we get to see the true color from those springs. I push my arm into the soft silt banks and find when I pull it out a rainbow of colors—red, light grey, black, coral, blue, yellow, soft green, and brown from strata high above us, and far away. Never will I forget looking into this living, opaque, turquoise jewel, then swimming in it, and I thank whatever powers let me see it, because I have a feeling I shouldn't be here at all, that I'm looking on something sacred. <END JOURNAL>

I was.

[Sally Bailey, a lovely Navajo lady I came to know, would sometimes come to see us off on the San Juan trips. She told this story shortly before she died trying to retrieve her whole Navajo wealth—her silver and turquoise jewelry—from a fiery hogan. Her speech, so clear in my memory, had the distinctive Navajo halting in the middle of her words, begetting a shamanlike authority to her story. I loved hearing her talk. She pronounced her own kind "In-nians."

Sally: "We were telling how the In-nians used to worship the wa'er ... an' we din' quite remember ... but it got to my mind and I said, Ohhhh, I think that's one time I heard how the In-nians they went to get their salt. And they had to worship the wa'er ... I din' know just where that is ... I think is way in Arizona, on the Colorado, or some-where ... and these In-nians they go over there and they come to that spring ... they have a li'l place, a hole in a rock where there's some wa'er w-a-a-y down in the rocks ... and they have to sing, and they have to pray to make that wa'er rise to the top ... so the wa'er pushes the salt up and the In-nians wade right into that wa'er and fill their bags full of salt. When they get done they sing and say some prayers. And that wa'er just goes away back down into that hole. That's the way the Nava-jos used to get their salt."]

Journal Note: June 18 (below Phantom Ranch)

My guitar comes out every night. I play for an hour, more or less, the folk songs I know, the river songs I'm learning—even feel a few of my own coming on. Hearing the soft strings of the guitar a mile deep in the earth, while looking back millions of years through time and evo-lution, is pretty inspiring; maybe I *will* write something before this is over. Somewhere in the Middle Granite Gorge below Phantom Ranch, where mules come down from the South Rim packing sore-butted tourists, Jim is hurled to the floor with such force I think he's going through the bottom, but he's back on his feet faster than he went down. The stern seat of the *Lollypop* (our boat) is flat with the river when a wave in Granite Falls rapid bucks us up and finally over the other side! Jim says, "Did *that* make a Christian out of you?!" He stands on the motor cover to see over the windshield when he goes into a rapid. After lunch we take on Lava Falls without stopping to look, because Jim says it's the same as last year. On that trip (the one I saw in the movie), Tad says, "He laid down on the back seat for about five minutes, then sprang up like he was stung and just took it!" Tad wants to photograph our run from the boat this time, but halfway through the mad turmoil he loses footing, the Bolex flips out of his hand, spins, and lands beside me on the stern seat! We stop below to wait for Bob—who seems for-ever stuck in there before his boat crashes up and out of the huge waves. We talk halfway through the night about life, the river, the canyon, the beautiful places—Toroweap, Nankoweap, Havasu, Shinumo, Thunder River, Matkatamiba, Vishnu, Kwagunt, Deer Creek Falls—the river, geology, star-bright sky, the river, people, history, moonlit water, shadow play, riveriveriver. … There's an art gallery in the Lower Granite Gorge where the river brings his finest tools of sand and silt to sculpt and polish quixotic, not to mention erotic, forms in the granite cliffs— configurations that would make the greatest artist envious! We see no other souls but Dock Marston's gang in their flat, waterbug-looking speedboats. (Dock: canyoneer, eminent river character, historian, documentalist, and agitator). They are at Diamond Creek, where we're initiated into the River Rats' Society. Dock talks with Jim and Bob for a while, then zips off. We hike to Emery Falls, which is now about a quarter mile away from the river due to mud flats built up by Hoover Dam. I have a shower under the spray falling from fifty or sixty feet. Too soon, Pierce's Ferry. What a nothin' place to end this most magnificent trip! How lucky can one person be, to have seen the Grand Canyon of the Colorado River from the bottom up? I can take a lot more of this. Yes, a *lot* more! <END JOURNAL>

Around our campfires and during the few stretches of quiet water, we'd talked about the traditions and superstitions that had come down from the bare beginnings of river running, and they were pretty bare—I was the 175th person to run the Grand Canyon after Major John Wesley Powell's first run in 1869 (according to Dock Marston's records), an average of two people a year in eighty-four years. But one tradition not mentioned, that seemed to prevail, was that women tended to fall for their boatmen, and sometimes the reverse. So that's what we did. Anyhow, that's what I thought back then. In reality it wasn't the boatman who got my love. It was the river.

Jim was all for muscling me onto Mexican Hat Expedition's oar-driven Cataract run a couple weeks later from Green River, Utah, to Lee's Ferry, with the approval of neither his partner, Frank Wright, nor any of the passengers who had already signed up. (The Cataract boat was a sixteen-foot wood/fiberglass hull designed and built especially for the Grand Canyon rapids by Norman Nevills; more about him later.) But I was smart enough to decline that offer, hot pants or not. I'd just been through a firecracker pinwheel of sensations on that river; had run an emotional rapid, tugging-swirling-blazing-whispering-caressing-howling-questioning constantly for six days and nights, and was still in shock. I needed time to absorb what had happened to me down in that great slice from Mother

Earth, time to sort it out. From that whirligig, my first river song literally erupted! It was about Jimmy and what he felt for that restless, haunting water—about my feelings, too, emotions stronger and maybe even more lasting than his ... "The Boatman's Song."

That fall of '53 he came to Los Angeles for a semester of pre-med at UCLA, which gave us weekends of water skiing on Lake Mead; time to work on the two Chriscrafts that were dry-docked at the Boulder City, Nevada, airport; time to ferret out paying passengers and plan trips on the San Juan and through Glen Canyon for next year. For my part, I learned and wrote more songs. Best of all, I learned in greater depth a river I'd only plunged through for one short week.

When Jim, the crew, and passengers came off the Green River/Grand run in the Cat boats a month after my trip, I was at their farewell dinner in Boulder City with my guitar, singing their songs and mine, and they were singing with me. I'd been afraid that I would be out of place with all those veteran river rats—after all, I hadn't been with them on their trip, they didn't know me—but Jim had paved the way. He'd been their "singing boatman" since the forties, when he'd worked for Nevills (killed, along with his wife, Doris, at the height of his river-running career in a plane crash in '49).

Unknown to me, my whole future on the river sat at the head of the table that night—Frank Wright, the leader and co-owner, with Jim, of Mexican Hat Expeditions. Frank was to add the final dimension, to make it possible for me to heal my soul and know my *real* love—the one that has never died, or been replaced.

The river.

~

The Boatman's Song
Last night I lay in a restless bed
A hum-drum life pounding in my head
When out of the night came a mighty roar
The river calling me back once more.

Chorus:
My heart knows what the river knows
I gotta go where the river goes—
Restless river, wild and free
The lonely ones are you ... and me.

Today I know your magic call
Will lead me back to the canyon wall
And the music in your rapid's roar
Makes this boatman's song from his soul outpour.

Chorus:
Tonight, as on your banks I sleep
Like a woman, soft, you will sigh and weep
And I will dream of a sweet warm kiss
By a moonlit stream, and the love I miss.

Chorus:
Someday, before I'm old and grey
I'll find a woman who'll go my way
She'll take the rapids strong with me
And she'll blend her voice in a song with me.

One more chorus:

TWO

The Handshake

June 11–17, 1954, San Juan River:
Mexican Hat to Lee's Ferry, Arizona

Frank Wright is a slender, long-muscled man with sloping shoulders, and tall—a couple inches over six feet. His dark hair is close-cropped, thinning a bit on top with hints of grey at the temples. He is fifty-one years old, sixteen years my senior—a Mormon High Priest with wife and six kids. To many lady passengers he's a father-confessor, gentle and sympathetic. I soon learn he'll be the same to me. His hands are big, the fingers blunt, the hands of a farmer. But he isn't a farmer, nor has he ever been; he's a mechanic now, when he isn't leading river trips. Many years ago he was a music teacher, yet I've never heard him sing, though one of his sons tells me he has a fine voice. Frank just listens. Listens with dark, heavy eyebrows pulled down in concentration or lifted in amused revelation, a wide smile stretching out the bowed dip in the upper lip of his generous mouth. His voice is deeply placed and soft. I've never heard him shout (even when it was necessary), and his speech has that distinctive, rural, Mormon cadence. I'd know it anywhere. I suppose he's a white man, though it would be hard to say unless he removed his wide-brim Western hat, or for some reason undid more than the top button of his shirt, exposing the skin beneath the hair crawling up to his collar. The cuffs of his khaki shirt are buttoned down over his garments, leaving dark brown hands, neck, and face the only spots free to meet the elements.

We need a bit of river history here to clarify who did what for whom, and when. Back up.

Norman Nevills is credited with the first commercial river-running operation on the San Juan and the Colorado River through Grand Canyon. He built his first boat at Mexican Hat, Utah, in 1934; his first paid run of the San Juan was 1936. His Cataract boats—often called "sadirons" because of their square sterns and pointed bows—were designed for heavy rapids and used on his first commercial run of Grand Canyon in 1938.

Frank and Jim had taken over Nevills River Expeditions after Norm's death in 1949, had renamed it Mexican Hat Expeditions and worked hard to make a four-months-a-year operation pay. They were the only commercial outfitter back then offering an eighteen-to-twenty-day trip through the Grand Canyon, yearly, around the first week in July. They ran the Green River, San Juan, and Glen Canyon until the water dropped so low it was better to walk. All the trips were oar-driven until Jim came along with the idea of the two Chriscrafts in 1952, but the power cruisers only lasted for three or four years. Frank never thought them a "practical" way to run the Grand Canyon, and he was right. When Rigg and Wright split the expedition's blanket, Jim took the power boats, Frank the Cats and San Juan boats.

The only method they had to garner paying passengers was to get a group together in a large city—usually through the efforts of former river runners—and show the river movies, like the one that nailed me. Now and then they would get lucky with an article in a newspaper or magazine travel section, but the cost was up there in the box seats. Most young people who'd really love to have gone could ill afford it. When Frank came to Los Angeles on his publicity trip, five months after I'd first met him in Boulder City, he stayed about a week, showing the movies every night to a different group: one night at my place to a group of writer-actor-directors; another couple of nights in Beverly Hills and North Hollywood.

I went along and sang some of the songs, and here is where I began to know something about Frank Wright. His love of music was our first connection. I had no idea how much he'd been affected by the songs (hellzbellz, I didn't even know how deeply I'd been affected) until he wrote me that spring of '54, "… one doesn't sing as you do unless there is understanding and a deep feeling to be drawn upon. 'Muddy River,' as you sing it, is so full of feeling that everyone who hears it can't help but notice that there is a heart tuned to the song. …" Yet I was inspired to write "Muddy River" before I ever *went* on the San Juan. I'd gotten it all from one Grand Canyon trip, the movies, and the stories of Frank and Jim.

～

Muddy River
Now if I had Mexican Hat I wouldn't put it on
 I'd jump right in from its broad brim
  And swim down the San Juan
And if somebody made for me a good old Gooseneck pie
 I'd rather float on down his throat
  In a river boat, says I.

Chorus:
Oh-oh-oh, Oh-oh-oh, Muddy River
Oh-oh-oh, on your way down to the sea.
I'll take your rapids and your roar
Like they ain't never been took before
And come a-runnin' back for more
Cause you don't worry me!

There is a stretch at Piute Farms that sorta makes me doubt'cha
 Your throat will parch from this death march
  And take the starch from out'cha.
And then the San Juan flows right on to meet his blood relation
 And if your ear is tuned, I fear
  You'll hear this conversation:

Chorus:
Oh-oh-oh, Oh-oh-oh, Muddy River
I'm the Mighty Colorado, that I am
You mud with me, I'll mud with thee
We'll send our flood down to the sea
I'll meet'cha there for a big party—
We'll bust out Boulder Dam!

Then Lee, he built a Ferry there and Brigham Young did boss it
 He spent his life to pay the price
  For all his wives to cross it.
The Little Colorado has a habit quite peculiar
 She'll turn her hue to a turquoise blue
  My gosh! I hardly knew ya!

Chorus:
Oh-oh-oh, Oh-oh-oh, Muddy River
Oh, Little Colorado marry me
And over Hermit we will forge
We'll snuggle up in the Granite Gorge
And on to Lava we will roar
Just crash along with me!

Oh, the mules work hard at Phantom Ranch
   But the deer are really livin'.
      Just have a seat and a buck will eat
         All the buckwheat cakes you'll giv'um.
At Toroweap I went to sleep a dreamin' of an actress
   I woke up there in great despair
      The air gone from my mattress!

Chorus:
Oh-oh-oh, Oh-oh-oh, Muddy River
Oh-oh-oh, on your way down to the sea
At every turn you give a show
And may you, crashing, ever go
"As long as our rivers shall flow"
Hey, you can carry me!

At Lava Falls the roar appalls and no words can define it
   We stood on shore for a week or more
      And swore that we would line it.
"No guts!" I heard a boatman say as down the tongue he rowed it
   He pulled ashore with a broken oar
      Some forty miles below it!

Chorus:
Oh-oh-oh, Oh-oh-oh, Muddy River
Boiling, seething, churning to the sea
Your rapids took me, and your roar
Like I ain't never been took before
I ain't so sure I want some more ...
A Christian you made me!

The Piute's River. The Navajo's River. The Fun River. The Sandwave River. The Air Mattress River. The Gooseneck River. The Stand-up-in-the-middle-and-walk River.

The San Juan River.

Out of snow melt, down from the majestic San Juan mountains in Colorado, it tumbles, gathers, meanders, flows, flattens, and carves its way to the Colorado River in Glen Canyon, Utah. It was June of 1954—a year after my Grand Canyon powerboat run. I had been invited by Frank, personally, my way paid, as before, with guitar, playing and singing by a driftwood fire at day's end.

Six San Juan boats, decked over blunt stern and bow, carrying twenty-six folks from Mexican Hat to Lee's Ferry. Wow! Jim was one of the boatmen, of course, but I hadn't seen him since his dad removed him from UCLA to a pre-med school in Denver. By then our little romance had scaled down to the plaintive sound of a thin reed—a little on, a little off music, mostly off. But to hell with that, I was on a river again, and so was my good buddy Tad. Hollywood and all its glitter, competition, and bullshit was out of sight, out of mind!

What knocks me out about our western rivers is their *smell.* The only way I can describe that smell is to call it more dry than wet, more dusty than dewey. Pungent, earthy, *not* fishy. A clean-dirt smell, strongest on the upstream wind when the rivers are nice and silty. I call it The Great Mother's cologne. It enveloped me when I walked down to the boats near the suspension bridge at Mexican Hat, and it kept me wrapped in its aura the whole trip—a kind of synesthesia. My ears *felt* it, and I certainly *tasted* it. Even back in Hollywood, I would sometimes smell it in my dreams and wake up smiling.

There were long, clean beaches full of the San Juan's little secrets—pinecones from the snowcap, every kind of driftwood from twelve thousand feet on down, smooth-as-a-baby's-bum rocks and tiny pebbles in rainbow-colored spectrum from the wild southeastern Utah strata, little marbles of deer droppings and sheepshit, and chocolate *mud!* O-o-oooo ... so fine ... so smooth ... perfect to take a mudbath in ... let dry ... and draw ... and crack, like the medicine it really is when baked on your bod in the hot sun, then peeled off, leaving your skin like satin.

But not with twenty-six passengers and five Mormon boatmen. I learned about that a few more riffles down the line.

Frank was the undisputed leader of that trip—my first on the San Juan—with almost half of the others repeating the run. The river wasn't very high (1,900 cfs), but the rocks were, which made it a kind of pinball game for the boatmen. I spent a lot of time riding the sand waves and swimming, floating in my life jacket or on the air mattress, learning to read the water, feel the currents, figure where the flow would go around the next bend, or *not* figure and get pulled in behind a rock and dumped. We slogged, pushed, and pulled the boats through Piute Farms, where the bottom comes up to meet the top and the river is over a mile wide. I made the mistake of getting in *front* of the boat on one of these maneuvers, up to my ankles, hauling with all my might on the bow rope. Next step I was out of sight, with the boat on top of me!

Journal Note: June 13, 1954 (Third Day Out)

Wonderful, wide beach for camp tonight just above Piute Rapid—from here it sounds like a conversation with intermittent laughter. I walk down to the lagoon and take yet another bath. The moon rides in and out of fleecy clouds, sliding shadows along the walls that make the cliffs look as if they're moving upstream. Well, here I am, *me* again—even singing at night, I don't feel "on." Everyone just leans back on their bedrolls and listens, or sings along with me. Some tell me how much they like the songs, here especially, with guitar. How nice! Jim won't sing at night—he sings on the boat or hiking up a canyon, even running a rapid, like he's singing to the river, not the people. Maybe he is. Frank says there'll be a place for me on any of his trips that have room. Holy Moses! It give me chills to think I can come to this place every year. Why do I feel so *new* here? I don't mean new to the place; I *myself* feel new, fresh, innocent. (That'd make lotta folks I know laugh if they could read this.) Well, I don't know how else to say it. I know I have to get out of Hollywood pretty damn soon. I can't stand television, radio is dying, movies give me a pain in the butt, and there ain't no theater. Nightclubs scare me, but where else is there? ... I can go ask the river swirling around down there ... maybe he knows. Egad! I must be getting dingy! <END JOURNAL>

A week before I left for this San Juan trip, I had a session with my venerable friend and mentor, Burl Ives. I asked if he'd please come to Cabaret

Concert (our co-op theater, managed by various artists and directors) and watch my performance. I needed his advice. He graciously did so, after which we went for a drive.

"Darker'n a bat's ass up here. You sure this is the way?"

"Yes, Kathryn. I told you, I've been here before."

"So have I but it was twenty-five years ago, and I'll bet it's still loaded with poison oak. Poison oak *loves* me. How much farther?"

"Bitch, bitch, *Bitch!* About fifty feet on your left I think there's a big rock for me to sit on."

Pausing for a minute to get his bearing, he asked me to carry the bagpipes. I was all duded up from the stage, wearing a full skirt and those high heels we women execute ourselves with, walking a trail overlooking the twinking, trailing lights of the city. Here and there searchlights fanned upward, pooled against the fog, and moved along the tops of the hills, offering a faint glow.

Olé! Found your rock.

He felt for the contour he wanted to cast his bulk upon and sat for a few minutes catching his breath. I handed him the bagpipes.

Then, on the midnight air, over Mulholland Drive in the Hollywood hills, floated an altogether alien sound. I think he said they were Northumbrian pipes. I stood there, rapt, hearing melodies we both knew and played on our guitars, but the drone underlying them put them back on the Emerald Isle.

"How the devil did you learn to play that thing, Burl?"

"It's not hard. All you need is a lot of breath. The pipes were given to me by a friend in Ireland—figured the least I could do was learn to play them. Christ, I *love* that place. You know, I sailed over there last year. I'm thinkin' of buying a house on the coast. By god it's a wild one, that North Sea, like your river you've been telling me about. Kathryn, you are ready to *get the hell out of here.* This town is full of clowns showing off for each other, too phony and full of themselves to appreciate what you're singing."

"But, Burl. Nightclubs ... I can't ... "

"The hell you can't. There are people out there who want to hear your songs, the way you sing them. Clubs, and especially coffee houses, aren't what they used to be; they're like your Cabaret Theatre. People listen."

"But, Burl, my material isn't ... "

"Your material's just fine, *Sergeant!* (another pet name he'd added to *Bitch*). Christ, but you are stubborn. Just go!" He started pumping the bag again. "You're so damned worried about your material, when you come back from your river, we'll go through your repertoire and I'll help you pick what's best. All right, Kathryn?"

~

Being on a river with so many people left little time to explore the side canyons or do much hiking. I mentioned the San Juan was mean, low and rocky. The boatmen were anxious to get to the confluence, about halfway into Glen Canyon, where they would pick up more water. But we did walk up Slickhorn and Grand Gulch a way, stick our noses into Desha and Nasja Canyons on the Navajo Reservation side of the river, and fill our canteens while standing under icewater falls in Redbud—a heavenly little grotto, verdant with that delicate tree and banks of dripping maidenhair fern, scarlet monkey flowers, and most enchanting of all, the magic flutelike song of the canyon wren.

Journal Note: June 14, 1954 (Fourth Day Out)

I'm just bobbing along in my life jacket, letting the San Juan have its way with me, when I feel a change, a kind of nudge in the current. On the surface the color turns a darker red, a boil bubbles under my chin, and I hear a whisper in the water as it swishes between my legs. Then the current dances me in a tight do-si-do like a square dancer, lifting my legs up and down to its rhythm. It would be useless to argue and foolish to resist this new dancing partner. *He* is the Mighty Colorado River! <END JOURNAL>

I do not forget that meeting at the confluence of the two big rivers. Nor can I explain why it was different from others, more exciting, more enigmatic, both before then and after. I *can* say it was somehow an understanding, an agreement, a handshake. We would know each other. Yes.

And maybe more.

One of the highest straight-falls in the Glen, from Navajo cap to riverbed, was less than a mile below the San Juan confluence. The walls seemed more massive there, double strength, to hold the combined rivers' flow. Desert varnish streamed down the cliffs, flashing iridescent blue-purple in side lighting; black, maroon, and deep rose in the shade. The two rivers mixed their muds, intertwined their currents, and traded gossip from the ranges up north from whence they spring. Looking down from the top of that great rim, as I did many times in later years, it was wonderful to watch them play, easy to read the anecdotes they told each other, and delightful to eavesdrop on their whispered and chortled conversation.

Journal Note: June 14 (Continued)

Hidden Passage. Exactly. If the shadow that reveals the passage isn't there—if you come upon it in bright morning sunlight, or late afternoon, or on a cloudy day—you'll miss it, most likely. The Passage, pulled from the slickrock, grain by grain, eon by eon, is smooth from the rub of rushing water and funneled winds. On its bedrock it twists, curves, and bowknots gradually upward to falls that can be navigated by one if he's agile, two if not, and maybe three if the one between the puller and the shover is chunky. (We have some of those on this trip.) A mysterious quality hangs over it that I can't explain. Maybe ghosts convene here. Our voices, though muted, rise up ringing, only to dissolve before forming an echo, and once around a bend you can't hear or be heard by anyone. All the river parties stop here. It's one of the best, even though most hiked of all, yet there's no indication of that once you're inside. I suspect even a modest rainstorm could wipe it clean of all but tree trunks and boulders.

This afternoon I am privileged to sing in my first *real* church: Music Temple, named by Major Powell in 1869. I can see why. A song can be heard from beneath that dome to the river, nearly a half mile away. A nostalgic spot, so full of whispers of the past, so lovely—the pool, the stone estrade, the bank of ferns and columbine backing the pool, hanging baskets of them overhead clinging to a seep, and the sandstone spire twisting mysteriously out of sight way above, from where pours a crystal ribbon of water that drops musical notes into the pool. <END JOURNAL>

I sang in Music Temple every year for ten years. In all that time, I never heard anyone shout. Kids didn't race about; no rough-and-tumble, no games. It seemed like when they turned that last bend under the dome and looked upon the scene before them, they treated it like a holy place. None of the guides said anything but, "We'll stop at Music Temple, where you can see the Powell party's names and dates carved in the sandstone." So it had to be the secret of the sounding rock itself that spoke to their subconscious reverence.

Journal Note: Still June 14

Why do these giants, rising on both sides of our tiny boats, feel like a protective cape drawn around me? What is the intimacy with *this* water all about? Was I once a fish? I'm in the river more than anyone else. I seem to have a need to know what's going on under the surface. I want to feel the tug and push of the current. We float from Music Temple to Forbidding Canyon (Aztec Creek) in moonlight so strong it seems to have a *sound*. Under its glow every harsh, jagged edge (and there aren't many of those in the Navajo formation) turns soft and sympathetic, inviting even. A shadow falling across two towers makes me want to go nestle between them. When we aren't singing, we hear only the squeak of an oarlock or water dripping from the blades. The river whispers or giggles or growls over a rock bar, and I swear I can hear him burp! We beach at Forbidding Bar and, after unloading, trail off to find our special sleeping places—the boatmen usually where they can get quickly to the boats if need be—some in groups, some couples, some separate and apart. I'm one of the latter now, way apart. Full moon tonight. Will I get a full-moonburn if I fall asleep face up and … uh … exposed? I hope so. <END JOURNAL>

Journal Note: Next Morning, June 15

Frank and Tad (the one who got me into all this, bless his heart) try to prepare me for the Rainbow Experience. They don't. In this life I never expected to stand on top of a rainbow frozen in the sky (much less walk across the bow to where the next step is the fast way down), see other partially formed rainbows from my seat in the blue, and watch our party of ant-people below picking their way up Bridge Canyon. But I do it all. From here it doesn't feel as if this stone rainbow is attached to the ground. This spot is pure magic! All of nature's intelligence, her artistry, and crying beauty are visible … Jim, Tad and I are the first up and the last down. I swim *all* the long serpentine pools, 5 miles, back to the boats.

Again the moon is brilliant, with strip-lace clouds crossing her face. I write by the light … Art Green in the *Tseh Na-ni-ah-go Atin* comes up from Lee's Ferry to dump his little gift package for us—two more of our River Rats, who'll finish the trip with us. <END JOURNAL>

My god, that boat was an interesting piece of architecture. *Tseh Na-ni-ah-go Atin* in Navajo roughly means "place where the bridge crosses over." She was a flat-bottomed aluminum hull, more or less eighteen feet, with an airplane prop and engine mounted at the rear. Art, who owned and operated the boat and Cliff Dwellers Lodge about ten miles west of Marble Canyon bridge, piled as many as 20 passengers into her and planed them up to Forbidding Canyon for the hike up Aztec Creek to Rainbow Bridge. It was an overnight trip in spring and early summer, so Art had a permanent camp set up on Forbidding Bar—just a semi-circle of rocks and logs, no civilized junk. He gave me a five-minute ride in that sucker once, and it nearly tore my ears off. Jesus! What a way to experience Glen Canyon. I couldn't imagine anything worse.

Nor can I imagine why we went from Forbidding Bar to West Creek Canyon in time for lunch—there were seventeen explorable canyons between them! But those folks weren't granted the favors that later came to me. They signed up for a 191-mile trip encompassing seven days, and the boats were oar-driven. For that alone they could be thankful.

After we'd hit the confluence, I kept asking Frank, Jim, or Tad whenever we'd pass a little niche in the wall, "What's in there? What's it like?"

"Don't know. Never been there."

After running this river since the mid-forties, they'd *never been there?* Seems after Norm explored several of the more accessible canyons, and took his passengers to the same ones every trip, *Mexican Hat* just followed suit. Jim had poked into a few others, but they still weren't on the regular agenda.

Hmmmm. In just a couple more weeks, Jimmy and I had two successive Glen Canyon trips signed up—nine days each, 162 miles, from Hite to Lee's Ferry. Frank would be on the first one, my Hollywood movie friends on the second, and it would me my *first* Hite-to-Lee's Ferry run.

The agenda was about to be amended.

~

THREE

Harmony

July 4, 1954

From Blanding, Utah—and *bland* it is—westward, over part of the old Mormon Trail, blasted from the side of a thousand-foot sheer rock wall, we rode with Frank in his "outfit," towing a new San Juan boat with our gear, while Jim, an hour ahead of us, towed another filled with supplies for a nine-day run.

Pale, buff earth and sandstone, yellow earth and rock, pink earth and walls, deep maroon earth and mud-bubble goblins cast in stone, soft mounds of strawberry, blueberry, caramel, grape, and lime that look like melting ice cream. Together they form mesas, buttes, synclines, anticlines, monoclines and talus slopes, canyons and cliffs, on the way down to the blushing, sensuous flesh of Navajo sandstone that embraces most of the river in Glen Canyon. From tall pines above the Bear's Ears, to the sloping juniper-piñon shoulders of uncountable canyons, we drove on a red and dusty road, neither seeing nor passing anyone; across bare slatelike rubble, devoid of any vegetation; through dry sand washes, over slickrock, across alkali flats, and past ancient cliff houses—stopping now and then to take photos. Almost four hours and some ninety miles later, under a cloudy, midafternoon sky, we dropped into Farley Canyon—a sudden paradise that offered us a clear stream, bordered by clacking cottonwoods. Then up it came: that wild river smell.

In front of Woody Edgell's store/post office, a mile from our starting point at the Hite Ferry, we tumbled out of the wagon and dashed inside for Popsicles! Beer! Sody-pop!

Suddenly, the old hand-cranked phone on the post office wall rang, startling me. Why that sound in this faraway place? I knew that Hite had no connection to the outside world. Turned out to be the "peanut can"—the ferry phone. Somebody wanted to cross over to this side. We drove down to the river, boarded that wondrous contraption, and ferried over with Woody to get the guy and his truck. It wasn't a fast ride, so Woody had time to tell us about other ferries that preceded the one we were on.

"This 'er's a floatin' Cadillac compared to summa them early ones. 'Er name's *Annabell*—the engine, not the ferry."

The Colorado River's last public auto ferry was a real iffy-looking thing with wooden planks atop a gang of fifty-gallon oil drums and a couple of bridge pontoons. On the upriver side of the planks sat the skeleton of an old Chevy/Dodge/Ford truck. (I heard all of those over the years). The cable that pulled her across was attached to the rear wheel, or a drum, so when Woody reached into the cab to turn the key, release the brake, push the clutch in with his hand, and slip the gear shift into low, the axle turned, winding the cable around the wheel, pulling the ferry forward. On the way back, he shoved it into reverse and it wrapped the other way.

[A year later, a spring flood scattered the oil drums over the water like peas out of the pod. Temper temper, Mr. River! Never mind; by fall she was afloat again. I remember the oil drums when we crossed that day, but it was all pontoons soon after that. I don't know how many times, from '46 to '64, the old Colorado gave *Annabell* (and the ferry) a bath, but it was more than Woody ever said. She was a fat old thing, and they couldn't always get her high enough up the bank to save her ass.]

"You wouldn't believe," Woody continued, "summa the rafts 'n' stuff that was built to haul equipment fer mining and makin' roads into this place. The *old* road come down Trachyte Creek from Hanksville. Take a look up that canyon sometime. Yipes! She's a mess!"

He said that during the ferry's earliest days, Cass Hite, who had strung the first cable across the river there, built a log raft, looped a couple of ropes over the cable from both ends, and had horses pull it across in low water, then (get this) swim it over when they couldn't touch bottom. He also had a couple of guys with oars moving it across when the load was light.

I got to liking Woody's stories best because they seemed so far out. But a few years down the line I saw old photos of two guys rowing on each side of a raft, while two others looked to be moving the ropes along the cable.

Art Greene once said to me, "Be careful who and what you believe when it comes to stories about the river." Then, on down the line, someone else added, "Yeah, especially if the story is one that *Art* tells ya!"

~

History … stories false … stories true. I don't have to believe them, I just want to hear them. Like meeting someone interesting, asking questions about their past—where did they come from, what did they do?—looking for clues to what made them the way they are. So it was with me when I met the river. How was this canyon made? Why? When? By what? Even by whom? Such stories gave the canyon and the river character. If they had a different beginning, or middle, or ending, I couldn't have cared less. Whoever said "never let the truth get in the way of a good story" said it.

Most historians agree that Arth Chaffin built the first *auto* ferry—it began operating in September of 1946, when the road was officially opened from Blanding to the river and from Hite, on the other side (now up North Wash, not Trachyte), to Hanksville. He was still the official ferryman …

… "Sorta," as Woody pointed out. "I take over when he's diggin' at one of his gold mines downriver. You'll prob'ly see him down there summers. Him 'n' Frank is good friends."

Arth was an old man, and my link to the historic past of Glen Canyon, when I met him in 1954. A year later he wrote to tell me what he knew about Hite's early history.

Cass Hite came to the Colorado in September of 1883. I knew Cass when I was a young fellow and many, many times I went up river by boat, by horse back and by walking, to get the mail which came from Hanksville and Green River, Utah each week on horseback to Hite.

Cass Hite came to San Juan River in the early 80's and hunted for the Peso-La-Ki silver mine. Hoskinini [Chief of the Navajos] befriended Cass and got him to leave the reservation lest he might get killed [for sticking his nose in their silver business]. He then came to Hite with a "pack outfit" and several other men—when arriving at the river he was in the lead and rode across, called back to other boys saying, "Come on boys, she's a Dandy Crossing." It took that name for several years, until Cass got a mail route established from Green River to Hite—then they named it "Hite" after Cass.

And another letter from Albert R. Lyman. Blanding, Utah, April 22, 1963.

My father discovered and named Dandy Crossing in 1884. Later Cas [sic] Hite began a ferry there, and changed the name to Hite. I remember seeing Cas Hite in 1883, and in 1891, Homer Hite, Cas' nephew, was operating the ferry.

The actual Dandy Crossing was a mile or so upriver from Hite and the ferry that Arth built, and of course the Anasazi, the Mokis, and whoever came before them, knew about the crossing several centuries before any of these guys showed up.

By five o'clock we had our two boats stocked, the gear loaded, and all passengers aboard. I tell you now, no matter how close it got to dark, there was always an urge to get *on the river* before anyone or anything could interfere—a hankering to be out of sight around the bend of the Dorothy Bar. Somehow that was the portal to another world, where we popped down the Rabbit Hole and could no longer be found.

A couple years after this first Glen trip, Tad, Frank and I spent several hours on Dorothy Bar taking photographs and building a crazy mobile out of old rusted pieces of metal, gears, pipes, and sprockets, which we hung over a shaft on what was left of the old hoist. We'd gone down the Rabbit Hole, you see; we could be children again—just one more of that river's many revelations—with time to let our imaginations build dreams about Dorothy ...

... of Dorothy Bar. Did she once sleep here in this old iron bed now rusted out of shape and tilting into a badger hole, under a roof of corrugated tin in a half-gone house of rough-hewn boards? Was she one of the Gearharts who staked the claim on the bar, dug all these holes into the mountain by hand, built sluiceways, waterways, and corrals, and dragged all this massive mining machinery here from hundreds of miles away, for a few ounces of gold? She taught school at the first schoolhouse at Hite, that we know. Did she cook for all the miners as well? And wash their clothes in this old tin tub? Probably. Were there any other women around to talk to, commiserate with, or enjoy? Probably not.

Journal Note: July 4, 1954 (First Day—10,000 cfs)

At last I'm on a small, laid-back float trip, just six of us—two veteran river rats, one greenie, myself, and two highly qualified boatmen to guide us, teach us, feed us, and get us to Lee's Ferry in nine days. At sunset, only a few miles downriver, we make camp under a half-cloudy but rainless sky. In the afterglow, Arth Chaffin himself comes upriver from

his claim and stops to talk with Jim and Frank. Everyone listens in as the talk turns serious. I've heard rumors about it from Jimmy, and I think it's just talk, but Mr. Chaffin is taking it to heart. He tells us that up and down the Glen, wherever there is a sign of uranium, the miners are desperately trying to prove out their claims so they will be compensated when the reservoir drowns them. Reservoir? Here? (He says the river will back up some 280 feet above Hite). But I can't see that happening. The government owns the land all along the river and leases it to private parties for claims. With this part of the canyon being in the Shinarump and Chinle formations—both rich in uranium ore, ore that our government needs and wants—it would be stupid to put it all under water, like cutting their own throat. Anyhow, I've got some particulars now from Mr. Chaffin and will draft a letter to our senator, Barry Goldwater. Surely *he* won't go for such idiocy; he's been down this river and knows how fantastic it is. Tonight Frank informs me the Reclamation Bureau wants to dam Dinosaur Canyon on the Green River! Holy shit. They can't do that! It's a national park—a *thou-shalt-not,* just like Rainbow Bridge is a national monument, another thou-shalt-not. There'd be water clear up to the Rainbow's buttresses if they put a dam down near Lee's Ferry!
<END JOURNAL>

And you know, not *one* of us believed that a dam would ever be built in Glen Canyon, because, "It is the intent of Congress that no dam or reservoir constructed under the authorization of the Upper Colorado River Project Act, shall be within any National Park or Monument." Amen.

That was the LAW. The law would save our canyon.

~

It takes a couple of days for river trippers to lose their city scales and turn into the beings they really are, though that's hardly true of Frank. He may be the only person I've known in my life whom I haven't had to re-think, whose personality hasn't altered over the years, and he exudes a sense of peaceful purpose that, even with jumping jacks like me, has a calming effect.

He told me he'd always hated the study of history, which surprised me, because he knows a lot about it—should, after all. His ancestors came west in the Mormon wagons, down through Hole-in-the-Rock and across the ruddy Colorado, on account of where Brigham said "go," they went. And they went the *hard* way—beneath the Kaiparowits

Plateau off of Fifty Mile Bench, and yet another thousand foot drop to the river through a slit in the sandstone wall, where they hacked a series of steps for their animals, put them in their traces while the men held back on ropes behind, drove them down one at a time, floated them across the Colorado, and hauled them up near the mouth of the first canyon downstream. The year was 1880 and it took several months to do the job. I always thought it was a bad choice for all concerned; surely there was an easier way—Dandy and Halls Crossings, Hansen and Stanton Canyons, probably—but I wasn't there. And I'm not a Mormon.

Whether Frank liked history or not, by the time I got to the river he knew the names of all the geological formations, knew where many of the ruins and picture rocks were located, who the historic figures along the river were, and what they'd done. I gobbled everything he said and asked for more. But *why* didn't they find out what was in those mysterious, inviting, sometimes dark and twisting, sometimes stream-trickling, sometimes dry but waterstained, hundreds of feet deep, often a mere shoulder's width, fluted, water-carved and wind-etched, cool, earthy-smelling crevasses? "No time to," they said.

~

From Hollywood I'd taken one helluva leap into another reality, and as I relaxed in my sleeping bag, watching clouds strip and tear themselves apart, I tried to figure the luck, the fates, the timing, that had brought me here. This place insisted on entering my being in a way that hundreds of nights outdoors, in as many other camps, had not. I couldn't get it. I'd stayed up with Frank long after Jim and the others had sacked out, telling him things I tried hard not to *think* about, never mind discuss. He knew as much about showbiz as I did about raising llamas, yet I felt he'd understand. ...

... The Old Story:

Small-town girl comes to Tinseltown to make it big ... and trips over dissolution. University graduate with B.A. degree in drama leaves rural Tucson ranch life for marketplace to act in movies, theater, radio—to sing, play guitar (no dancing), and smile-all-the-while, all-the-while, all-the-while. After six years dedicated to the selling of her artistry—being "on" day and night, working for a "name," going for auditions, interviews, tryouts, dressing for the cameras, swearing, living on cheese and crackers, doing benefits, staying off the "couch," holding back insults-to-idiots, learning the ropes, cussing, being nice—and smile-all-the while—she makes it!

Folk music is in bloom, the public eye nigh ready to focus on it; "rock" hasn't avalanched on us yet, and television is a mirage in the distance. Hollywood still retains a few old customs and courtesies—it's not *all* dog-eat-dog. Radio still attracts a large audience, and live performances keep the pot boiling.

Why is she starting to have doubts about her plan?

My acting career had blended with the musical one, and I had running parts on three national NBC shows, along with roles on stage, in movies and even the new spook, television. Nice. I'd left old Arizona to be a movie actress, but I found movies and television to be something of a salad bar, very unlike the stage. Little bits of this, little bits of that, nothing carried through from one scene into the next, everything hacked to pieces—gives a stage actor indigestion. At least when I sang I was responsible for delivering the whole story, which had a beginning, middle, and ending. Another thing: On stage we *all* worked for perfection of the *whole*—that's what good theater is all about—but there in Bleached Blond City (yup, me too) there was the star system.

~

The Great Gildersleeve. One of NBC's most highly rated weekly radio shows.

I appear as "The Girl in the Wood," an acting/singing/guitar-playing role that brings some five hundred cards and letters to the agency that manages the show, all asking, "Who is Katie Lee? When will she appear again? Where can we find the song she sang? What a lovely voice," etc., etc. Well, wow-eee, I finally made it! I'm in seventh heaven.

Why isn't the agency all hyped up about it?

Their first excuse is that they don't have time to answer all that mail. Give it to me, I tell them. I'll *gladly* do it. When will I be on again? The fans want to know. Are the writers working on my next appearance? How soon can I see the script?

They hedge any commitment, giving all sorts of weird reasons.

One day about a month later, Betty, the secretary, takes pity on this poor dumb child and sticks my nose in it.

"Katie, this agency *never* gets five hundred pieces of mail for a show. *Even for the star.*" She lets that sink in for a minute, which it doesn't.

"But, Betty, the show was wonderful! *Everybody* thought it was. Even PeeBee, and LeRoy, and Carmen Dragon [the actors and orchestra leader] said "The Girl in the Wood" was ... "

"Katie ... "

" ... an absolutely great song."

"Katie ... Willard Watterman—*Gildersleeve*—is the star of this show. *Not you*. He's upset."

"I don't wanna be the star, I just want to have a running part, come back; be me, sing and bring some nostalgia to the ... Why in hell should he be upset? I'd think Gildy'd be pleased that we got all that mail ... I ... "

"*We* didn't get all that mail, Katie. *You* did."

I called it the Star-crossed Lesson.

~

There on the shore with Frank, over the sounds of a river polishing his stones, disappointments, regrets and wishes were confessed, fears were mollified and possibilities brightened. That special "riffle" sound became a balm to my tired soul—and in the same way that I learned to speak with the river, Frank and I discovered ways of feeling each others thoughts without talking.

Journal Note: July 5 (Second Day)

Clouds are gone. It's hot. We've hiked a mile or so up Ticaboo Creek (Ticaboo means "friendly" in Ute) to the site of Cass Hite's old cabin, just a chimney and a couple of graves amid parts of a stove, some rusted cans and pots. A huge rock covered with petroglyphs stands nearby, indicating this was camp or home to the Mokis, who were here long before Cass arrived—reason being, there's a spring not far up the trail that probably flowed a lot more then than it does now. <END JOURNAL>

More from Arth Chaffin's letter:

It was Cass who really started the placer gold rush in Glen Canyon in the late 1880s. In Green River, Utah, at the old Railroad Boarding-house, in the year 1891, Cass killed a man named Kohler in self defense over a claim dispute. He was convicted by an all Mormon jury to twelve years in jail, but was pardoned within a year on a promise that he would stay out of Green River ... Later he returned to Ticaboo and started his little ranch, farming in summer and placer mined on the banks of the river in the winter. He lived there until his death, about 1915, was found by a friend named Lon Turner who was working at California Bar downriver. He notified Bert Loper and Bert took the word to Cass's brother Johnnie who was running the Post office at Hite together with Fred Gibbons. Cass's grave is one with the cedar posts around it, other is Delaney's grave, an old friend of Cass's who died at Red Canyon and had requested to be buried by Cass at Ticaboo. He was taken and buried there in 1932 by his son and Billy Hay.

Journal Note: July 5 (Continued)

Again I'm on and off the boat, in and out of the water all day. A silty moustache forms on my upper lip after two or three strokes. We stop for lunch on the left bank, where we climb up a slippery cottonwood trunk to inspect a granary—a mud-and-stone structure the Mokis built into a crevasse and sealed to keep the varmints from their grain and corn.

Left Bank: River people never say east, west, north, or south bank, only technologists who like to complicate everything. The way it flows is the way you goes, ferkrisake—DOWNSTREAM. Whatever the meander, the *Right Bank* is on your *right*. And flip-flop.

Most of this upper Glen is rife with mining sites, and Frank even knows who owned some of the old, more extensive, gold claims. What he doesn't know, or Jim either, are the *names* of these side canyons. These guys know where they are, but I don't, and we've no map with us. A USGS Plan & Profile map like the one Jim put together for the Grand Canyon would be handy. He cuts them up, pastes the whole river on a roll of butcher paper so he can unroll it to any section. [In those early days they were just black and white contour lines revealing little more than a few miles of a side canyon beyond the river, most of them bearing no name at all.]

Night of day two: Wow-eeee! I have never heard such a sound! Wake up to spooky stillness, like being in a vacuum. Then down-canyon I hear a kind of moaning—sounds like a wounded animal—a sigh, then a cry, then a pulsing sound like a heartbeat. Frank's and Jimmy's heads pop out of their sleeping bags. They rush madly for the boats, pull them way up on the sand, throw the kitchen gear into boxes, and rock everything down. The pulsing begins to sound like a far-off cannon. Ros (one of the seasoned river rats) sits up, listens a second, grabs everything within reach of her bedroll, pulls up the zipper and dives like a mole for the bottom. I start to get out as Jim races by, hollering for me to grab anything loose, stuff it in with me, and zip up. He and Frank run for their bedrolls and do the same. Then it hits! The booming has changed to an openmouthed howl, then a scream, and now a sound like something frying. If you've ever watched a sand-blaster take paint off a building, that's what's going on here. A bucket rolls over me and on into the willows. I'm having a hard time breathing, so I stick my nose out the lee side just long enough to suck up a snootful of the beach. Now I'm hot, sweating—my bedroll, my hair and eyes are full of sand, and my ears have boulders rolling around in them! I begin to itch. Sonofabitch! After about fifteen minutes the wind dies from a moan to a wheeze, but the rain doesn't come. We lose a bucket and somebody's shorts, and I'm now initiated into one more aspect of the river's character: The higher the wall, the narrower the canyon, the harder the wind roars through the tunnel, taking the earth with it! <END JOURNAL>

I would learn to know that sound, and better yet, by its pitch, sense how long it would take to reach my camp.

~

Now, as I write, every mile of that canyon, and what was hidden in the side ones, is incised on my memory, complete with remembered conversations there, with smells, with springs, with redbud trees and heron nests; with owl perches, pink lizards; with good camps, bad camps. Was there ever one? Of course, but I'm trying to relate how it seemed to me before I really knew it. What fascinated me? Enslaved me? How did it, and why? On this trip I meet the canyon that begins the book—the one I see each morning in the photograph on my bedroom wall.

Journal Note: July 6 (Third Day)

The canyon a few yards farther downstream is called Forgotten Canyon by Dudy Thomas and Dick Sprang of Sedona, Arizona, because it was left entirely off the old Plan & Profile maps. It has been explored by them and Harry Aleson as far back as ten miles. There is a capped jar in a cairn for names, asking us to record our trip also. There are some old initials on the canyon wall—DER WB LHB FMG—below which we find a *metate*, broken pottery, and flint. Also there are petroglyphs on the wall, a clear-running stream winds with the canyon, and there are big cottonwood trees at the mouth of the canyon, before it narrows down. <END JOURNAL>

I *looked*, but didn't *see* it, didn't *feel* it. Its aura escaped me. I hadn't befriended it or learned its secrets—its persona was no more evident than that of a stranger I might meet on a bus. Aside from a handful of history gatherers like C. Gregory Crampton, the few who've published anything about Glen Canyon went through it like a dose of salts—once. Dick knew it like the back of his hand, and loved it maybe even more than I, but he finds the memory too hurtful to recall, let alone write about. Nor did the extractors care for it all that much, I'll bet. Ain't many have a life-long passion for the business end of a pick and shovel.

As I quickly scan my notes, I have to laugh at things that were wholly unrelated to the place: We come back to the river before noon ... start at 7:30 and get there about 10:15 ... we beach at four o'clock ... it takes us about forty-five minutes ... we can only spend about half an hour in here ... take twenty minutes to walk the trail ... still pressed for time, campsite will be after seven o'clock tonight.

Jay-zus, I was wearing a WATCH! Must have had an interview with said canyon at 2:45; another to see a director about a part in a cotton-wood tree at 11:30; an audition at 3:30 for a duet with a canyon wren. I remember now, just for the river trips I bought a waterproof Timex. Dear god, how we are stuck in it! There's much ado about the heat, up-stream wind, and this one grabbed me: "A cool, circular, clear pool fed by a seep overhead, where Ros and I bathe and wash our hair."

Oh dear, sorry, but that was once upon a then. There were hundreds of untouched potholes, pools, and sluices in the sandstone bottoms, on the cap, in crevasses, everywhere—and many *un*touchable ones out of reach, glistening deep and inviting. As for the river, we drank it, swam in it, washed in it, fished from it, cooked and built driftwood fires be-side it; never gave it a wink. Furthermore, we sank our garbage out in the middle. It acted as a disposal, ground everything to bits in the space of a few silty miles—cans, bottles, the works—and we cussed the dudes who buried their crap on the banks for the coyotes, foxes, badgers, and other wild critters to dig up and strew about. My present-day camper friends tend to choke on this logic, but try to visualize how *few* of us there were in this true wilderness, compared to the masses hardly able to find a place even half as pristine now.

I don't know when the *harmony* of the Glen began to dawn on me. Everything fit. The willows hanging over the water, the banks of young shoots running parallel to the water's edge in strips, as if planted there by hand instead of a receding tide. The heron roosts where leaves and branches were splotched white with years of birdshit. The way sandstone walls curved gently down, or stabbed into the river's edge; the immense talus slopes acting as buttresses for the varnished cliffs rising hundreds of feet to a cobalt sky. Row upon row of multicolored green trimmed the base of massive orange walls. Pink and white sand islands, like dabs of artist's paint, looked to be floating on strips of blue or coffee-colored ribbon, and rock fingers poked into the water, ruffling its flow. The eye was led from one faultless design to the next, moving in beauty, no colors colliding—a 360-degree cyclorama with a soundtrack from the river, narrating.

Only one element seemed in conflict. The scale was so huge that a photograph couldn't describe it, and I would try placing a person in the frame somewhere to give it perspective. In the end I gave up. WE were out of harmony.

Journal Note: July 8 (Fifth Day)

We tie the boats together and again do my favorite thing, float in the quiet dark with the night sounds—riffle talk from the river, a great horned owl's deep yodel, the smack of a beaver's tail on the water by the bank, catfish flipping near our boat. Our "silent time," everyone thinking his own private thoughts—tuning into the river and the canyon.

The river curves past Keyhole Rock; suddenly the wilderness is gone! Our intended camp on Forbidding Bar swarms with people, half of them Boy Sprouts. Another dozen in two rubber rafts led by a hairdresser, Johannous, from Sacramento—his accent from Prussia. (I stoop to mention the name here because of where we found it later.) Some teachers from Missouri, two Navajo boys, a young married couple, a nurse and a guide named Ken, all hiking to the Rainbow tomorrow!

Oh sh … nuts! I explode, barely catching my favorite four-letter word in mid air.

"Ocean nuts? What kind of nuts are those?" Frank grins at me, his teeth sparkling in the starlight. He then smoothes my ruffled feathers with, "This is the only place it happens—and won't you please sing tonight … *way* up the bar … far from all these people?" Still smiling, he wiggles his ears. (Some folks can, y'know).

I answer with what is now only a half truth. "Of course I will, Frank. Remember? That's what I came to do."

But we are not as far away as we think, because several people quietly wander to the edge of our firelight, stand or sit to listen, which somehow makes me feel resentful.

My god, that's a new twist, after spending more than a decade of my life trying to get people to listen to me.

What is happening here? <END JOURNAL>

[The guide named Ken, who would become a dear friend, was even then a true champion of Glen Canyon and avid fighter against the dam to come. I never met him on the river or saw him again until the seventies. Why our paths did not cross, I still don't know; maybe because I refused to run a river—any river—from 1963 to 1974. Then, one day, I found Ken Sleight in Escalante, Utah.]

FOUR

Eddying Out

Ros and I were riding with Jim next morning, when a couple miles below Forbidding Bar I spotted a narrow, mysterious gap in the right bank with a tiny cove at its mouth; a nip-'n'-tucker to get into because the water was fast.

"Hey! Hey, Jimmy, bet'cha can't pull in there."

That was all he needed—and Frank followed right behind. No one in our party had ever been in the canyon, or knew who had. The entrance, not twenty-five feet wide, was piled head high with driftwood. We debarked and scrambled over it, trying not to fall through. Under it ran a crystal stream and just ahead in the only shot of sunlight stood a radiant redbud tree, backed by a rose-colored wall dripping with desert varnish. Paradise.

Journal Note: July 11 (Eighth Day—8,600 cfs)

Great alcoves, ceilings several hundred feet up, overhang giant thumbs that poke from the snaking canyon's opposite side. It is dizzying to look up at a winding blue river in the sky, see a paint-spill of darker colors dripping from the rim over rose-colored walls, and feel the presence of those huge upstanding thumbs as we walk around them. They are so smooth, almost velvet to the touch. Sensuous shapes. Like giant phalluses. Mother Earth has many lovers!

Then comes the deep, cold, black pool that ostensibly ends the canyon. We can't get around it, nor the fall that slithers into it. I take the fever here. Explorer fever. I feel the peristalsis in the snake's throat pulling me in farther ... there is so ... much more canyon ... to be *eaten* by ... I can *see* it up there, but here's this clot in its throat. Damn! <END JOURNAL>

We called it Driftwood Canyon. Turned out aptly named. Only one year out of ten thereafter did I see its entrance minus the old Colorado's woodpile, and that was after a torrent from the Kaiparowits Plateau had "'flashed" it away.

"You're learning many things from this canyon, aren't you?" said Frank.

"The history of the place, the miners, the Mokis? Oh yes," I said.

"I don't think that's what I mean; something else. I've had many passengers who go hard after the history, prehistoric and modern, but you … you, I don't know. I'm not very good at expressing myself. You seem to *stick* to the canyon, or it … uh … wraps you."

I laughed. "You mean I *wear* it, Frank? You're right. Look here!" There was mud all over my legs and thighs, I had blood on my knee, scratches wherever I was bare, and my hat was conked in on one side.

"No"—he shook his head—"no, it's deeper. You're finding things in this canyon that I never knew about, or maybe never paid attention to, and I don't know just what." Then he lit his face with that wide grin and added, "but you sure look different than when you came."

"Well, I hope so! Don't we all?"

"Not the same way," he insisted.

I didn't know. I was too engrossed in what I saw, and the effect it was having on my everyday attitude, and too damn busy sucking it all up to bother analyzing it.

Journal Note: July 11 (Continued)

Across river, very shortly down from Driftwood, Jim pulls into another gap. We beach the boats and disappear into the cool maw of yet another miracle. Outside the sun is scorching and we are down to little more than swimsuits, but very soon we're confronted with long, dark, cold pools, god knows how deep, and walls so tight against us we can't swing our arms for a stroke. Then the gravel, then bigger and sharper rocks— on the tennies, off the tennies—now a streak of sun where we shiver and try to get dry. On to more stringy pools, up over boulders slick with algae, into an immense cathedral. A stone altar stands dead center under the dome, something like the one in Music Temple, only here the light seems to come through blue-purple-rose–stained glass high above. It filters down onto the altar, on top of which lies an eroded sheaf of rocks resembling a gigantic book with the pages open! There are *three* of these cathedrals, each with its stone altar beneath the overhang, each with the eerie light from the nave. Our "ooohs" and "ahs" blend with the whispering water.

Jimmy, Ros, and I outdistance the others and forge ahead ... to a twelve-foot jump! Here it takes two to get one up—me. Ros and Jim stay below.

Now another facet of Explorer's Syndrome takes hold. No one can follow you. No one's in front of you. And maybe—just maybe—no one's been before you. *You are alone.* Something clicks inside. Your heart rate quickens. All senses sharpen. You are out of earshot. The only sounds are those of the canyon, the essence of it, pure, distilled.

I race ahead to the next long pool, slide in and swim. So-o-o cold ... woof! ... out. Walls make a V. I see sky, no more overhang; sunlight ahead, and a bright green cottonwood smack in a bulge of the snake's throat. Warm water slips gently across bedrock into a shallow pool, chasing bubbles along the sandy bottom. Now, a flat sand and gravel floor, another bend, and then another. I run ... know they're waiting for me, worried probably, but I can't stop! Up, on up. A pool that I can rim without getting wet, one more pool, and then ... a boulder the size of a car blocks the passage. With help I can get around it, but it's too dicey to try alone. (Later on I take this as a sign—a protective one, a subtle or not-so-subtle way of telling me I've had enough, physically, emotionally, or both. It's time to turn back, turn around and rest, think awhile, take it *all* in, not just the pieces. A place to leave myself and take the *canyon* back with me).

Jimmy is waiting for me alone at the falls. I expect a reprimand. Instead he smiles a crooked little smile that says "now you know," and tells me he'll probably catch hell from Frank for letting me hold up the party. Then he gives me a hug, says, "We'll call this Katie's Canyon. You've seen more of it than anyone else," and starts downstream.

For no reason I can explain, I begin to resent his being in front of me, where he's always been before—me following in his footsteps without giving it a thought. But now *I've* made the first tracks into mystery; I have a right. Quite suddenly he stops, gives me that funny smile again, pushes me ahead of him and follows me all the way to the boats. <END JOURNAL>

My journals say I wasn't interested in having the canyon named after me, that I wanted to call it Cathedral Canyon, but was sure someone else had already named it. Apparently not. Cathedral it is to this day, and I can't tell you why I didn't want my name on it, or on any of them, really. Must have been instinct—not wanting to be drowned.

Frank was not upset with me. He said we'd make it up by "night fly-ing." Like Jimmy, he was a pilot of small aircraft, but what he referred to was "night floating" with the current. I changed to his boat and we had a chance to talk. He pulled gently on the oars, putting us into slower current as Jim's boat floated past, taking its murmuring conversation slowly out of hearing. Stars pitched and glided on the black wavelets. There was no moon at all. Frank could feel the river with his ears.

He said, "When I was in Los Angeles last winter, Katie, I knew from our conversations that you've been through some rough water these last few years. I sure hope these river trips are making things a bit easier for you, even for the little time you're here."

"Holymoses, Frank. You've got to *know* they are! Being here is like having a new lease on life."

"My lease on life's a lot brighter too. You've given us a lot of pleasure with your songs and your singing."

"I'm so glad. I can almost forget I've got troubles in this incredible place."

"Troubles sometimes have a way of shrinking when they're put in the proper place for the proper length of time," he said.

Oh? I thought. How Christawful long was that length to be? So, be-tween Klondike and Wildhorse Bars—nine quiet, drifting miles—the river and Frank got the whole story about my son, the ten-year-old boy I so longed to bring to this river. Impossible now. The scenes of injus-tice were still etched on my soul, and beneath them the muddy waters of anger and frustration swirled.

Frank was quiet for a long time after he'd heard my story. Finally he said, "It puzzles me to see how you can sing, and to all appearances be happy, when I know you have been hurt very deeply. Maybe the answer is, you *are* happy while you're singing."

Strange, something that simple I hadn't thought about, but I answered, "You're right, you know. I *am* happy when I sing; it's getting myself into a position where I can make a living at it that poses the cliffhanger."

In the quiet we glided beneath a willow. As a frond brushed softly across my cheek, I set my thoughts afloat on the water. Look how this river has picked me up in its current and shown me harmony in all its diversity—first muddy, then clear; gentle, then ferocious; it finds an eddy and circles back on itself; cuts through hard rock, spreads and relaxes in the shallows;

carries its burden, then *leaves* it! Well, my life is like this river, moving through triumph and sorrow, good times and bad. So, I'm going to leave some heavy driftwood at the high-water mark, and if I'm lucky, the burden of my lost son will stay there, at least for now ... on the bank.

Journal Note: July 11 (Last Night)

It is pitch black. Not even an ember glows from the campfire. I'm getting to love the nights this way, more than under a full moon. The river is more articulate, probably because in darkness our other senses sharpen and we hear better, the birds are quiet, the wind is still but for intermittent whispers, and nobody is talking.

Talk covers up what nature has to say.

For almost an hour Jimmy and I sit on a sandstone bench a few feet above a riffle, listening. Just listening. (Until now, I wondered why he went down to the water just before sack time—not to take a piss, he'd be gone too long for that; so he tells me he goes to talk to the river). In that hour he proves that the river *does* talk. You learn the language and keep still until you do; later you can start asking questions. After Cathedral today, he must figure I'm ripe for learning.

So I listen, and after a while I hear the talking. *I distinctly hear words!* But I don't know the lingo well enough to ask questions. Not yet. <END JOURNAL>

When we returned I was surprised to see Frank standing alone by the campfire, staring into it, hands braced in his hip pockets. Jim went for his toothbrush, saying goodnight. Frank laid another chunk of drift on the fire and looked up at me, shaking his head.

"It's amazing to me that you've accomplished what you set out to do in less than a year." (He was referring to the May issue of *Arizona Highways* magazine featuring my story, "Folk Songs of the Colorado," essentially about last year's Grand Canyon trip with Mexican Hat Expeditions, which I hoped would fill this year's passenger list.) "You must feel great satisfaction with that article. I know *I'm* really proud of you."

I *was* pleased to have done it and said, "Frank, there had to be some way to repay you for opening up this new world to me besides just singing a few songs. The article seemed like a good one, and now look what else you did—you unveiled a talent I didn't even know I had."

It was the first writing for a publication that I'd ever done, and frankly I was surprised as hell that they took it.

"I know it's not practical," he said, "but I wish you could be on every single one of our trips. Everyone should hear you sing those songs."

"I don't believe in going for free, Frank, and you're a dear and thoughtful person, but maybe everyone doesn't feel like you do about the music."

"Then they'd better get used to it, because I've got some other tricks up my sleeve. And *you'd* better think about the possibility of the Grand run in the cat boats next year."

So that's what he'd stayed up to tell me. Yipes! "But you don't know if there'll be a space."

"Wanna bet?" And wiggled his ears.

~

A kind of peace had settled over me, something I was utterly unused to. (I always worried about my next buck and where it was coming from, but now it didn't seem to matter at all). I talked with Frank about my career misgivings almost abstractly, a thing impossible before this. It all seemed so far away, and yet more clearly defined, like looking through the wide end of binoculars at a bug, every hair on its legs visible.

It's obvious that I'm living in two separate realities. Not just separate, but diametrically opposed. Tinsletown—the totally fake; and nature, the river—totally real. A double life. Where's the harmony in that? For a year, while pushing relentlessly ahead with my career, my one consoling thought in the rat race has been this river paradise, so when I'm here I try not to think about my career. But with this new peaceful feeling, a kind of eddying out, my thinking has cleared. I'm not only hearing what Burl Ives has told me, I'm understanding it: Get the hell out of Hollywood and take your songs on the road.

~

I have forgotten my first face-to-face meeting with Burl—we talked a lot by phone before we ever met—but after we'd known each other for a spell, done several radio broadcasts together, he asked me to pick him up one afternoon at Warner Brothers. For some reason he didn't have his 1926 Willys-Knight; said he'd take me to dinner if I'd drop him afterward at the Montclair Hotel, where he was bunking.

This, I *do* remember.

Sometime during the evening I said, "Burl, I think you are one of the all-round greatest artists on the scene today, *the* folksinger, actor, storyteller; you're even an artist at living. There's so much I want, and need, to learn from you, I hardly know where to start. I have to pick your brain. We are not going to fuck."

Long silence. "Hm-m-m-m. All right, Kathryn." Another long silence. "Anybody ever tell you, you're a consummate bitch?"

"No, not to my face."

"Well you are. You're a real bitch, and ... "

"Hey now, wait a minute ... "

"And you're too dumb to know that's a compliment."

"Doesn't sound like one to me," I said, trying for a brave front, but certainly my tone sounded hurt.

"I said you were dumb. It's a compliment. Trust me. Bitches have spirit. Bitches have passion. *Some* bitches are good in bed, but you probably wouldn't be ... probably talk too much."

"Fine. Now we got that cleared up, how in hell do I sing *folk songs* for a sophisticated nightclub audience?"

"God-in-heaven, girl, whatever gave you the idea they were sophisticated?"

I was so naive back then, I didn't realize he was trying to set me up for a future folksinging career. I knew he'd done the same for more "hopefuls" than he could count, but why was I one of them? I thought he probably just wanted my bod, which wasn't unusual in those days (an *older* Marilyn Monroe, he called me), but I was totally wrong. He stuck with me until I was well on my way, bless his huge and beautiful soul.

A few days later he had to go to Malibu on some business and asked me if I'd like to come along. Every time I climbed into that classic Willys-Knight beside the beard and bulk of Burl Ives, I slid back some twenty-five years. It was just like the one we had when I was a kid— barely room for the two of us in that narrow front seat.

He handed me a box tied with a blue ribbon, about a ten-inch cube, light in weight. Flowers? I couldn't imagine what prompted this; seemed unlike the things I'd come to know about him.

"Open it, Kathryn."

I was hesitant and kinda embarrassed. "To what do I owe ... "

"*Open* it, Sergeant."

"Yes*sir*!"

Inside the big box was another box, also tied with a ribbon, this one pink. Then another, and another, and another, all tied with different colored ribbons. As the boxes got smaller, visions of the gift got bigger, down to the last one of about three inches. Inside was a note. It read:

"You deny a man a great deal of anticipatory pleasure when you tell him right off, we ain't gonna fuck."

I called that one The "Box" Lesson.

Journal Note: July 12 (Last Day)

We pull into Wahweap Creek, rowing upstream behind Sentinel Rock to look at Bert Loper's inscriptions tallying his trips—probably not all of them over the years, but these are a few feet above the high water mark: 1907–08, 1911, 1912, 1921 (two that year), 1922, 1929, 1930, 1934, 1944. [Bert, a legend in the Glen, went *up* river as many times as he went down—working the eddies, lining or poling from the bank when rowing was impossible—to improve his claims, to visit, take supplies or bring things home to Red Canyon. He died in 1949, on a trip with his friend Don Harris, through the Grand. Died of a heart attack in 24.5 mile Rapid, they say—died the way he wanted to ... on the river. His old boat lies there still somewhere on the right bank, two or three miles above President Harding Rapid—a monument to a man who loved the old Colorado.]

A bit farther down we stop to look into the beginnings of a diversion tunnel. My god, is Arth Chaffin right? Can these Wreck-the-nation idiots be serious? (Purblind, we refuse to believe, because in Marble Canyon they've been "monkeying" up and down, running an elevator and cables, testing, drilling, and marking up the walls for several years; now it's all abandoned). Through binoculars we see three lone figures high on the rim opposite Sentinel Rock—survey party, tripod, and plane table. They call to us and some call back. Not me! We note contemptuous scribbling near the site from other River Rats who are livid about its possible construction. I've got some hot things to add, but Frank stays my hand. <END JOURNAL>

There's no way anyone on our trip would have answered the Bu Wreckers if we *still* hadn't been certain, by law, that nothing would destroy our Glen Canyon, nothing as unspeakable as a dam—even with such dumbfounding evidence before our eyes. (Interesting word, *dumbfounding*— *dumber* than dumb it found us.)

But I was starting to panic.

I'd just found a place on earth that could save my life and some blackhanded bureaucracy was already clawing to take it away from me!

FIVE

Tinseltown Transformation

That night, July 12, we had our usual farewell dinner at Art Green's Cliff Dweller's Lodge. There was much talk about the looming black cloud of a dam just fifteen miles upstream from Lee's Ferry. Art spoke of "concessions" on the "lake," about marinas and buying property upstream from the proposed site—at least *he* wasn't going to be left holding the bag when everything concerning river trips in the Glen was over.

I was mad. "It won't be a *lake*, Art, it'll be a goddamned *reservoir!* And they can't dam it anyway with Rainbow Bridge ... "

"Well, I ain't bettin' they won't. I've heard 'em talkin', seen how they work. Some of the surveyors is stayin' here y'know. It's political, Katie, not logical."

Next morning Frank flew back to Blanding. He had a San Juan trip hot on the tail of this one.

Jim and I, Joan Nevills (one of Norm's daughters), and Bob Rigg, who'd come to pick us up, trailered the boats back to Blanding through the Navajo Reservation on what was then called "The Trail"—unpaved, all of it. A nightmare trip in any kind of weather, and clouds were building. Talking among themselves, not to me, they spoke a been-there-first, done-that-already lingo, which I learned from my friend Dick Sprang was actually caused by a disease known as *canyonitus*. Learned also that sooner or later we all get it.

I turned my attention to the scenery, rewarding in a different way altogether than the river's. I'd been through Monument Valley several times before this, but without boats. The sand traps, especially after Red Lake and around the Elephant's Feet, were something to squabble with. We all got out and pushed. (How many who roll through it so easily in air conditioned cars today *see* anything but a few monoliths, orange sand, and junipers?) Consider the Monuments back then in July. You couldn't even hold them in focus—they waved like giant red flags in the heat mirages. Or consider trucking through in fall, as I often did later, when the wind tore the tumbleweeds from their Russian roots and sent them bowling into an arroyo that we had to cross. They'd pile higher than the cab's roof and we'd drive through with the windows rolled up, praying the tailpipe wouldn't set them all on fire!

It had rained here and there, *not* where it was sandy and we needed it, but rather at Chinle Pass, where we didn't, where it made gumbo of the Chinle shales. Two miserable hours to deal with that. It was long after dark when we drove into Blanding, all of us asleep except the driver, and I wasn't too sure about him.

Next morning I had a hangover.

Not from booze. That you can't buy in this good Mormon town, and there was never any on our trips. Nor did I want any. From my first day on the river, I learned what intoxication was all about. Nothing could have made me drunker than that canyon, those rapids, and my binge with nature. The hangover was from an overworked brain; what was to be done about the impending threat to our river?

That dam.

One reason I was so shook on the trip back to Blanding was that I couldn't get anyone in the car to do anything but joke about it when I tried to tell them they had a problem. This was going to change *everything;* didn't they care?

Jim and I had three days to prepare for my Hollywood passengers who would be flying into Hite. Activity in bland Blanding was in overdrive— cleaning and restocking the boats, airing bedrolls, washing sheets, checking for leaks in air mattresses, buying food. No time to talk with Frank, busy outfitting his own trip. No time to think river, but merely what to take on it; study lists, check things off, and make myself as useful as possible. Only at night, stretched out on Frank and Dora Wright's cool green lawn under the elm trees, where a quarter moon squinted through, did the music of the river come back into my head to put me to sleep.

In the morning before breakfast I took out my notebook and began a letter to our Arizona senator, Barry Goldwater.

~

At first curious, then fascinated, I began to watch the impression these river trips made on various people—even played a guessing game about their reactions before they got there.

My three Hollywood friends—a director, a screenwriter, and a script girl—would see the Glen from a whole other side than mine, naturally. Cosmopolites—New York and L.A., witty, hip, sophisticated, used to working on location sometimes far from the U.S.A.—they'd seen many and varied kinds of scenery, but how would they take to this wilderness? It's mostly what we bring with us that determines what we see and feel.

I needn't have worried. Danny must have shot twenty rolls of film; he was the director. Sy caught between six and a dozen catfish and chub every couple days; he was the writer. Sylvia, one of those hard-to-get-out-of-high-heels types, was the script girl. She played chess and poker with the guys whenever they felt like settling down. This was her way to relax, which she enjoyed doing more than hiking a lot of the time. She didn't say much, but I kept her in the corner of my eye, and my bets are that she sucked up more peace, joy, and serenity as a buffer to closed-circuit Hollywood than the other two would guess. She called me Pocahontas, her trusty Indian guide.

When Jim and I met them at Hite, I felt I'd stepped into a new role—not just a passenger anymore, and certainly not a guide, but they would be asking me questions because they knew I'd done this before. Ambivalence. A sense of importance that I *did* know some things and a sense of inadequacy because I didn't know enough. I should worry? Jim is the real expedition leader, one of the best with his love of the canyon, his ease, humor, and the security he provides. I'll just add another dimension to my knowledge while he keeps them astounded.

Another new thing was added. They'd asked us to bring beer. I remember that Jim had to go all the way to Monticello for it, 25 miles—it wasn't always available at Hite. Well now, if you've never drunk Utah 3.2 beer, here's what you get: a lotta wet bubbles with no effect, except a lotta the same comin' out the other end without even a color change. The trio made cracks about that until the middle of the trip, when there was no more, and they neither missed it nor pissed it.

Journal Note: July 17, 1954 (6,000 cfs)

Around the Dorothy Bar ... heh-heh, we're gone, and I am in *familiar* territory! Trachyte Creek fades from view. We have a map, so I can put the names on the terrain. It is raining, and we're all laughing. First rain on the river for me. No music tonight; we are camped on Monte Christo island (mile 152.5). Every now and then Jim likes to make it more exciting, like when the weather is stormy, you don't camp on these islands, right? I ask him about it; says it's moving on east and nothing to worry about. Considering the speed of his movements, I've no doubt he can get us and all our equipment off of here long before we'll be high-watered. <END JOURNAL>

Journal Note: July 18 (Morning, Second Day)

We come upon Arth Chaffin at Ticaboo Creek, loading a jeep onto a raft to cross the river and get down to one of his claims on the other side. There's a half-assed trail on the right bank from Hite down as far as Seven Mile Canyon—albeit rougher'n a cob and impassable after storms or big river water—as well as myriad abandoned wagon trails, slickrock, and stock trails woven through the upper Glen, most of them hardly visible. But more than you'd think are still in use and were undoubtedly *made* by Arth. Only god knows how many gold claims he has on the river; nobody else knows. Gold is his life. No, probably not—the *search* for gold is his life. [I could tell he was shy about talking to women, as our correspondence starting after this trip proved, but I got great tidbits from other riparians. When he finally left the Glen and moved his body to Teasdale, Utah, later that year, his soul did not go with it, any more than the souls of Bert Loper and Cass Hite, and other souls, like mine, who went there to dig or boat, to explore and be amazed, and found it wouldn't let them go.]

Everyone else is taking a siesta under the willow shade on Good Hope Bar beside a five-foot bank of sand that the river has cut away at some higher stage of water. The crossbedded pattern is like a cutaway picture. Various velocities of wind have shifted and lifted, swirled and drifted the grains. Rains have come to harden them; they've dried. More winds, and they've piled one atop the other. Dunes in the making. Now and then loose sand slides from the top of the bank, forms a small slit in the cliff, and piles up in a cone at the bottom.

I look up to the outer walls of the canyon and see a duplicate of this miniature! Same colors, same cross-bedding in the high sandstone walls and in place of the cones on my miniature, huge talus slopes buttress the cliffs. Creation! Before my very eyes. Here's a whole Sahara, covered over, pressed down and solidified by tons of water, surfaced again, maybe baked in some grand oven and left here to be worn down again by all the elements and a mighty river—not to forget man's little hatchets.

Well now … that puts a whole other perspective on things. You do not—*we* do not—just arbitrarily cover this creation over on the whim of a few piddling politicians. Goddamnit!

This dam, 139 miles downstream, will encroach not just on century-old history, or on the prehistoric, nine to eleven centuries. This dam will encroach on antiquity—Triassic, Jurassic, Cretaceous—a *geological age*, ferkrissake! These guys (the Wreck-the-Nation-Bureau, Floyd Dominy, our senators and so-called representatives) aren't just moving a few rocks around; they are going to alter, destroy, drown, two hundred miles of an *era* that nobody knows how long it took the planet to assemble (we can't even think in that kind of time), and they're going to fix it all up to suit each other—not you and me—in *six or seven puny years!* The kind of time we *can* understand.

Playing god in Glen Canyon! I bloody well don't think of politicians in such lofty terms—I agree with e.e. cummings, who says, "*A politician is an arse upon which everything has sat, except a man.*" <END JOURNAL>

I said before that I was on familiar ground. Only my second time in upper Glen, and I could predict what was coming around the next bend. How could that be? I'm moderately observant, but that was a bit much—over 175 miles with the view changing every spin of the boat, every meander in the river?

Only in retrospect do I realize that the river, called inanimate by many, was becoming "someone" to me, not just a place that I passed through. This river had a personality shining through his power. Walls were no longer just walls; I could see how they were the result of something that had been in progress for eternity. Often they had friendly, amusing faces that I could touch, and I had ceased to look upon the river as mere adventure, no matter the new and different side canyons, trails, waterfalls, ruins, petroglyphs, pictographs, springs, arches, domes, and alcoves. I was learning how miracles turn real.

Historically, I was at "a pause in the river's occupation"—mining was done, the people-crunch not yet underway. There was *time* to form an alliance. I wasn't in a hurry; neither was the river. In Glen Canyon the river rested, seemed almost in a coma—which gave me time to put thought behind what I was seeing, time to engrave it on my memory screen. On the Grand Canyon run adrenaline had rushed like a waterfall, making it tough to comprehend what I saw.

Journal Note: July 18 (Afternoon, Second day)

My senses undergo a changing of the guard when I return to nature—to the river. Freed from smoke, smog, and city gases, I'm able to separate and identify animal scents, the meaning of a shift in the wind by its whisper in my ear, its brush on my skin after twilight, after dark. Such things matter here. Like a windborne smell that will evince the kind of weather we'll have. Hearing and sight followed the same pattern; even the sense of touch is more sensitive, and my bare feet have a tougher sole that actually lets them feel more, now that they're no longer sore. I hardly use my tennies any more, and I'm only wearing two strips of cloth on me bare bod. Gonna be the same color as the rocks before long!

I row now and then, learning to read the water. Short chop, long chop, diagonals, swirls, and ripples tell what's underneath—sometimes—until the inevitable upstream wind wipes the lesson off the water. I'll never be like Jim and Frank. They can read with their ears; not being able to see even two inches below the surface doesn't bother them. Ahead, I see some water that puzzles me. I roll off the deck to feel with my hands, or feet, what makes the surface act that way. Oops ... the river and I are stuck together, belly-to-belly.

Tapestry Wall is three miles long, most of it a thousand feet high, with sheer drop to the water part of the way, the remainder buttressed with talus slopes. We camp tonight at the head of this incomparable sounding board on a ledge above the river bordering Warm Spring Creek. Both the river's babble around the ledge and the creek's giggle as it slips over its cataracts can be heard, one at a time at the turn of my head. I was going to have a talk with Mr. River tonight, but he's deep in conversation with this creek, and I don't wish to intrude.

I sing for over an hour, my voice coming back to me from the great wall. Sy catches eleven fish tonight and cleans them for breakfast. The three play poker, Jim and I walk up Warm Spring Creek. Clouds part and moonlight patches the canyon with black and silver, making us look as if we were bathing under an infrared light. <END JOURNAL>

Journal Note: July 19 (Morning, Third day)

The river is red. Nobody has to tell me why. Rain up north last night cut into the Moenkopi and Organ Rock maroons, and they're now bleeding down our way, blotching the surface with little sticks and foam—he rose some eight inches in the night. We poke a stick on the shore at water's edge before we go to bed, then we know: Is he up, or is he down? His conversation with Warm Spring Creek is entirely unlike the one he was having last night—sounds like he's got a hangover, or a cold, with his throat full of mud.

～

Syl says, "I just figured it out."

"What?"

"Why it *looks* like you guys wait for us to find our sleeping spots, then just plop your bedrolls wherever we don't."

"That's right," I explain, "you're the guests, you get to pick your spot first."

"Nya-a-a. I pick a nice cool place, and every morning when that sun slams over the rim, I'm the first one in the Kleigs, while you guys are still in the shade of the old apple tree, or somethin.'"

I nod and smile. "You got it, darlin', but wasn't it nice to discover the big outdoors all by yourself? You can ask me where the sun'll come up when we camp tonight and I'll find you late risers a nice cool bedroom. Okay?"

"Okay, smartass. You do that." <END JOURNAL>

[Know what's queer about this? I don't remember a damn thing about Danny, Sy, or Sylvia *off* the river—what movie or television sets we worked on together; wouldn't even remember Syl's name if it wasn't in my journal—but I remember her on that trip, her attitude and how she fit. It didn't turn her into a wilderness buff, that I know, but she was no wimp, and like the others she had a super sense of humor.]

Journal Note: July 19 (Noon, Third Day)

The Bennett Wheel.

Who was Bennett? And why is this riverside mining operation still here a mile or so below Warm Spring Creek on what's known to us as Olympic or Olympia Bar? Built on a cliff that overhangs fast water, the frame that holds the water wheel still stands, hand-hewn from logs and twice the height of a tall man. As for the wheel and buckets, they're long gone; but lying about are many other implements—an oar cart, sluiceway, flumes, wheels, chunks of iron, bolts and cables and a trestle for the carts to dump the oar into wagons.

How'd they get all this stuff in here over this rock-dune country? Dumb question. Miners can get *anywhere*. There are books, surveys, hundreds of reports, U.S. Geological Survey papers, photographs, and historic journals that give extensive accounts of Glen Canyon and its gold rush, but I don't want to read the stuff—not just yet. I want to walk around, hike up on the cap, check the side canyons, and feel it out for myself. Anyhow, history is just a boiling cauldron of obscure antics mixed with dates and semantics and flavored to taste. <END JOURNAL>

When I did start reading and asking, one source said the Bennett wheel used to be ten miles upstream on Good Hope Bar, and that Mr. Chaffin kind of, ah … sort of moved it down here. Nobody said it was his, but nobody said it wasn't either, and whatever Arth did, I figured he deserved the fruits of his labor. The bugger was forty feet in diameter, lifting water from the river to a flume that carried it to other parts of the gold operation.

When the rush was on, I'll bet there was a miner (or group of miners) with pick, shovel, pan, or dredge on every sand and gravel bar in the Glen. Probably could have formed a human telegraph from Lee's Ferry to Hite by just hollering the news to each other up and down the river.

Cut back ten centuries into the prehistoric, when there was *really* a human population here. They got the news by other means, no doubt. Drums? Flutes? Runners? Their picture rocks don't say.

Only Kokopelli knows … and plays his music stick.

A wanderer through the lives of the Ancient Ones and into ours from the rock art, always an enigma, teasing us. A mythical creature, or real person? A clown? A lover? A vendor from faraway lands to the south with rare gifts in his pack? Or a deformed, magical musician? We called him the Humpback Flute Player. Our guides didn't use the name "Kokopelli" for the many glyphs that illustrated this figure of renowned sexual prowess. They never mentioned that prowess, either. Possibly he used his flute to charm the ladies. In one place he's "pict" delightfully relaxed, flat on his backside, flute raised to his mouth and one leg crossed over the other knee. Maybe this was his "come on" pose. In mythology he's known for his charisma, musical magic, and endurance—not honesty. It's wonderful to me that we will *never* know. We're left with our imaginations.

Wherever I came upon the Flute Player, I stared long, ran my fingers over his form, trying to pull him out of the rock. I wanted to know how he made out, musically. Where were his gigs? How large an audience? What were his tricks? Had he ever played in Music Temple? Somehow I believed so. I've heard his flute on the wind—too much melody for a whistle through some crevice in the rock. Yes, Kokopelli was here.

Journal Note: July 19 (Afternoon, Third Day)

MUD. The river's ultimate and most refined element, his favorite toy; thick, thin, smooth, rubbery, cool, warm, downy, and pure-smelling.

Why do I like mud so much?

Aside from pulling the fire of sunburn out of your skin for many hours after treatment (a painkiller discovered by the Old Ones) and working as a cosmetic and curative, a potter's element, a paint, a building material, a material to be used in games, wars, and who knows what else—there's something else about being all wrapped up in mud, something to do with our mysterious beginnings. Didn't we crawl out of this stuff somewhere along the evolutionary line? Didn't we live in it, belly up to it for a longer time than we've walked on these funny sticks? It gives me the feeling of being a part of the pure Earth, and smelling like it too.

Here and now, mud is about to make Syl and me beautiful. I lead her to the salon. We strip and slather on a hot chocolate sundae, a quarter-inch thick, all over our bodies except the hair on our heads, do each other's backs, and stretch out full length in the sun.

What follows is a sensation not easy to explain. It tickles; it doesn't quite itch. It feels cool in some spots, warm in others, and as it dries, it draws. That's the object of the exercise. It pulls at the pores of our skin like a hundred million little suction cups, all our body poisons being pulled out of us. When I move a muscle it feels as if my silk stocking has sprung a run. I hear a few garbled words from Syl, then a giggle. "Shit! My face just cracked off!"

"I told you not to wiggle, giggle, or move, Syl." But it's too late. She's laughing so hard her belly jumps up and down, and mud cakes flip all over the ground. *I've* done this before, so I know the next sound will be ...

"E-e-yow! You didn't tell me this treatment would remove all my pubic hair!"

Now *my* face cracks off. "Not to worry, Topsy. Go sit in the river."

"How'n hell do I get there? Every move I make pulls out another wad. Some beauty salon ya got here. I want my money back."

"You should be grateful to me. Think of the money you *save*. Elizabeth Arden charges an arm and a leg for her mudpacks, and no scenery mixed in." By now we both look like Frankenstein's monster, bursting out of our plaster, and we can't stop laughing. "God, Syl, you're never satisfied. Look, all your pimples are gone."

"Screw you, Pocahontas. I never had any pimples."

We lie in the eddy and let the river slowly melt what little chocolate remains. Syl dries off, runs her hands over her skin and looks at me wide-eyed.

"Ooooh, wowie, is this ever velvety! You were right, Pokie, it does something neat to your skin—feels like my fingernails after I put polish on, smooth and slick."

It's like her to make that analysis. I say, "How about smooth as the inside of a virgin's thigh?"

"Dunno. Not a whole lot of them where I come from." <END JOURNAL>

Journal Note: July 22 (Sixth Day)

Jim tells the Hollywoodites there's a canyon we call Driftwood that hasn't been explored yet and, with a wink, silences my correction. A storm over the Kaiparowits has erased our footprints from eleven days ago, making him appear honest, which he halfway is, since no one's been able to get past the big jump. He goes downstream, finds a crack, puts his booted toes onto something no deeper than the petals on a rose, ascends the lip, and disappear into the sky. Rocks slither down, sounding like he might be slithering with them. We call; he answers "Okay," then there's utter silence. He's out of hearing and beyond echo.

We wait ...

... and wait.

Danny, really turned on by this canyon, wants desperately to follow him, and so do I—the "syndrome" again. The canyon has Jim by the throat and won't let go. But I'm afraid to take the responsibility of getting Danny up there. To rattle his frustration further, he runs out of film and is ready to make the hike back to the boat when Jim returns. He cools Danny by telling him it's just more of the same and, from where he stopped, another waterfall he couldn't get over. By now I've learned to read Jim pretty well, and his shit-eatin' grin tells me he lies.

I will get into that place soon ... at all costs!

Tonight we treat our guests to a night flight. I pull out the guitar and sing for a two-hour drift to Navajo Bar. The wind is up, the clouds hide-and-seek, the watch (which I still have) ticks to an hour past midnight.
<END JOURNAL>

Journal Note: July 23 (Seventh Day)

The names—the names—the names. Ros told me she was the first one of a Nevills party to discover it. They lunched at its mouth one day, and while the others were napping she took off to investigate. It got a little dicey for her taste, narrower and more profound, so she went back to wake one of the male passengers to come with her. Together they walked about three miles until it ended in a crevasse—an exit for ravens only. They decided to call it "The Devil's Corkscrew," but Norm, who liked doing the naming jobs himself (even "Catacombs" wouldn't do), insisted on "Labyrinth," though there's a repeat in the lower Grand. It isn't a labyrinth. You can't get lost—one way in, one way out—but simple walking is not the mode of locomotion.

~

We slip-slide to the entrance of the trough, where a stench of very dead animal rot pervades. Jim and I take a few tentative steps in; the others balk. Standing there, we describe what they're going to miss.

Me: "It's like this, guys. At the end of this trench we crawl up through a little bitty hole called Fat Man's Misery, after which is a very long 200-foot-deep, shoulder-width, fluted rift that slants so much you need your hands, as well as feet, to negotiate it. Its best to have gloves and jacket, otherwise you exit with sore hands and elbows."

Syl exclaims, "Great! I got no gloves so I can wait for that. I'm so bruised up now, when I get back to the set they're gonna think I've been in a train wreck."

"Shows you've been somewhere, Sylvia, besides sittin' on your duff on a movie set."

"True ... true, Pokie, but will they believe me when I tell 'em where?"

"Don't bother, just tell 'em you fell off your director chair."

Jim muses, "Too bad they have to miss the Devil's Slide, though."

"Yeah, man," declares Sy, "but before we get to all that neat stuff, we have to go through this scumpot. Bet'cha if I threw a hook 'n' line in there I'd pull out half a cow's guts!"

Jimmy tells them, "We're just unlucky this time. I've walked through here when it was all dry, nothing in the bottom but cracked mud."

"Don't forget the little pink Glen Canyon rattlesnake," I remind him.

"Ee-e-ek! That does it!" squawks Syl.

"I pass," says Danny. <END JOURNAL>

~

Two years later, Frank and I explore Labby, hoping to get beyond the "exit for ravens."

Journal Note: *October 12, 1956*

The mephitic odor of dead things in the winding trench beneath Fat Man's Misery is gone, as are the dead things. No wading, only a little mud, and unlike other trips, it is *quiet*, with time to look, feel, study, and observe. I now see this canyon to be so exaggerated in every aspect of rock formation that it borders on kitsch. A vaudeville burlesque. We, the clowns, must perform nearly every kind of rock traverse known to canyoneers—bridging, crawling, sticking, slantwise and athwart—everything but chimneying. (Somewhere in here we cross from Utah into Arizona.) This great oblique rend where we side-step, hand-walking on one wall much of the way, is a mile-long crevice, averaging a foot or two wide, winding like a snake through solid rock with few places to stand upright—no trees, no brush, *nada.* It reminds me of those old horror movies where the villain pushes the button and the walls come together ... slowly ... oooh ... soon the hero will be crushed to death.

Yipes! We're out! The rend parts at a wide sunlit corridor, six hundred feet high, and confronting us, on a straight sheet of pure gold, is The Devil's Slide—a black-as-tar strip of runoff stain from top to sandy floor.

"Well, Bigfeets, Ros got her Devil's name in here after all, but I sure don't see any sign of him, do you?"

"Nope. But it looks like he burnt his tail coming down."

A few yards beyond we come to the raven's exit—a dry watershoot with a hemstitching of Moki steps near the wall. The steps follow an intrusion in the sandstone over several high rises to disappear an aggravating fifty feet above us. Attrition has reduced the upper ones to little more than shadows on the rock, leaving the intrusion sharp as razors— a grisly place to land, should we fall. We can probably get up, but getting *down* ...

The pick.

Cautiously, Frank negotiates the depressions to the first rise, turns and shakes his head. "I don't think so, Katie."

"I don't either; you've got nothing to hang to while you chip."

Backing down slowly, making it look easy, which I know it isn't, he says, "This isn't practical with just the two of us."

"It's maddening," I groan. "Jim's been up there, and Hugh Cutler, Harry Aleson ... "

"They probably had a rope."

"A rope! Why didn't *we* think of that?"

He gives me a Cheshire-cat grin and says, "You see a sky hook to tie it to?" (I don't know why we never thought to take a climbing rope into the canyon. It just wasn't a thing many people did back then.)

Going back, for the first time I carefully examine the many places where faint etchings of Moki steps run up and down the sides in Labby. We figure they were chipped here for a logical reason: to get out in case of flood. From the bottom we can't really see if they go anyplace; we'd have to be above the rift to know if they connect with others. But if they used the canyon for access to the river, to get water, to hunt or fish, even if they traveled much faster then we do, they had to be in the rift at least half an hour before reaching safe ground. My god, a flash flood in there would rise a hundred feet in five minutes! I think about this on the way out when we hear a plane go over. It, too, sounds like a gathering of the waters, and with a sonic boom, more than the devil would slide. Brr-r-r-r! <END JOURNAL>

Journal Note: July 24 (Last Day of 1954 Trip)

More of Sy's fish for breakfast this morning, his last catch. Going on down we see something that looks like petroglyphs in a shallow, arched cave back behind some willows on the right bank, mile 21.8. Petroglyphs and histoglyphs. Many, many names, some indistinguishable. The cave must have had a floor at one time a lot higher than it is now for the names to be scratched and carved here, and there's campfire blackening six feet above our heads. Historic names, for sure! They date way back; the oldest, G. M. Wright (relation of Frank's?), November 18, 1892—and J. C. Tipson, same date—were they together? The names are far apart. One Thompson (probably A. H.), February 28, 1901, who was with Powell on his second (1872) trip (and came back again, just for fun? Sure, why not? We do). R. Monnett, November 1907, of Russell & Monnett's documented trip that left Green River in September of that year in two steel boats. The Kolb Brothers, who did the surveys for the USGS maps, all their dates, 1911–1921, 1923, 1928. One of the many Bert Loper inscriptions, this one 2-2-08, and a charcoaled longhorn cow's head that looks to be fading away. All that and much more.

Sylvia taps me on the shoulder. "Pokie, why're you writing all this down?"

"'Cause I can't photograph it; too dark in here."

"But why?" she insists. "You said you liked this canyon for it's *mystery,* and all the things you had to guess about."

"Well, dearie, these inscriptions don't throw much light on the mysteries … "

Jimmy adds, "No, they just sorta validate a lot of information that's found in journals and books about the miners and other folks who ran the canyon." Danny asks, "Then are these guys important to the history of the river?"

"Yeah," I tell him, "most of them … except these two assholes down here." I point to some gaudy, chipped-in names dated only last year and ask Jim if we can obliterate them.

"Lets! There's a weatherproof cairn with a notebook right here, and plenty of other such ledgers all through the Glen for anyone who cares to be noted. No need to decorate the walls."

"This place got a name?" Sy asks Jim.

"Some people call it Loper's Cave to sort of distinguish it from Outlaw (Galloway) Cave, downstream a ways."

About four miles above Lee's Ferry, it begins to rain and my movie friends kinda glum up. Suddenly Jimmy starts singing, jumps up on the stern of the boat, and before long gets everybody laughing and dancing on the decks, acting like they don't want the rain to stop. Then we get a theatrical performance, with sound effects, that brings the curtain down to thunderous applause! Colors deepen under the rain. High, sheer walls seem to *suck* color into their flesh … Then, from their tops pour a hundred silver veils from rim to river … a thousand-foot drop! The walls glisten under a late western sun, turning the veils to fluttering pink tinsel. Thunder rolls … booms … crashes against the cliffs, sounding and resounding up and down canyon. Water falling from so high makes its own kind of thunder. The river turns a dark red … scummy … swirling … mean-looking. Everyone's in high spirits as we nose into Lee's Ferry and the rain stops.

Syl, Danny, and Sy have had the vacation of their lives. They've never known anyone like Jim before—unflappable, funny and ingenious, he turns every sticky moment into a laugh or a song. When a guide has that special knack, it's worth all the gold in Glen.

Good-bye, Muddy River, until next year. <END JOURNAL>

SIX

Induction by Fire

Back to the salt mines!

My desert cooling system was a complete drenching under Art Green's hose, a cool seat under me and a wet towel over my head. A repetition of this act at various service stations along the way would get me to Tierra Linda, my mom's ranch home on the outskirts of Tucson, where I'd spend a couple of weeks before returning to Hollywood.

Mid-July. Northern Arizona. Driving with windows open beside the streaked and bubbling red lead of the Echo Cliffs.

Hotter'n'hell.

Navajo,
    Kayenta,
        Wingate,
            Chinle,
                Shinarump,
                    Moenkopi,
                        Organ Rock Tongue,
                            Cedar Mesa ...

... and sometimes on top of all that, farther north ...
    Entrada,
        Carmel,
            White Navajo ... I knew them all now.

Belched from the earth, the top five of those formations tilted northward; between them and the highway, a few hogans and some patches of Navajo corn scalloped a dry wash. I was having a problem keeping my eyes off the rock and concentrating on the white line.

Coming out of wilderness is like coming off a drug. A heady feeling of still being there keeps returning, making reentry into the mundane world slow and troublesome. I only half-hear what people say. My answers are vague. Looking at people, I see a river flowing over their faces;

across a page of script, a sandstone cliff looms; down the asphalt, a narrow fluted canyon twists; in traffic I hear a rapid's roar, forget what I'm supposed to be doing. I haven't come down yet. My wilderness high would last for weeks, and even after it began to fade, in quiet moments I could call it up and make it last long enough to regenerate my spirit. When I could no longer do that, I used the memory as a bromide to put me to sleep. After that, Frank's letters, and those of River Rat friends, always helped me through.

Whatever rain we'd had in the canyon hadn't managed to dribble down into the lower Sonoran desert, and when I turned into Tierra Linda, the old saguaro, with twisted arms that in spring held out bouquets of waxy white flowers, now held wads of dried and ravished seedpods. The clean, open desert, where I'd spent most of my years, shimmered in a heat of dolor.

In many ways I was reluctant to return. I felt I'd grown up to outgrow the ingrown Republican politics in that house, which had led to a kind of cul-de-sac in my relationship with my mother. Just off the river with a fistful of new decisions, my world felt like a pinwheel spinning out of control—too many changes, too fast. I was heading for a whole new place, unfamiliar, even scary. Tinseltown had given me pretty much what I'd sought, but in the process had pointed to paths undreamed. I'd made the transition—from stage actress to movie-radio-television actress—and ultimately to singer-actress—pretty well, I thought, before the realization bloomed that I'd also waded the waters from singer to *folk* singer, opening a potential I *didn't* grasp, or even attempt to explore at the time.

To be politically naive is one thing. To be plain dumb is another.

~

Back up a couple of years: By 1950 nearly all the folkies were my friends, and I had invited most of them to sing at our Cabaret Concert Theatre—Woody Guthrie, Burl Ives, Josh White, Cisco Houston (whom I dated for a while), Terry Gilkyson & the Easy Riders, Freddie Hellerman, Ronnie Gilbert and Pete Seeger of the Weavers, Dave Zeitlin, Peter LaFarge, Ramblin' Jack Elliott, and a host of others now long forgotten. The hoots, usually at someone's home, were where I learned all the different strokes from different folks on my guitar, the place where we traded styles, beats, lyrics, and sundry versions of songs. To me it was like going to an easy-learning school. Most of them had been at it way longer than I. I had much to learn.

To my surprise, they were also people who Senator Joseph McCarthy had his fanatical eye and ear trained upon, along with Hollywood writers, actors, and directors.

I didn't read the newspaper (except for the want ads and reviews) and rarely listened to the radio, but by mere osmosis I should have sniffed the stinky wind of the House Unamerican Activities Committee. Neither Burl nor Josh had said a word about it to me, so when I discovered that both of them had been called up, before I'd ever met them, I began to get inquisitive. Like what in Christ's sweet holy name was *un-American* about them? Hell, Woody even wrote songs for them about their damn dams! When Cisco finally laid it out to me, I got really pissed. This was not the way I learned it in school. Now, quite plainly and for the first time in my life, I smelled evil in the seat of what I'd always thought was an honest "do-gooder" government.

Inside grew a tiny bud of fear.

If my singing friends were being sought out, what about me? In Arizona's big outdoors, where I never even heard the word "politics." I *had* listened to the radio. Not the news, but serials. "G-Men," the detectives, our protectors. The FBI.

Here comes the dumb part.

I did an ass-about on the old theatrical chestnut, "don't call us, we'll call you":

Listen, I said, I'm from Arizona. I make my living here as a part-time secretary for Mary Pickford Productions, a part-time picture actress, a part-time folksinger and radio actress. I don't know beans about politics, and I could care less. All I want to do is sing my songs. Because there seems to be some stigma against folksingers, and because we are becoming more popular, I just want your office to know I most certainly am not involved in anything un-American. You can check my background any time.

I gave them my address and phone number and figured that was the end of it. At least they knew where *I* stood.

Did they ever!

Sometime later—it could have been weeks or months; I'd forgotten all about it—I get this phone call:

"Miss Lee, this is so-'n'-so from the Federal Bureau of Investigation. You remember talking to me a while ago?"

I was set back a notch, but said, "I do."

"I understand there's to be a party, I believe you call them hoot ... hootin ... "

"Hootenannies."

"Yes ... in Topanga Canyon this weekend at Mr. Dehr's, Rich Dehr's home. Are you planning to go to that, uh ... gathering?"

The hair started rising on the back of my neck and arms. Was the FBI going to tell me I couldn't go to a hoot without being suspect, couldn't sing with them anymore? I was close to tears when I stammered, "Wh ... why? Why d'you want to know if I'm going? I took special care to tell you that I'm not involved *at all* in whatever their politics are. Are you going to tell me not go to hootenannies? I don't sing political or protest songs ... I ... told you ... "

"No. Oh, no, Miss Lee, not at all. Of course you can go. In fact, we hoped you were. We just want you to tell us who's there."

There was a long pause before it hit. Under my breath I whispered "ohmygod!" and sank down on the floor asking myself, "What have you done? You stupid, stupid, *stooo-pid* woman!"

Mr. So-'n'-so asked again, "Will you be going, Miss Lee?"

After taking a minute to collect myself and keep my voice from shaking, I answered, "Yes, I *will* be going to that hoot. But *I am not an informer,* and I will not be telling you who is there. I did not phone your office to offer my services as a spy; I called to tell you that I'm apolitical. You have your lists and probably know better than I who will be where and when—but you won't be getting information from *me.* Please don't call me again. I'm sorry I ever contacted you. *Good bye!*"

I told Woody about what had happened. He gave me a typical Woodyism with that dip-in-the-top-lip smile, cheeks rising over a grin, his dark eyes sparkling: "You tell the Fellatio Bru-ho of Instigation to go to hell. Sing your songs to the people, Kaylee, and heal their hurts by telling them how it looks to you."

I told Cisco, who shook his head and groaned. "You dumb shit, why would you do something like that?"

"Because I ain't too smart, that's why, but I'm learning."

Burl said, "Look out for those people; they're devious."

Joshua felt the calluses on his fingers and frowned. "Goin' before that committee damn near ruined my whole career, to say nothing about my life."

[I did not hear from them again, but *my* file probably started then and there. By now it would contain several protest songs—heh-heh—many appearances at rallies and marches against nuke tests, mines, dams, air pollution, gravel companies, uranium dumps, wilderness depletion, tire burners, chaining, logging, paving, fencing ... Hellsfire, you name it. Now the *whole earth* needs our help, not just my poor old rivers.]

~

As I drove up to the house, I thought—a different person enters here— how do I explain myself? I don't. I just act like the old me, and nobody will notice, right? That river (with a dam I couldn't, *wouldn't* envision) was on my mind. All the way from Art's I'd been mulling over how to complete the letter I'd started to draft on the Wright's lawn a couple weeks ago—the one to our senator, Barry Goldwater. A letter that would be my induction-by-fire to politics and persuasion, at age 34.

But I wasn't the only politically naive fighter for Glen Canyon. So many of us underestimated the power of the Reclamation Bureau, the tricky payoffs and playoffs of our representatives, the deals that go down and the boondoggles that float to the surface as a result; so naive as to think a LAW was THE law, that the manipulators couldn't just up and change it if they didn't like what it said or what it protected. I'd yet to understand one doesn't write four-page, single-spaced, epochal, passionate pleas to senators and expect them to be read ... yet Barry read it.

The pith of it stated that I figured Barry, as a photographer, knew and loved the country he photographed; that the majesty of Glen Canyon did not deserve a watery grave; that I'd spoken to our Governor Pyle, who didn't seem to know much about the proposed dam; that I was bewildered over his support, even as a politician, because he lived here, knew the canyon and had run the Grand ... a law protected Rainbow Bridge National Monument.

Glen Canyon is already a recreation area, where people can go to see a little of God, regain their perspective on life ... it is eye-searing beauty to be forever carried inside and be called upon in moments when there's no relief from the drab, common plots man has made for himself. [My, how I did ramble on! And this is only bits and pieces, but I've just come off the river, remember, and I *know* what I'm talking about!]

Why is it that the very last vestige of natural beauty must be tampered with? Because the great conceit in some men must be identified with a thing they can barely understand any more, nature herself, so they seek to improve upon something that cannot be improved upon ... now or ever ... and one day we will all come to know this.

Now in the face of politics and your prestige as a dam builder, I suspect this moves you not ... A further redundancy would seem to include the government which now seeks the power of the atom along the banks of the Colorado; [This part was for Arth Chaffin.] *literally hundreds of uranium mines will be covered over if the dam goes through. Hydroelectric power, in a few more years will be senseless in the face of atomic power, which can produce the same results at less cost for a longer time and more efficiently than a huge dammed area ever will.* [Ouch!]

[About here is where I started to piss him off, not just bore him.] *I was surprised to learn that you had made an attempt to purchase property at the proposed water level of the new Glen Dam on the left side of the river. If this is not true, I stand corrected. If it is, I can only muse that perhaps you need to get away from Washington and go on another river trip to recapture your sense of values and to remind yourself that you are Barry Goldwater, Citizen of Phoenix, extra fine photographer, golfer and preserver of the natural beauties of your state as well as the industry; not Senator Goldwater, politico. ... I expect to get a very polite letter from you, but I don't expect it to contain any sentiment, that is probably gone from you now. I wish only that you could come with me and stand in Music Temple or Hidden Passage again, and listen to the river whisper of the still living legends of strength that made America and Americans. Don't let them drown it ... please don't let them drown it all!'* [Copies went to the House and Senator Thomas Kuchel].

Within five days I had a page-and-a-half answer in which Barry Goldwater explained that his desire to retain the area in its present condition was outweighed by the hard, cold fact that Arizona would need power and water for its future use; that a lake that would afford transportation to more people to view the upper side canyons (wall-to-wall water inundated well over half of them!), that the Glen Canyon Dam was being constructed for power and silt control; and that he had never attempted to purchase property at or near the dam site:

For years I have operated Rainbow Lodge on a year-to-year permit from the Navajo Tribe ... so it won't affect me, one way or another, except to take away any chances we ever had of making a go of transporting people to Rainbow Bridge by mule ... In closing you mention one possibility that I firmly believe has a good chance of becoming a reality, and that is the development of atomic generating plants to the point that we might never have to build dams in this country again for hydroelectric power.

What irony! The one place we agreed, we *both* were wrong. What I should have done was send him the lyrics to "Muddy River." But what the hell, that wouldn't have helped either.

~

I stayed at the ranch only a couple weeks, that late July of 1954, because along with my other problems, I was stony broke ... again. I needed a bundle of jobs to catch up, to pay for my fabulous fling in the wilds. It was a month before the old momentum kicked back in. I knew why.

I still had Glen Canyon and the river in my eyes.

I was slacking off, not pushing hard enough or concentrating, *willing* those in the seats of power to hire me. (Producers, casting directors, agents, all have this uncanny knack of forgetting your very name if you don't fit your face to it and show up on their thresholds every few days.) Then, there was all this push-and-tug going on in my mind about my career. Muddy waters. In my dreams the clear blue streams I was swimming in would turn shallow and murky as I walked *upstream* against the flow.

~

I did my acting, my radio spots, and sang my songs. Scots-Irish-English ballads, early American, songs from the Appalachians, the Tennessee hills, songs of love and hate and incest, outlaws and murder, with characters who rose from the dim mists of legend and fantasy ... far, far in the past. Songs about labor, poverty, politics, and injustice rolled off me like water off a duck. *Wait a minute!*

Politics ... injustice ...

My river was about to be unjustly dammed ... politically damned. Songs about my river! Songs of *protest! Folk* songs! Holy Mother! There it was! It hit me like Lava Falls at 100,000 cfs!

I had a cause! A cause that didn't center on me-me-me; one that asked nothing of me, really, yet was far from mute. I'd never had a *cause* before, but now there was a *place*, almost a person, that needed my help—a very valuable place that couldn't speak for itself. I could be a voice for it.

I knew what I had to do—get out of Tinseltown, take me and my songs afield, across the land, anywhere and everywhere.

The dream waters cleared, and all the tugs turned to shoves.

Burl, as he'd promised, went through my repertoire with me and picked the best for clubs; called his agent in Chicago and had his public relations gal arrange a press party, where I'd be interviewed by all of Chicago's important columnists. That was just for starters.

All I had to do was get there.

I'd had the great good luck to meet, talk to, and get to know Carl Sandburg during these last few months. He especially liked a historic poem I'd cut and set to music, called "Lasca." This greatest of American poets said it needed to be *sung* now, because no one listened to poetic recitation any more; that he would certainly see me in Chicago, and we'd have lunch together at his old writers' hangout, the Dill Pickle Club.

Josh White told me of a wonderful radio show, hosted by a guy named Studs Terkel, that we could be on *together*, when he got to there for his gig at the Black Orchid in late November.

My aunt wrote from Chicago, saying I could stay with her until I wanted or needed an apartment of my own. I set the date to leave: end of September, before the rent was due.

When I crossed my river way down by Yuma, Arizona, he sure looked sad. I said, "Pore Colly Raddy, yer just lookin' for a sea ... wonder if yer mama ever told ya what sea it oughta be."

Heh-heh ... Turned out to be my first *protest song*.

~

Pore Colly Raddy
High upon a snowy crag was born a ripplin' baby.
"Will I be big and strong one day?" And his Mother Earth said,
"Maybe."
There is a way down to the sea, my son, if you are clever,
You'll go ahead and make your bed, to lie in it forever.

So the Colorado baby went along his lonesome way
He huffed and he puffed and soon enuf, he heard a loud voice say,
"Hey! Where d'ya think yer goin'? You'd best keep offa my toes,
I'm Gunnison, the Son-of-a-gun, and what I say here goes!"

Chorus:
Pore Colly Raddy, just lookin' for a sea
His mama never told him what sea it oughta be
Now this may take a little time, but I'll betcha if I tried,
I could dig a well right through hell
And come out on the other side, Oh Glory! What a ride!

Colly Raddy bounced the Gunnison just like he was a feather.
"Hey, easy lad, don't get so mad, we're in this thing together!"

With noble savoir faire he picked up Miss Dolores;
He next was seen takin' Miss Green and heading for the forest.

He took 'em through a canyon where he'd built some cataracts,
They split their girdles on these hurdles, pret' near broke their backs.
Then he cut a canyon one mile deep, and made his grandstand play:
From a lava dyke he took a bite and spit the rest away.

Chorus:
From there on it was easy and to the sea he ran
When he arrived no one denied that river was a MAN.
So now you think my story has surely got to end;
But humans came to stake their claim and call that river, "friend."

They checked his endless labor with a big cement creation
And he said, "Well, now what the hell, I can't fight Reclamation.
I'll just sit here and chew away at this concrete foundation
And one year soon, in the month of June—
they'll have *free irrigation!*"

Chorus:

SEVEN

The Pagan

Entrenched Meander

October 5, 1954—Denver
  October 8—Chicago
    November 29—St. Louis
      December 18—Tucson
        December 20—St. Louis
          December 28—Chicago

February 3, 1955—Hollywood
  February 6—Chicago
    March 4—Duluth, Minnesota
      April 21—Chicago
        May 8—St. Louis
          May 21—Chicago
            May 24—Denver
              May 27—Art's Cliff Dwellers
                May 28–31—Blanding, Utah
                  June 1–7—San Juan River

Ten working months between river trips put my head in a wholly different place and took me all over the map!

~

Bits of a letter from Frank, October 27, 1954:

You have made some quick moves, haven't you gal? Tucson didn't hold
you very long and L.A. didn't do much better. Ros told me of your move
to Chicago ... I can hardly keep from laughing when I think of the
weather change you got yourself into! [snow] ... Regardless of
regular or special trips, I wish I could promise the Grand, but at this

*point there are more who have asked than there'll be room for. But you
are officially invited on the San Juan, the Glen, or both ... I hope for
one with fewer people, where we will have a chance to talk and see what
all this river travel has done for you. Is it the river or the people who
have been on it? ... Anyway, how was the opening at the Stream Liner
last night? I know they loved you and that you were frightened ...*

Frightened! More like scared shitless!

In Chicago's oldest, hippest *jazz* club, with jazz combo and two superb jazz singers (Carmen MacRae and Lucy Reed), this little guitar-
playin' folksinger opened her first eastern gig ever, got up on the stand
all by herself in a big full skirt, sang "John Henry," that great black folk
fable about the indestructible steel-drivin' man, hoping nobody would
walk out ... and he knows they loved me!

I think they were in shock.

At first I thought Burl's agent (now mine) was off his rocker, but that
club date lasted a month. Every few days there'd be a write-up by one of
the columnists, or a favorable review about the "new folksinger in town."
Burl had told me, "If they like you, you'll get the best press in the country. It's a great newspaper town, so be nice, *Sergeant,* and sing sweetly." Yes,
daddy-o! His press party had paid off a hundred-fold, and I was off and
running; running not away, but with it, not scared anymore.

~

As for what all that river travel had done for me, I knew for certain it
was *not* the people. If asked, I could pour out a torrent of words about
its effect on me in the same way a person talks about a new infatuation
or a love affair. But in truth, I couldn't fathom the mystery or the power
in the potion I'd taken. In that place where no bombardment of unwanted stimuli could enter my sight lines, it was possible to savor the
overview. "The overview," said Isak Dinesen, "is the one thing of vital
importance to achieve in life." I'd gone there, gained some perspective
(the overview was yet to come), and when the water in this peculiar double life of mine muddied up, I could go back and gain some more. That's
one thing the river had done for me.

Another, it had helped me leave a lot of the phony me back in Tinseltown—the motion picture me, the I-know-what-you-want-so-I'll-be-it
me. I returned to my roots, to songs of the West, to cowboy and Mexican and border songs that you couldn't have paid me to sing in

movieland—they were pure corn; none of that floppy fringe for me! I hadn't even considered them folksongs.

But a subtle change was underway. I sang now of things I knew about, and I began researching all my songs back to their beginnings, so they would ring with authenticity. I plowed through the libraries of every town I played in and bent the ears of my peers for anything they might add. Josh White was teaching me the blues. Harry Belafonte and his guitarist were doing their best to show me how to sing and play calypso. (I'd met them that November of '54 in St. Louis, where we became friends. When we worked the same town together, I traded songs for techniques.)

But I leaned on the river for songs that eddied in my soul.

For Frank, I wrote newspaper articles about Mexican Hat Expeditions, talked about the river and the canyon whenever I was interviewed; showed slides, sang river songs wherever possible, certain that if more folks saw the beauty of that place and understood what would be lost to everyone, there'd be no way the Wreck-the-nation Bureau could build their damn dam. *The people would not let them.* I was blindly unaware, of course, that I was pooping in my own parlor, introducing a multitude of strangers to my wonderland, where I didn't really want them at all.

The ecological Catch-22: Saving a wilderness takes enough people to ultimately ruin it.

~

Along the artistic way—the showbiz path—I had learned some basic principles of "getting there." I don't recall who voiced them, but they sank in like mantra, and because I was lucky in my time and place, I was able to put them to use. I'd hate like hell to be a young performer trying to use this advice on the ladder up today.

Never go to some underling in second or third place down the line. Go to the Top Banana. They have the advice and the help you need. So it had been with Burl Ives. With Josh White, instinct told me just to go knock on his dressing room door; it was that simple. Fortune smiling, I met Carl Sandburg at an after-concert party. Writers of *The Great Gildersleeve Show* passed me on to Gordie MacRae and *The Railroad Hour*, where I joined him and other famous folks for his Summer Series. Carmen Dragon and Leo Reisman, composers/orchestra leaders for many NBC shows, touted me to Ronald Coleman's *Halls of Ivy*, *The Roy Rogers Show*, and the longest-running serial on radio, *One Man's Family*. It becomes a chain-link situation, like most things in life—the names a kind of strata from the world of make-believe.

Still, I'm certain all of the above could not, and would not, have happened to me if I hadn't been blessed with the bedrock that my parents laid for me.

In the years before the Depression I got piano lessons. Hated them. Didn't want to *read* music. If I *heard* it, I could play it—find it on the keys quicker than that old *do-re-mi, e-g-b-d-f* junk. Boring! So I learned to play by ear. My mom nurtured the artistic side and taught me the basic principals of singing. She had wanted to be a singer herself. That failing, she watched it happen in me. Even before the Depression eased off in the mid-thirties, they somehow managed to give me private dancing and dramatic lessons. Ballet made me dizzy as a coot, but the dramatic lessons turned the tide of my whole life. Finding that talent made me sure of what I wanted to be, what I *would* be. An actress first ... later a singer. My daddy, little kid to the very last, kept me outdoors, cherished the tomboy in me, taught me to shoot, hunt, climb, swim, hammer nails and saw wood, made certain that both feet were on the ground, physically in contact with the honest world of nature. Cowboys l'arned me how to ride a horse, but they never l'arned me to trust one, and to this day I don't, nor do I like them much. I'd rather just sing about them and watch somebody else get throwed.

And Arizona? Arizona taught me to *love* running water, because there war'nt hardly none of it in our riverbeds, except when there was too much, and real quick!

~

It's the night at Cliff Dweller's Lodge with Art and Ethel Green, a few days before the 1955 San Juan trip that Frank promised me the previous year. After we ate dinner Art launches into this tale:

"So they watch the old prospector walk down the San Juan beneath the bridge leading a couple of burros with his usual sad, beat-up old gear..."

"Wait a minute, Art. *Walk?* How? On water? There's no trail down there."

"Who sez there ain't? There is ... fer a mile or so ... left bank. But he walked down the *middle* of the river."

I wait. He lights a cigarette.

"Walks right down the middle 'cause the old San Juan has gone completely flatass dry!" He tips his cowboy straw back off his brow and grins—four front teeth missing, his fangs tobacco stained.

"Really? How far back was this?"

"Hell, I dunno. Prob'ly a summer in the early 1900s when they was all gold-fevered down there. Frank Barrett, old placer miner up to White Canyon, told me this. It's true, y'know."

"Sure, Art. Go on."

"So, the old man's downriver coupla weeks. When he comes back he passes right through Mexican Hat without stoppin'. Month later he shows up with all *new* gear, new panniers, two *mules* instead of burros, sashays through *under* the bridge and disappears again."

"River still dry?" I ask, dryly.

"Yup."

"Nobody follows him, huh?"

"Hell, I dunno. I wasn't there. Guess if they did nobody found 'em. But they was suspicious; you know how prospectors is. Next time he come up just ahead of a *big* storm, which is about to make heavy water in that streambed. Besides, he's dry as a popcorn fart, needs a drink of whiskey, and stops in Mexican Hat this time. They get out of him that the river, in places only he knows about, has neatly sluiced out gold dust and nuggets just like it piles up sand. His claims is staked, and nobody else can do nothin' nohow because the storm *does* come and river *does* rise."

"Runs a-bankers again, just like now?"

"Yeah ... a'course." He puffs a billow of smoke toward the ceiling.

"So," I add, "he comes back next summer to haul out more gold, but the river ain't dry. He waits another year, and another, and after eight, nine, ten years (depends on who's tellin') he goes looney, jumps off the Goodridge Bridge and drowns."

"Aw-w-w-w ... you should'a ... "

"And the very next year the old San Juan goes dry once again. Did I get it right, Art?"

"Why'nt ya tell me ya heard it b'fore? An' who told ya?"

"I don't remember now—maybe Jim, maybe Woody. I think Norm used to tell it to his passengers. I'm always hoping to hear a new slant, or the actual name of the Old Prospector. Until then, Art ... "

"Well, Frank Barrett knows who the guy was. Ask him when you git up t' White Canyon. But it's true what happened."

"Well, if it's not, I know how we can find out for sure—wait 'til the next time the San Juan goes dry."

Ghosts of the Old San Juan

There's a legend they tell of treasures galore
  Along the Old San Juan
Where there's long lost plunder in deep hidden store
  Along the old San Juan
    Well, them that searched have come and gone
    There ain't nothin' left but the old San Juan
    And the ghosts of a wild old river.

Oh, the Spanish came, all lookin' for gold
  Along the Old San Juan
Seven shinin' cities, so the tale is told,
  Along the Old San Juan
    Now the plundering Spanish have come and gone
    Ain't nothin' left but the old San Juan
    And the ghosts of a wild old river.

Then the Piutes came, all lookin' for spoil
  Along the old San Juan
Where the waters burn and the whirlpools boil
  Along the old San Juan
    But the warring Piutes have come and gone
    Ain't nothin' left but the old San Juan
    And the ghosts of a wild old river.

So the prospectors came, all lookin' for ore
  Along the old San Juan
But died 'fore they got what they's diggin' for
  Along the old San Juan
    Oh, the prospectors now have come and gone
    Ain't nothin' left but the old San Juan
    And the ghosts of a wild old river.

Then the dam builders came, a'diggin' a grave
  For the swirlin' old San Juan
They stilled the waters and filled the caves
  Of the glorious old San Juan
    And the river met with the dam head on
    Now there ain't nothin' left of the old San Juan
    But the angry old ghosts of the river.

So, stranger remember when you pass this way
   Where flowed the old San Juan
That the gold lies deep and the devil's to pay
   For damming the old San Juan
      For dam builders come but soon they'll be gone
      To join the ghosts of the old San Juan
      The angry old ghosts of the river.

Journal Note: June 1, 1955 (San Juan—4,200 cfs; high!)

Boatmen:
Piute—Frank Wright
Nokai—Willard (Frank's son)
Moonlight—Duane Bishop
Wahweap—Big John Harper
Four San Juan boats—14 passengers (sadly, not the "fewer people" run). I'd go down this river with Frankenstein and King Kong if it was the only way, but Reet and Becky, two yearly Rats, are on board the *Piute* with us, and that's good. Wind is blowing a good fifty, it's cold, but I don't care. It's a *real* wind that carries my personal river smell, not an icy-toothed, too-many-people smell off Lake Michigan's black water! Sally Bailey, with her long green-and-gold velvet Navajo skirts and shirt, is most likely the only warm one as we leave her under the bridge at Mexican Hat. Sand waves are like ocean breakers, foam blowing off the tops. We nearly tip over in a couple, scrape bottom in the troughs more than once. Wild, wild San Juan; I don't recognize you from last year. Lunch at Honaker Trail. Lunch? Seventeen miles from Mexican Hat! Camp is a mile above Slickhorn Gulch—thirty-eight miles in one day, when it's usually fifteen to twenty. But it fits my mood 'cause I haven't slowed down either—not yet.

Tonight the river songs are where they belong, echoing down the fading light—no spots, no smoke, no babble but the river's, and no applause. I ask them not to applaud because it seems so inappropriate here where the real performers stand like mime statues in their great theater-in-the-round. Frank goes around camp before dinner to see if everyone is happily sacked out. I ask him, "Gee, Frank, you have to baby-sit them too?" I figured he did enough just getting them down the river.

"You'd be surprised at some of the strange things city folks do out here. Norm and I took a couple of *bi-i-ig* fellas down the river once—250 and 290 pounds. After about three nights, we suspected they weren't getting much sleep. They didn't complain, but something wasn't quite right. When we finally checked their setup, we couldn't keep from laughing. Those two huge fellas had blown up their air mattresses, put them inside their bedrolls, zipped them up, then tried to squeeze in! So, I like to make sure folks are comfortable when they go to bed." He chuckled and continued his rounds.

Rather quickly I get a new picture of the life and times of a river guide, and it ain't all that grand. <END JOURNAL>

Journal Note: June 2 (5,200 cfs)

There's some disturbance in the atmosphere. Wee spatters of rain, cotton-ball cumulus float over the rims, dress up the river and canyon like a photographer's dream and disappear to make water elsewhere. Not a soul in Slickhorn's big pool. Do handstand dive off the high rock ... cold! Clean and clear, can see the bottom, deep and mysterious down with the elfinks—deeper I go, colder it gets! ... <END JOURNAL>

Journal Note: June 3 (5,500 cfs)

There are rapids—*rapids*—in Piute Farms; no more improbable, I suppose, than Art's story of the dry time. (Piute Farms began at Clay Hills crossing, where all San Juan river trips *end* now—about mile 57—and covered five miles downstream to mile 52). Piute Rapid, a half-mile long, is roaring! All passengers out. At Redbud, I'm filling my canteen at the falls when a canyon wren lights on my head and gives me the whole verse, bridge, and chorus, with a coda. Gawdamighty! How many people know what it's like to have a canyon wren (or any wild bird) *light on their head and sing an aria for them?* What serendipity! <END JOURNAL>

Journal Note: June 4

Nearing the confluence I slide off the deck to do my dance again with the Colorado, but Frank asks me to get aboard. He says the whirls and boils are already strong against the blades and I'll be far from the boat before either of us can make a move. Wish I could see us from above— four little white tops spinning to the touch of the big river's current as if some kid had wound a string around them and thrown them down on the water.

Music Temple. Ahhhh ... <END JOURNAL>

If anyone should ask me
   where I wish to sing;
I know a place where whispers rush
   to join a bird on wing.
Where silence is cacophonous,
   where even thoughts are heard
And all words come together
   To form the only word.
Beneath this wind-sucked arch-dome,
   Time-hollowed out of stone—
I have sung in solitude,
   yet never sung alone.
My notes rose up in harmony
   to join the Shaman's flutes
That played the night for ancient rites
   And chanting multitudes.

Journal Note: June 4 (Afternoon)

We *row* into Mystery (mile 73.6) for lunch, hike to its "stopper"—an impassable fall and deep, aqua pool—return to the boats, and go down to Twilight Canyon (mile 70.8) for the afternoon. *Big* ruin, many petros and pictos, and a floor of big baked spuds. Real ankle-breakers, hell to hike. Very narrow, average fifteen feet, stingy with sand, generous with pebbles and rocks; looks like an insane wiggle-worm on the maps. No running water in here; most unusual, because obviously when it comes down it's akin to a horizontal geyser—a beautiful lesson about how these side streams are made. At bed level in the bends are deep caves, some thirty feet floor to ceiling, that look like they'd been bitten out of the wall. Storm water comes down here at one helluva rate, rolling and smashing boulders into the walls so hard, apparently, they've no time to take on a smooth surface. Someone aptly named it Boulder Canyon, but Norm, who's said to have walked five miles up, claimed it was always Twilight in here. [That more picturesque name stuck until it became Navajo Valley on the new quads—who knows why? There are many Navajo something-or-others along the corridor; this one is not even on the Reservation side of the river]. We gather driftwood from the beaches and benches, stack it on bow and stern for our campfire at Forbidding; the one place in all the Glen where there isn't any wood. <END JOURNAL>

Two things became evident on that trip. First, I wanted more solitude—more of the quiet healing the Glen made possible when first I came two years ago; discovery-of-self time, therapy if you will. For instance, mule skinner lingo had nothing on me. I could out-four-letter-word the best of them; a lifetime of showbiz and cowboys can do that. The Glen was where I detoxified my tongue and dumped the trained behavior patterns relevant to my job so I could let nature back in. That requires solitude. Hm-m-m-m ... some of Frank's less guarded remarks added up. *A trip with fewer people ... boatmen have very little time to themselves ... responsibility and the untangling of personalities sometimes overshadow the beauty of the canyon and the time to enjoy it.* Yeah ... fewer people ... the fewer the better. By then I understood the value of the gifts I'd been given and knew how close I'd come to the *real* Eden in those intimate side canyons.

Second, canyonitus was setting in. I couldn't abide those who took the place casually. I was even taking canyonitus a step further. I wanted to belong to the Glen, rather than feel it belonged to me; wanted it to breathe me in, suck me through its sandstone pores, let me course through its veins, be part of the canyon's circulatory system, so to speak.

Ongoing ... never ending ...

My parents never made me feel shame about my naked body. They were not nudists in any sense of the word, but neither did they make something rare, unusual, or unhealthy of my brother, me, or them in the nude. Up through my teens, we lived mostly in the desert, where we could go about uncovered during the heat of the summer without offending anyone or creating a spectacle. I spent my free time in the canyons of the Catalina Mountains, outside Tucson, in private nooks far from hiking trails and the eyes of the curious, where I swam free, bare, naked, *tout ensemble*, buckass, nude, birthday-suited, in the altogether. There I learned that if I cared to feel nature's pulse, be heir to her gracious gifts, I had to go unencumbered to her living streams and rivers. When propriety forced me to be clothed in those waters, I actually felt *un*natural, or *shamed*—as they say Eve felt when Whatsizname pointed to her pudenda, making the poor thing self-conscious, along with her boyfriend. As for me, I didn't always grab for the leaf when a boyfriend (mine or someone else's) entered those waters.

Because of this holistic attitude, I've been a magnet for many names, from obscure as well as familiar sources. They'll say I'm a nudist, a show-off, or an exhibitionist; I'm immodest, a heathen, a pagan (I like that one), indecent, risqué, and a host of others.

All of the above are in the eyes of the beholders and have nothing to do with me. Except pagan—that's true.

Journal Note: June 4 (Evening)

The traffic has begun! Forbidden is a hornet's nest ... five blubber rafts fulla Boy Sprouts. I don't sing tonight; everyone's bushed. We hike to Rainbow tomorrow. I look for my special place way up Forbidden Bar, find it, tell Frank, and after dinner he comes to sit on the edge of my tarp, his big feet stretched out on the slickrock in hightop, laced boots that (wet or dry) never come off until bedtime, and we finally have a chance to talk.

"How're ya doing, gal?"

"I'm *here*, and you ask me that?"

"I could tell it was taking a bit more time for you to unwind," he says. "Just making sure you're all right."

"Godamighty, I'm the *last* person you have to worry about. I'm in *paradise!* I swear, Frank, I don't see how you keep all these people happy. Every minute of the day you're stoically answering everyone's questions, like you'd never heard them before. You amaze me."

"Hmmph ... You get up and sing the same song over and over to hundreds of people and make it sound like you'd never sung it before, and I don't see how you do it."

"I'm faking it."

"Oh-ho no, you're not."

Hesitantly, I come out with, "Haven't I heard you, kind of off-hand, mention a *small* Glen trip, Frank? Like, three or four souls. I could sure go for that. Souls that don't make waves, who want to explore, take it easy, photograph—Tad, for one. Maybe take three to four weeks?"

A long pause, while he looks out over the river, tilting his head slightly and squinting, as if he can see just one boat with three or four people, then—"I'd like to be able to get away for that long without a big hulla-baloo, but right now it doesn't seem practical ... though, uh ... it *might* be possible later in the season, in the fall." He whooshes a big sigh, looks at me and smiles. "I can dream, can't I?" He looks at the river again and adds, "Water'd be awful low then."

"Who cares? For once we wouldn't be in a hurry. Just *think* of the nooks and crannies we can explore! Even with all the trips you've taken, Frank, you haven't seen a tenth of them."

"Hmm-m-m ... wouldn't be a whole lot of people on the river then, either. You'd like that, wouldn't you?"

"Oh, boy, would I! By the way, *mañana,* Becky, Reet and I are going up Aztec Creek, not to the bridge. Okay? We'd like a bath in clear water, and I'd like to stretch full out under the only spotlight worth a damn and feel it all over me, not just parts."

He gives me his lame excuse for a lecherous grin and wiggles his ears. "Better post a lookout," he says.

"Na-a-ah, everyone else is going to the bridge. I checked."

"Couple of my boatmen might not." He's really grinning now, teasing me.

"They're not going to hike three miles up Forbidden Canyon for the tenth or twelfth time just to spot three little maids at the bawth."

"It's Forbidd*ing.*"

"Who? What? Us? The boatmen are forbid ... "

"No ... no, the name of the canyon is Forbidd*ing.*"

"Forbidden, Forbidding, Aztec. ... dernit, why don't they make up their minds?"

"I'll tell you why. The *creek* was named Aztec—by prospectors probably, who thought the ruins here at the mouth were built by Aztec Indians. The Navajo, who knew about Rainbow Bridge long before white men came into this country, considered it sacred. At Mexican Hat, where Norm knew many of the Navajos, they said it was mysterious, full of uneasy spirits, a *forbidding* kind of place."

"Ah-haa, there are spirits in there, all right, but I can't commune with them through all the chit-chat of the nonspirits, so I'm going up Aztec *Creek* in Forbidd*ing* Canyon—after I play with the little green turtles at the junction of *Bridge Canyon,* and let old sol paint my white spots *red.*"

He pulls his feet in toward him, presses himself up and stands. "Ha-ha ... you gonna sit on your air mattress all day tomorrow?"

"I'll probably *float* on it most of the way ... hot side up. It'll be worth it."

"You gals feel free to do whatever you want; nobody's going to bother you." He digs both thumbs into his lower back, braces backward, says, "Sleep tight, gal ... Oh, almost forgot what I came to tell you. If you can make it, July 13 there'll be a space on the lower Grand run."

He turns and walks down to the river before I can gasp, squeal, or poop me underwear! <END JOURNAL>

Journal Note: June 6 (*cfs dropping*)

Reet, Becky, and I walk nearly two miles up Aztec in our bare buns, sliding into pools deep enough to swim in about every fifty yards. Forbidding

has no footprints or human sign past Bridge Canyon junction and no
sounds but our splashing and laughing, birdsong, the whisper of flowing
water, and our "ooohs" and "ahhhs" as each turn of the canyon reveals
more and more beauty. Lunch under a redbud in full leaf—the Glen
Canyon Tree. Trees of a million emerald hearts cling tenaciously to rock
and crevasse in the side canyons, where flash floods work to cut them
loose, but seldom ever do—high water is marked by drift some fifteen feet
above our heads. The trees seem to flourish best up these narrow, shaded
tributaries. Not found on sunny slopes, they hug slickrock, splash it with
pink-purple blossoms in spring, heart-shaped leaves in summer that turn
up to light like the supple hands of a Balinese dancer, thus giving them an
oriental look.

BOOM!! Eardrums ping! For a second the canyon feels like a vacuum, its air sucked to the sky.

"Yipes!" yells Reet.

We're on our feet before we hear another bang and clatter up canyon.
I scan the walls for exits, or higher ground, but having learned to note
such places in case of flash floods, I know there are none. I see a contrail
crossing the blue narrows overhead, and mutter, "Bloody jets! Those
sonic booms are going to kill someone in these canyons one day!"

"Yeah, why can't they play their games somewhere else," grumbles
Becky. "You hear that rock-fall upstream?"

Reet grabs her clothes. "Not a big one, I hope. We better get outta
here, babe."

I wise off. "Look at us ... three lovely Eves expelled from Paradise by
man's destructive thunder ... Sheee-it!" <END JOURNAL>

~

The next morning I was so high with the news that I'd be running the
Grand Canyon in the Cat boats in a few short weeks that I hadn't even
gotten my bowels in a uproar over the filthy camp left by the Boy
Sprouts on Forbidding Bar. The place was butchered—boxes and crates
all over, willows cut down and strewn everywhere, trash half-buried in a
pile of rock or under a couple shovelfuls of sand.

So it only happened here, but ...

I'd gotten here barely in time for the last of the *best*, eight years before
the impossible *worst* would come.

~

EIGHT

A Storm Moving In

The Fates have just stuck their hands in again, thank you very much. While waiting out the July 13 date of my Grand Canyon run, I stayed with friends who were managing Mystery Ranch in Sedona, Arizona, only to find that it was owned by Dudy and Dick Sprang, the explorers who'd named Forgotten Canyon in the Glen! I could have spent hours talking with them about the secrets of the canyon, but that was impossible for Dick. The man was nailed to his drawing board, from which emerged the famous antics of *Batman* and *Superman*. For them to take a month on the river, he was working double-time. But when he learned of my yearning for Glen Canyon, he found enough time to share more of its wonders and to assure me that the very best time to go was in the fall.

~

Ta-vwoats. God of the ancient ones.

Divider of continents. Splitter of mountains. Carver of canyons. Almighty plumber of rivers. Conjurer of miracles. Diviner of mysteries. Guardian of the afterworld.

Nu-ma, a mighty chief, had lost his beloved wife and would not cease to mourn for her, day or night. Where had she gone? To a happy land or sad? He could not tell, nor did she reveal herself in dreams, nor in the Shaman's Smoke of Mysteries, even after many moons.

Ta-vwoats wished the great chief no more suffering. He appeared to Nu-ma and offered to take him to that happier land where his wife dwelled so the chief might see for himself that she was content, and thus make a promise to cease his grieving.

Nu-ma agreed.

Through the mountains between the balmy regions of the west and the great dry deserts Ta-vwoats cut a canyon path and led the chief to that happier land.

Nu-ma was convinced.

Upon returning, Ta-vwoats extracted a further promise from the chief that he tell no one of that place, lest through discontent with this world, they should wish to go to the other. The divine one then made certain no others would follow. He rolled a mighty river into the gorge, a river of mad, raging water that would engulf any who might attempt to pass through.

Journal Note: July 14, 1955 (Bright Angel Creek,
Grand Canyon—8,750 cfs; low!)

Boatmen:
Sandra—Frank Wright
Doris—Duane Bishop
Norm—Willard Wright
Mexican Hat III—John Harper

My legs are so sore I can hardly move from my sleeping bag, much less get up and start packing things into the boats nosed in the eddy above Bright Angel Rapid. They look like four little white birds pecking at the sand. Four of us walked down the Kaibab Trail yesterday at dawn, and my hold-back muscles are telling me all about it! My sixth river trip, but first in the Cats. I've heard of their quick response compared to the powerboats, and I've seen them before, on the water and in the movies. Now I'll feel how they ride the rapids. In the *Sandra* with Frank, I ride the stern deck, "fish-eyeing"—which means lie on belly, pelvis over the hatch, chin over stern, twelve inches from the water; grab ropes encircling top of stern deck, spread legs on either side of splashboards for bracing.

Come to Horn Creek rapid midmorning; cadre looks it over carefully. Very messy in such low water—rocks are all we're afraid of in our pretty little boats, especially designed for the Grand Canyon, with seven airtight compartments and perfectly balanced sixteen-pound oak oars. Horn, a series of steps (four holes in line). Passengers walk around. Willard gets too far out in center stream at the head, misses the tongue, comes down *between* the rocks, cracks the bottom with a jolt that knocks him off the seat, puts a hole dead center and another right stern, both small, but ... boat repairs after lunch.

Granite Falls Rapid: The difference between powerboats and the Cats is easy to explain—like the difference between the Queen Mary and a dingy, a log and a leaf. Explaining the experience of riding the stern of a flat, hug-the-water, instantly responsive Cat—weighty, yet highly maneuverable *if the boatman knows how*—is more difficult. Much of the time I am kissing the river; in Granite *he* is kissing *me* ... HARD. Using Norm's technique, we head in stern first. I can feel my heart thumping the deck. The tongue is smooth as silk, rocking a little as it licks us down ever faster, ah-h-h-i-ie-e!, into a deafening mass of booming, curling, tossing, angry waves. Frank quarters left; a corner of the stern cuts through the top of a ten-foot foaming curler, spins me around, washes me half off the deck. I scream, hold to the rope; while the boat, with my butt and legs over the side, goes into a trough. He pulls back, angles into the next wave. As we rise in the curl, it picks me up with the boat, heaves me back on the deck, slams down on top of me, knocks my wind out and replaces it with half the Colorado. We're full to the gunnels; I'm choking, but bailing like a stern-wheeler! Oh, Lordy, what a ride! ... can't tell if I'm laughing or crying. On shore I shiver, but it's hot as hell. Adrenaline lashes my veins like an out-of-control fire hose. YA-HOO-OO-OO!

"Did I get you wet?" asks a grinning Frank. <END JOURNAL>

Some months before this first Cat trip, I bought the USGS Plan & Profile maps and was astounded to note, really for the first time, how many dam sites there are between Bright Angel and Grand Wash, 169 miles downstream. Pipe Creek, Ruby Canyon, Hakatai, Big Bend, Specter Chasm A, Specter Chasm B, Havasu, Prospect, Diamond Creek A, Diamond Creek B, Travertine, Bridge Canyon, Spencer Canyon, Devil's Slide, Flour Sack, Pierce's Ferry, Grand Wash. Seventeen of the dam things, plus seven more from Lee's to Bright Angel—total of 24! The Bureau beavers were a busy bunch, for sure.

Journal Note: July 15 (Second Day—8,190 cfs; dropping!)

Rapids for Today: Hermit Falls, Travertine, Boucher, Crystal, Tuna Creek, Agate, Sapphire, Turquoise, Ruby, Serpentine, Bass, Shinumo, Walthenburg, Garnet.

We line Hermit and I can see why the boatmen, even some passengers, hate it! A three-hour job with all gear out. After the line job, I walk up the beach with Becky (happily, she is again on this trip) to a hundred-foot-long, six-foot-high driftwood pile for my initiation into The River Rat Driftwood Burner's Society. Setting the *whole thing* on fire with only *one* match are the requirements; no altering the pile, no matter how large. Looks like I'm their newest member! <END JOURNAL>

Hard to believe, now, that the Park Service *asked* boating parties to do such a thing, but it once was *de rigueur*. Why? They didn't want all that drift messing up the head of Rez Mead, nor did we. We had to pick up our tow there, and drift is hell on boat propellers. What we really needed was Art Green's *Tseh Na-ni-ah-go Atin*—fly right over the stuff, but don't forget your earplugs!

Dock Marston once told me of his strange experience with Mead's Medusa-head of drift:

They got to the head of the dead water late in the day and found, an hour or so beyond Separation Canyon, a blanket of driftwood across and down the reservoir as far as they could see—forget their estimated time of arrival! They bulldozed ashore, ate, and sacked out with the very unpleasant thought of having to plow through it the next day. Their world was a furnace—no wind, no breeze, not enough friendlies from the Bat Cave to eat all the mosquitoes—and of course, it stank. To boot, during the night there were some very strange sounds—bumping, groaning, sucking, and a weird bubbling.

Dock was up before first light, trying not to think about the day ahead. As it got brighter, he saw the smoky light of dawn across the water. Water? Dock thought he was hallucinating. The surface of the reservoir was as smooth and shiny as sheet metal!

"Where'd it all go?" I asked.

Dock just shook his head. "Sank, I guess."

"All in one night?"

"What else? There wasn't any wind the night before or that morning. And on the way to the dam, no masses of it, just the average stuff that we all expect. It just disappeared."

~

Did I have quiet moments to talk to Frank, like we had on the Glen? No way. At night the crew was physically and mentally exhausted just thinking about the dropping cfs, rocks popping up like grizzly teeth, more each day. The passengers were pooped from sheer exhilaration and the wild beauty of that phenomenal place, and though it was a much slower and more revealing trip in every way than the Power Run, it still was so high-key that relaxing was impossible. Few were the side canyons we had time to hike, or even step into, and I knew from the Glen that those canyons were as inherent to the character and mood of the place as the raging water that carried us through it.

And something else was missing. A feeling? A sight? A sound? Something I couldn't put my finger on. Hm-m-m.

The night above Deubendorff Rapid I sang everyone to sleep. Heh-heh. Everyone except Frank, that is. He handed me a canteen, took another for himself, and we walked a quarter-mile down to the clear water in Stone Canyon, where we filled them under a little waterfall. Then we sat on a ledge and began to devise plans for what later became the "We Three" trips in Glen Canyon. We would go, as Dick had advised: (1) in the fall, (2) for the purpose of exploring side canyons, (3) to photograph places we'd long wanted in our collections, (4) plan ahead and take two or three weeks, and (5) with only me and Tad (who would be our teacher and who also wanted time to use his tripod and do things *right!*)

We Three had never enjoyed such a mini river trip.

Journal Note: July 17 (Fourth Day—7,620 cfs; lower!)

Tapeats Creek. Sweet Mother of Jesus! There they are, all over the beach like ants—the garbage scows of Georgie White and her swarm of passengers! (These are not boats, understand, but big, black neoprene rafts, inflated rings with soft, squishy bottoms. They look so ugly—like turds in a punch bowl—that we beg Frank to leave and put them out of sight.) Below Tapeats, I swim the granite narrows, which average 60 feet wide, the river quiet as a pond. At 66,000 cfs the powerboats got dashed all over here. Lunch at Deer Creek. Willard and I walk behind and under the falls, pouring from the wall 75 feet above. The torrent hits our heads, *blam!* In spray this thick it is hard to breathe, but we make it out the other end. Why is everybody hollering the water's so cold?—feels just right to me. Hike to Surprise Valley, a twisting labyrinth carved from Tapeats sandstone by the little stream that obviously roars at times, judging from half a huge cottonwood wedged into both sides.

Back to the river to take some photos of our pretty little boats from above, and ... Jeeeeeeezzzzzus! There they are again, those goddamn blubber rafts plastered on both sides of our little swans—three bridge pontoons upstream and three baloneys below us. For three years Georgie White glued her unwanted self to Mexican Hat Expeditions—in case she throws all her passengers in the river, I suppose—and now has the balls to tell Frank we should all celebrate! Celebrate what? The meeting of the garbage scows?

Scow Passenger (grinning): "Guess you didn't think you'd have thirty people walkin' across your camp tonight, did'ya?"

Becky (burning): "I sure as hell *did not!*" She turns to me and adds, "How does an ego get that fat ... and ugly?"

Poor, gentle Frank, who knows his cast and crew are upset, goes to talk with Dan Davis, the park ranger she has in tow, and finally to the Garbage Woman, who condescends to move her pontoons from above us so her flock won't have to walk back over four Cat bow ropes with all their gear, and through our camp. I hope Dan gives her a chewing out. I'd like a go at it, but Frank won't let me out of his sight. He says she'd probably flatten me, and he's probably right, but up to now river folks with more sensitivity than a dead pig in the sunshine have managed to stay out of each other's way! I don't think there's ever been that many people through the Grand in a single party before. No doubt I'll dream of carving White meat tonight.

Enough g-r-r-r-r for such a gorgeous place! I walk to the pool for a night bath to cool me off, inside as well as out. Standing beside the great dignity of Deer Creek Falls, regardless of its power, I feel a soothing effect. <END JOURNAL>

~

Mexican Hat Expeditions gave each passenger a deluxe eighteen-inch-square bedroll, zipped on three sides, containing an air mattress, clean sheet, and waterproof ground cloth large enough to make into a "wet roll" by pulling half over you and tucking it in along the sides, should it rain. There were a couple of foot pumps in the boat for those who didn't fancy using their own hot air, but if you laid your mattress on one of the Grand Canyon's egg-frying rocks only partly blown up, by the time you went to bed it would be full. I never saw a tent in the ten years I ran the river. Who needed it under that shimmering river in the sky, or between moon-drenched rock towers, pinnacles and spires, beside an ever-changing dervish of dancing lights reflected off the water? Who would want a tent when they could watch a thin line of silver moon-paint trickle slowly down a dark cliff's edge? Anyhow, it was way too hot for a tent.

Random Journal Notes: July 18 to July 23
(7,580–6,140 cfs, Deer Creek to Diamond Creek)

Up at dawn to leave the garbage scows behind; twenty miles to Havasu tonight. Riffle above Kanab Creek gives us a good dousing, but at Kanab we didn't even get wet. Major Powell quit here in 1872, walked up Kanab and out. Two fierce and very big holes at the bottom of Upset lie waiting for their lunch, so we line fifty feet and run the rest. As we get the last boat down, along come the hippopotami. Georgie looks it over this time because last year it flipped her and spilled passengers all over the river. We pull out, letting her worry about it, and take our boats up Havasu Creek (safe for a while at least; she can't get her scows in here). Before dinner we play in the icy-looking travertine water (not really cold, but colder than the Colorado's), where lime deposits that haven't crystallized are soft as silk and very sensuous to sit in. Havasu's ledges down by the river are *hot* for sleeping, but oh, such lovely berths. My ledge, as close to the water as I can get, cools down around midnight. Again, that feeling of something missing ... something along the river. What?

Easy day to the Black Plug (Lava Pinnacle) through the high and mighty Redwall scenery; a lot of singing, a lot of swimming, a lot of easy little rapids. A sandstorm at Red Slide Canyon gives us a stinging lash about the waters, where the garbage scows again come cavitating up behind us. We quickly pull ashore to let them pass. She beaches a mile below us; we row past her *again* to camp near the Pinnacle, now standing some fifty feet out of the water. Is this a damned game of touch tag, or what?

I am deep in my sack tonight. For some reason it's cooler. Singing is not in it—we all know Lava Falls, the fire-eating dragon, is a mile or so downstream. Here in camp the ground shakes, not like a quake or any kind of metronome rhythm, but to the river's special cadence with his adversary, the lava wall that dammed him millennia ago, and which he is still arduously chewing away. With my ear to the Earth Mother I catch a sense of what's happening down there—the surge, the pitch and dive, an occasional timpani, its boom echoing back to me. Gnawing away at this intrusion, *Ta-vwoats* is intermittently pissed, then indifferent, before he takes another chomp at those damnable black volcanic rocks! Too bad, rocks. Time ... time is on his side.

I've run Lava, but at 59,000 more cubes than this! Not a chance in hell we'll do it tomorrow at this low stage. Frankly, I just want to stand and *look* at it—the roaring, thundering power of it. Old Lava Falls ain't nothin' but rocks, some of them not even decent enough to be covered at 7,000 cfs. We line to below the big eater hole, portaging our gear and stepping around the hippo riders, who've come down to watch and take pictures of us. They think we're chicken, we think they're knotheads. Our last boat is lined and ready for the rest of the run when her barge, garbage scow, whatever-ya-wanna-call-it, comes through—three baloneys tied together with an outboard on the middle one.

Now I've seen everything! We laugh until tears stream from our eyes. They lumber, flop and slump, bump, ooze, slide backward, stop dead, squash, flap and boi-i-n-ng over every rock and into every hole in Lava. Norm once said, "There are rock dodgers and there are river runners." Wonder what'n'hell he'd call this. There's absolutely no *skill* involved— just point the thing and go. It wallows sideways, and one barge flips on top of the other, making a "people sandwich"—a Georgie White Special—with arms, legs, heads, and bodies sticking out the sides. She calls it (so help me, this is true) "thrills with safety!" We call it a freak show.
<END JOURNAL>

After watching the fiasco at Lava Falls, we created—to the tune of "Captain Jinks" ...

The Hippopotami

The Ghost of Nevills will walk tonight
And shake with rage at the awful sight
Of the craft and crew of Georgie White
On the river he loved so well.

If he were on this earth with us
He'd stand behind his oars and cuss,
"My God, a Hippopotamus!"
On the river I loved so well!

He'd stand and stare at the old sea cow
There ain't no stern and there ain't no bow
It looks just like a garbage scow
On the river I loved so well!

Aboard this thing it's hot as toast
At dinner Georgie will play host
Each passenger brings his own rump roast
On the river he loved so well!

The Hippos, boy, they smell like sin
They wallow and warp and bloop and spin
You bail it out and it bails back in
On the river he loved so well!

The thrill that made this sport a "wow"
Is lost and gone in a rubber plow
And anyone can do it now
On the river he loved so well!

Norm mutters a curse and turns away
And says they'll die to rue the day
And for this insult dearly pay
To the river he loved so well!

But Frank was not amused, and I knew why.

Georgie had broken every unspoken tradition on the river, with no thought for anyone but herself and her enterprise, and it was my opinion that she'd done it on purpose, though Frank, with his deep-seated reluctance to accuse, would not agree. Yet, he knew that his repeat passengers weren't going to enjoy that circus any more than he did, and since "flagrant disregard" seemed to be Georgie's password, such scenes were likely to be repeated—as indeed they were five or six times before the end of our trip at Temple Bar.

As the days went by with rapids sousing us, keeping us cool in heat above one hundred degrees, the canyon pinching our little brown strip of water to a narrow twining ribbon, the jagged rock towers rising closer and closer beside us, looking as if they plunged under us as deeply as they rose overhead, I finally hit upon the elusive thing that had been missing.

Green. No cuffs of vegetation beside the water. Quite unconsciously I'd been comparing it to emerald bands that bordered the Glen's every turn and continued up most of its side canyons. Secretly, I longed for the soothing, lounging shapes of Navajo sandstone—shapes I could press myself into and feel a part of. The Grand's rocks were sharp and dramatic, and in a way, cruel; hard for me to relate to. There was some green—the Grand wasn't all naked rock. Tamarisk and willow, rabbitbrush, saltbush, and cacti thrived on the long, half-mile or more beaches, but in the Middle and Lower Granite Gorge, what I write is what you got.

Granite—wall to wall.

Some of that polished artistry, at Rapid 232, got the *Doris*, impinged her upon slippery stone teeth, until a surge flipped her on her belly and sent her to be rescued below. Duane managed admirably, getting his passengers off the boat and onto those sculptures, where they clung until we beached the *Sandra* and got a rope out to them.

When we reached the dead water of Rez Mead and Jimmy came up in the *Lollypop* to tow us to Temple Bar, I knew there was another thing bothering me. I didn't like this nothin' place to end such a wild and rugged trip—didn't enjoy being towed across miles of funny-smelling, hot, glassy water. Furthermore, Her Crudeness had done much to tarnish the splendor of the trip.

Still more: Glen Canyon Dam was becoming a political war, in need of more of us to fight it down. Yet, even before it would obliterate two hundred miles of the Colorado above, and make it a crippled wimp through the Grand Canyon below, the old style of river running would be crowded out. With the coming of the dam would go seclusion, the untrodden beaches, the wildness of *Ta-vwoats*, the quiet, the peace—and saddest of all, our specially-designed-for-these-rapids, little oar-driven, two-passenger Cataract boats, which couldn't possibly bring in revenue enough to vie with all the Georgie Whites sure to follow. What was in the wind proved to be a storm moving in on us, tearing away the footings of tradition and replacing them with a landscape strange and busy—an instant city built on a wilderness waterway. The old, warm, silt road paved an icy, gunmetal blue; big floating condos, leased through a term we'd never imagined—"user days." New rules, restrictions, traffic, clutter, crowds, noise ...

I remember crying much of the time across that reservoir, though my notes say nothing about it. A letter from Frank, later, brings it all back.

Do you know how badly I wanted to talk to you while coming across the lake? But because of a gas-consuming, foul-smelling, noisy contraption called an outboard motor, there was no way. ... There is nothing I want more than to have the feeling I can help someone in some way if only by furnishing a shoulder to cry on.

I couldn't see that the trip I'd so looked forward to had *not* given balm to hurts and problems; yet, this gentle man, clearly from outer space, knew more about me than I did, and furthermore, wanted to help!

I'm very proud of the way you have handled some very bad situations. You are an artist, and artists are known to be "high strung." Your profession imposes great demands on your good nature. It demands that you set up a barrier to protect your feelings and personal rights. There is a conflict between the body and spirit when you sing under conditions where it would be natural to cry. No wonder to me that you love the country away from the big cities; no wonder to me that you are quick to be on guard when things don't "smell" right; no wonder to me

*that you are slow to let down the barrier just a little ways; no wonder
to me that you look back and ask what the thirty-five years have done
for you and what you have done for others. Maybe you will let down
the barrier in September. I am really looking forward to being with
two good friends on the Glen.*

On the Glen.

On ... on to the Glen!

PART TWO

~

*Getting in Step
with the Stone*

~

NINE

Tale of the Ticaboo

Hite, Utah—Thursday, September 22, 1955.
Pretakeoff, First Glen Canyon We Three Trip

The dew is drinkable as it rolls from the slender, yellowing willows into my mouth where I lie, snug in my bedroll, beside the chattering river. It tastes and smells like a lick of sandstone. Backed by the clearest indigo blue ever seen and weighted at the bottom with orange-maroon-yellow crenelations seared by a rising sun, this picture has to be in a dream. But this time, I know it isn't. Today my life support system goes into full effect. I am thirty-five years old.

I am here.

We are here ... two thirds of us.

We wait. As always. For Tad.

To know Tad Nichols is to love him. As one of my oldest and dearest friends, to love him is to know the true meaning of frustration. My Irish can really flare up at him until his utter defenselessness douses it. I think of him always as born with silver spoon in mouth; as never having had to *do anything*, and therefore *doing nothing* (unless he thinks he's about to miss something, like a good time, a new adventure, a photo/movie assignment where he can prove out the unique talent that is his behind a camera lens). And oh gawd, he is lazy! Says *I*. Took me some time to realize it's a combination of metabolism, preoccupation, and the "absent-minded professor" syndrome.

He stands well over six feet, is lean to skinny with long muscles, long legs, long arms, and slender fingers, a slightly bowed torso, and eyebrows so black and thick they look like two caterpillars fighting. To hike with him, when he's finally ready, willing, and motivated to move, is to trot ahead, then wait, rather than be stepped on from behind. If I do elect to stay behind his easy, lanky stride, sure enough I'll round a bend and run

Those Three

They came once a year,
    Those three.
The secrets of my hidden canyon
    were their treasured prize.
I raised my battlements and fought
    For naught.

They swam every pool,
    Those three.
Through the moss-green ribbons,
    depth unknown and stinging cold,
They sought a slit of sunlit sky,
    To dry.

Striving for the end
    Of me,
To tenuous cliffs of talus, to
    walls of shale they clung,
While boulders struck below the boom
    Of doom!

Hearts of conquerors,
    Those three!
Standing in my storm-born chimney,
    viewing their conquest.
Back into the centuries of time
    They climb.

So I coveted
    Those three.
I protected and held fast their
    footprints in the sand
To show them none had come that way
    Since they.

This they do deserve
    Of me:
To take with them a secret peace
    throughout a tortured land,
And know they've trod on virgin sod
    Near God!

smack into him, because his fine camera eye will have stopped him mid-step to case the scene, and there he'll be for no one knows how long. We've used each other as flotation devices, bridges, Tarzan vines, and footstools. Once I served as a log in a bog when he pushed me ahead, I fell, and he stepped on *me* rather than get his feet wet. Hike with us, you get a Mack Sennett comedy! He knows a lot about plants and bugs and rocks and constellations and sea life and, of course, photography. He has the tiniest widdo speech particularity, which endears him to us all in spite of his aggravating major vice: procrastination ... with a capital P!

He has a wife, Mary Jane, near as tall as he; same metabolism, of scientific mind, her eyes behind binocular lenses, studying, classifying, counting ... birds. They have traveled the world together, adventurers to the core. M.J. is not coming on the "We Three" trip—that would make four. She knows her man (better than he thinks), she knows me, and she knows Frank. It's Tad's trip, she said.

It is if he gets here.

~

I had been in Blanding at Frank and Dora's house since Monday evening, when Tad was *supposed* to call us and say where he'd touch down—Blanding or Hite. By Wednesday noon, nothing—we'd no way to locate him, and Frank was getting antsy. We stayed away from the house, with the excuse of getting supplies and running errands, but mostly so Frank couldn't be found and hauled off somewhere. At four o'clock on Wednesday, with still no word, he rounded up his youngest son and only daughter, told Dora to send down any message from Tad, put the boat behind the truck, and with four of us in the cab took off for Hite. I had research to do there, anyway, and the extra time was welcome.

~

I smell coffee. Movement beyond the willows, along with the resounding boom of cans hitting the bottom of *Tinny* tells me that Frank is organizing our supplies in the aluminum boat that'll be our water horse for the next two weeks. I don't know it yet, but I'm in for a new and different Glen Canyon. We arrived after dark last night, too late for anything but a rolled-out tarp and bedroll down here by the landing. The last thing I saw was a sky so dense with stars I couldn't find the planets among them; the last that I heard, a giggling sound from my river being tickled by the end of the Ferry.

I sit up, look across the water toward Hite and the gauging station, and am amazed to see rocks at least two feet beneath the surface! I've never been able to see my hand even one inch into the Colorado before. And the color overall is a frosty pea-green, not totally opaque. Like the tamarisk and willow along his banks, the river has settled out to his fall color. No more summer storms. Spring runoff, far away.

Now! Through the willows ... warm sack to cool river. Blam!

It ripples over my skin like soft feathers under air pressure. Almost cold. Ah-h-h-ah ... river. Cool and fleet. Water, the escape artist ... tranquil, mad and dangerous, caressingly sensuous. Fingers of moving water, touching and hugging me, welcome me back like an old friend I've waited to see for more than a year. Never mind that just a couple months back I was in another part of this same river. Now it is different, because here there'll be no interference, no distractions, no need to explain feelings or actions. We, of the same mind, will be FREE—free to learn the river, the canyon ... and ourselves.

Oh-oh! There's the rattle and squawk of Woody Edgell's old truck. Blessing the acoustics, I'm out of the river, clothed, and Frank is handing me a cup of coffee, when Woody clanks down to the landing.

"Hey, Chantoozie! Why'nt ya stop an' say 'hi' to a guy?"

"Middle of the night, man. You wouldn't like that."

"I heerd ya go by ... nothin' gets past me up there in Farley Canyon. Hi Frank ... y'all're comin' up fer breakfast, ain't cha?"

I look at Frank. He smiles and nods, which means he knows as well as I that Woody loves people to talk at, even though he claims that all summer long they've been like ants crawling all over, pestering him something awful.

Woody likes to spar with me in a kind of "hip" conversation when he thinks anyone is listening—because he likes me, I guess. I once heard him say to someone, "Got legs on 'er like a tap dancer an' a butt t' match; can sing an' play that geetar, too." Then stretching the truth, like always, added, "She does, y'know, every time she comes, special fer me." Actually, I'm kinda flattered, and as I've said before, he tells some great true/false stories.

"Who all's here now, Woody?" I ask.

"Lessee. Frank Barrett an' Slim Williams on this side, an' over there the USGS guy, Lawrence Lopp an' his wife, takin' the flows, an' Reuben an' Beth Nielson runnin' the ferry."

"Arth? Arth Chaffin's not running the ferry or messing around his claims? I sure need to talk to him."

"No. Did'n ya know? He leased it to the Nielsons; moved to Teasdale fer keeps, he says. Gettin' too old to mess around these back trails and waterways."

I find this hard to believe. He'll be back next summer when it warms up; just can't see him nailed down anywhere, especially that far from his beloved claims.

We ride up Farley Canyon to the store/post office with Woody in his "rattler," getting the latest exaggerations about the number of crackers an' nuts who'd run the Glen that summer in everything from a log raft with a chicken coop wired on top, *full* of squawkin' chickens peckin' at each other; to a couple in a kiddie pool with ping-pong paddles for oars, who got as far as the Dorothy Bar; to several on air mattresses. We finally make him confess that most of them only made it to Bert Loper's cabin at Red Canyon, twelve miles down.

Woody blurts out, "Musta been two thousand of 'em! [read: two hundred]. I'uz surprised them chicken-coopers didn't try t' drag it behind 'em, they was so damn stupid! Frank Barrett says when they gits out at Red Canyon, there's this wire cage with about fifteen drowned chickens in it hangin' over the side, an' one of the guys was dyed purple all over his skin from somethin', they never did figure out what!"

I can't help it; laughing like a fool, I say, "Maybe chicken poop is purple, Woody … when its wet."

Frank shoots me raised eyebrows and a pumpkin grin.

Woody assumes we are running a regular party, that more folks and boats are on the way, and wants to know when they'll be here and how many.

"Tad," says Frank.

"And … ?"

"That's it," I conclude. "And I guess we'll know *when* when he shows. He *should* be on the mail plane today, but you know Tad."

"Yup, I know 'um. He'll want a beer."

Only Tad is *not* on today's mail plane.

This afternoon I meet the entire population of White Canyon—the miners of old Dandy Crossing, Frank Barrett and Slim Williams, whose cabins are on the left river bank under big swatches of gossiping cottonwoods.

About sixty-five and handsome, Frank Barrett has the kind of face I look upon as aristocratic—slender, strong, with a well-fitted, hawklike nose. His shock of close-cropped white hair sets off lucent blue eyes that sparkle with sky and river; his tan face, neck, and hands jut from a blue denim shirt. What holds him up is a frame slender and straight as a saguaro trunk, and I suspect about as durable. The voice, way down there below a noble Adam's apple, wells up full of colorful stories, punctuated with chuckles. The accent is hard midwestern, the humor seemingly uncalculated, as the words come slowly and the punch line curves around to hit you unexpectedly between the shoulder blades.

He is telling me: "It was November of 1937. We were living down at Red Canyon where we'd only see about four people in four months. One evening, damned if someone didn't knock on the door. Scared hell out of us! I open the door and the guy backs up like he's scared as we are. Said he didn't really expect anyone to be there, just knocked out of courtesy's habit. He had a red beard and a purple hat and seemed sort of restless, or nervous. He'd flipped his boat the night before in Cataract Canyon. When he got himself and the boat to shore and made his camp, he happened to look above him on the wall and saw the carved initials of Glen and Bessie Hyde [the first husband-and-wife duo to attempt the run from Green River, Utah, to Needles, Arizona, in 1928—without life-jackets. They mysteriously disappeared in or below Rapid 232; I knew all about *that* one! Only their undamaged boat and gear were found.] This guy said it gave him a weird feeling to be camping there, especially after his first spill in Cataract. He was going from Green River, Wyoming, to Boulder Dam ... *alone*. He stayed with us for two days; said his name was Buzz Holmstrom."

There's the punch line. Buzz Holmstrom stands real tall in river lore, but almost no one knows he spent this time at Red Canyon with Frank Barrett. It didn't surface in Holmstrom's journals. And yes, he made it all the way to Boulder Dam ... alone.

Down the long bar near the end of the landing strip is Slim Williams's cabin. I got to really know Slim soon after this and I suspect he's worked in every mine within two hundred miles of Hite—the Happy Jack during the uranium boom, the Hideout and Shitamaring, and many placer claims throughout the Glen. Slim is from Missouri, and you *do* have to show him. Later in our friendship, something *did.* In a tunnel of one of the mines, a rock the size of a ten-ton truck dislodged, rolled over him, pushed him into soft dirt, kept on going, and didn't kill him. At that point in his career he figured somebody was trying to tell him something, which prompted him to work *at* mines rather than *in* them—an assayer, no longer a driller.

The two Franks and I walk through Slim's front gate under a six-point rack of antlers nailed overhead. The open front door reveals a bright and clean kitchen-sitting area; behind it, clear across the back of the cabin, is a screened-in sleeping porch. I notice geologic maps and mining books all over the front rooms, but what drives me simply wild is a whole wall covered with pasted together USGS 15-Minute Series Topographic Quads, from Dark Canyon to Lee's Ferry—1952! Why have I never seen these before? (Because Frank knows the river so well, he doesn't even think about it). Here is all of Glen Canyon *with the tributaries!* Through its maze the Colorado meanders blue, twisty and tantalizing; here, splitting like pulled taffy around sand islands; there, trenched by brown contour lines so thick they form blotches on the map. Myriad splats of green indicate vegetation in the side canyons, along the river bars, the benches, and at the heads of canyons—some named, some not, like Forgotten Canyon. Its entire length is drawn in, but *still not named.* On Slim's wall for 167 miles below the Hite Ferry (and about 130 more upstream), no road crosses this waterway! The handful of trails and overlooks that dare to touch its edge seem held there by some invisible force; dense lines meet them on the other side, thick as a ream of paper but not nearly so tidy. Ridges border miles of unmarked paper that are but bare rock islands hoisted in the sky thousands of feet above the ribbon. Where a canyon yawns at the river's edge—steep, deep, and narrow—its V runs quick to the crotch, much like a cowboy dressed in wild woolly chaps, standing with his legs apart.

Roadless! Trackless! Spacious! Wilderness!

Lemme at it! If I thought I wanted to know what lay up in all those crotches before, now I'm in a fever to hike, twist, crawl, climb, swim, whatever it takes to get into those otherworldly places. *I want those maps!*

Slim is talking to Frank, and I've missed part of it.

"He made money from the yellow sand and bought a ranch in Idaho. Wouldn't have anything on it that wasn't white—white house, white furniture, white horse, white fences, white everything—but he spent it all, ol' Charlie Gibbons. So, his White Ranch went kaput, and he became a freighter on the Hoskinini Trail. Next he ran a pool hall in Green River, selling bootleg whiskey. He was still freighting, but now it was strictly for Butch Cassidy 'n' the Robbers' Roost Gang."

I can tell Slim's addicted to punch lines, too—pretty much like all good storytellers. The best of the lot are men who live alone, who have time to work out the story until it sounds just right to them. Unlike most rural folks, he pronounces his "ings," and he doesn't say "kain't" or "hain't" or "thang," even when he's telling a tale. He's another tall one, a bit more fleshed out and bigger-boned than Tad and the two Franks, has a two-tone, blond/grey crewcut—wears a straw cowboy hat and tennis shoes and is actually tanned to the waist! Wa-hoo! Everyone else but me is covered up like they're on African Safari and might get sunstroke. Slim's eyes are blue and mischievous. Something's always going on behind them—nobody's ever sure what, usually something that couldn't be further from your mind.

Frank Barrett says, "What's the matter with your eyes, Slim? They look all bloodshot."

"Y'ought'a see 'em from *this* side" he says, quiet-like and offhand, staring out the front door.

"Little heavy imbibing in the red-eye last night?"

"Yeah, that poison musta been contaminated." Heh-heh … the straight man and the comedian. Those two know when they've got an audience.

~

Everyone at Hite, White, and Farley comes to our camp tonight for hot chocolate, cookies, and songs. Larry Lopp, the USGS guy, says the river's only running about 3,100 cubes and we can *walk* across the river upstream, where Dandy Crossing used to be. I'm gonna to do that tomorrow, because I hain't never walked across the Colorado River before and likely won't get to again.

Frank heats a couple of big rocks beside the campfire to put at the foot of each bedroll. How nice!

Later … beside the water … Talking with my river … Frank has gone to bed … Water colder than I've ever felt it, but never too cold for my evening bath. I reach across the surface to gather in the gently rocking stars—mine, all mine! I've stacked the other world and all my troubles away beyond these mudstone walls—my thoughts no longer in a tumbler, but recalling today when I didn't have one minute of anxiety or trepidation, didn't do or say a single thing that didn't come naturally. No holding back, no showing off, just flowing along with you, Old Boy; feeling the sun, remembering the air currents off the water, testing the mud, registering the new/old sounds and smells. Up to the ruins, down to the potholes, feeling the right and wrong pressure, the angle and balance with the balls of my feet, letting intuition tell me where the solid footing is.

Getting in step with the stone.

Hite—Friday, September 23

Tad isn't on the mail plane today, either.

We hike up to Woody's to have lunch, and we get a message from

Dora telling us he'll be here Saturday or Sunday by charter. (I'm thinking, holy shit, E.T., you're going to ruin this trip yet!)

Beth Nielson drove us up Trachyte Creek in the Jeep over what used to be the old way into Hite, and what surely was as Woody described it last year—a mess! Five murderous miles up to a tributary named Swett Canyon, the Jeep trail ended at a rock formation that Arth Chaffin named Hoskinini Monument—said it reminded him of the old Navajo chief. I couldn't see how, but who knows? More interesting were the petroglyphs and Beth's idea that they, and the early hieroglyphics of the Incan and Mayan Indians, were the story of the Book of Mormon! Since wise men don't discuss it, I let that one fly with a nod and a smile and amused myself by imagining what she'd have said if I'd told her my "Book," with *all* its pages, was down there between the walls of Glen Canyon.

Before we departed she presented me with a historic jewel—a poem Cass Hite had written, supposedly on the night of his sixtieth birthday, March 3, 1905—alone there in his cabin at Ticaboo. He called it "The Trail of Sixty Snows," a verse for every year of his life. Within the poem was enclosed another, titled "The Ghost of Hoskinini," written for Cass by a friend named Cy Warman, a popular songwriter of the time. It wasn't more than a few hours after I read Cy Warman's poem that the music started forming in my head and guiding my hands on the guitar for the song I call:

>
> **The Tale of the Ticaboo**
> They tell a tale on the Ticaboo
> Beyond the Snowy Range
> A story if it be true
> Is surely wondrous strange
>
>   They say at midnight when the winds
>   From out the canyon blow
>   And Colorado's foamy waves
>   Dash on the rocks below
>
> A horse of solid silver comes
> Whose feet are shod with gold
> And dashing o'er the canyon's walls
> Is reined by rider bold.
> The Ghost of Hoskinini
> With wild and wandering eye

Who comes to guard the pathway
Of the Hosteen Pish-la-ki.

The sheepmen tell the story
The prospectors who came
From Tintic mines in Juab
Say that they have heard the same.

That every night at midnight
When the winds go wailing by
Rides the Ghost of Hoskinini
'Gainst the Hosteen-Pish-la-ki

For here it was the Spaniards,
He said, made Injun slave
And maybe so the river
Flows sometimes by the grave
Of Hoskinini's old Grandmother
Who 'fore she came to die
Was made to dig the Peso
For the Hosteen Pish-la-ki.

But brave old Hoskinini
'Fore death his hands had tied
Said he would guard the Peso
Made paper-talk and died.

And even now at midnight
As we talk, you and I
Rides the Ghost of Hoskinini
'Gainst the Hosteen Pish-la-ki.

The trapper by the river
My guide the Navajo
Says that he has heard the story
And knows that it is so.
And that's the tale of the Ticaboo
Beyond the Snowy Range—
A story, if it's really true
That's surely wondrous strange.

When Slim went upstream to check his fishing lines at North Wash, we went along. As he hauled in each line, casually unhooking four catfish and giving us one for dinner, he answered a remark I'd made about Frank Barrett—that Frank was so poised, so unflappable, such a gentleman.

He "hmm-m-ed" with that tight little smile of his, only the corners of his mouth tucked back, and said, "Oh yeah, gentleman to the core. Poise of a priest. We took some supplies to a miner down at the Rincon this summer, and a'course when y'go down you've got to come back up, which isn't so easy if the river is low, and worse when it's high and rolling drift. That day it was just right until ... until we got just below the Dorothy Bar. Out of nowhere comes all this driftwood. Frank is cussing like a string of mule-skinners and dodging it the best he can, while I'm in the bow slashing away at it with an oar, not being very careful what I say, either.

"'Goddamit, Slim, where's all this crap comin' from, water's not even muddy!' he hollers at me.

"I was damned if I knew, and coming over Trachyte Riffle we dinged a few chunks—could've lost the prop.

"When we got to the ferry, we got the answer. There's about fifty Boy Sprouts on it and every one of 'em's heaving driftwood off the end, practically covering the whole channel with it.

"Frank makes a beeline for 'em. Passes within ten feet and yells, 'You goddamn bird-nest–robbin' little bastards! Cut it out!'"

~

I stand by the river on the cool, wet sand, watching the colors fade and breathing the river-scented air. Stars begin to arrange and concentrate their battalions in the eastern sky, sending out a few to reconnoiter before the troops advance. Beaver slap at their work, and birds make sleepy peeps and rustling sounds of settling for the night. Bats careen through pinkish twilight, silent of wing, dipping water that turns from salmon to silver-grey, in streaks and swirls, in circles and ruffles, an ever-changing pattern, alive and moving, breathing, throbbing, stroking ... encored with silt.

Wind changes from up-canyon to down.

Nocturnal sounds slip in to replace those of day, as the new moon, a golden eyelash awash in a sea of turquoise, drifts to the horizon and disappears. Sand banks fall to the shameless advances of the water. In the shallows where the river runs over smooth-as-velvet rocks, I hear his seductive night conversation.

Flecks of black dot his surface where driftwood bobs and floats—an occasional one sounding *Tinny's* bell, where she swings gently in and out, little chocolate waves patting her gunnels, shushing … muttering …

Not much time … not much time … not much time. Godalmighty, Tad, hurry; get your bloody buns in gear!

Journal Note: Saturday, September 24, 1955

Well, Long-lean-and-lanky finally gets here! Woody doesn't hear him come in, so Tad walks from the landing strip to the store and downs the beer Woody planned to bring him before we even know he has arrived. An hour later, after Woody's through bending his ear, they rattle up to the ferry landing, where Frank and I are *still* camped … and waiting.

Lemme say, we don't waste any time getting loaded and *outta here*. My waterproof Timex watch says 3:30. Watch! Never again. No way. As we slide through Trachyte riffle, I undo the band. When we disappear from sight of Hite around the Dorothy Bar, I fling it high in the air. It lands, splat!

"Of *Time* … and The River." Heh-heh.

[Camp—mile 154*] <END JOURNAL>

Journal Note: Sunday, September 25
(Morning, Second Day)

We are camped eight miles from Hite on a l-o-n-n-g willow bar. Brilliant sun here, popcorn clouds to the north. Last night grey-white-indigo thunderheads came down close to the river and snagged themselves on the Henrys. I thought we were going to get it, but only a few drops fell. So begin our joyful days—back to being kids again. In rhythm with the earth's turning. To bed at dark, up with the sun; I fall so easily into the pattern, here beneath big skies.

Frank's pancakes and syrup for breakfast. First stop Ticaboo—running water clear to the river now—cooler weather, less evaporation I suppose. Wish I had at least a picture of Cass's hand-hewn cabin where only the chimney stands now. Easy to see why he loved this place and to understand some of his loneliness, after reading "The Trail of Sixty Snows." But the funny thing is, he and Bert Loper would squabble heatedly over

---

(*Miles noted are not to the absolute tenth, but are within a quarter-mile of mapped distance).

politics whenever they met. Can't you just see it? The only two hermits for miles around, living three miles apart on opposite shores—see them nose to nose, then stomping away in a fit of pique until the next time they meet to have another go? I love it!

Tad and I wiggle in and out of Ticaboo's potholes on the way back for lunch at the boat, where we lie on the smooth, warm, curved-to-fit-us sandstone to dry and nap. Tad snores. Frank, down at the boat, monkeys with the little twenty-five-horse motor that we will use only to go upstream for something we've missed, or to make up the time we've lost in some canyon we couldn't bear to leave.

At mile 142, we find a spring (that cows have usually taken over), clean and full of watercress; I gather a bunch for tonight's salad. Just above here is the makeshift grave of a man who drowned in Cataract Canyon this April. The body eddied out and was found by Frank, half-buried in the sand, in early May. (I have to get all this from Tad because Frank won't talk about it; just being here and remembering has made him sick.) They found some identification and managed to place the remains in hard, shallow ground beneath piled-up rocks—to the misery of all concerned, except the deceased. If I should cross the Styx anywhere along this water trail, I want the river to have me, and I'll haunt them as tries to take me from it. Laws, rules, regulations be damned. Just push me into the current and let the river grind away. (I know several more who feel the same, like Bert Loper felt—no fuss, no muss, no costly, stupid, morbid rituals.) The crude cross they erected has fallen down; the rocks have been disturbed by small animals. Tad and I try putting the cross back, but a stiff wind will knock it down again. With any luck at all, some high-water year will wash his bones clean and welcome him to bedrock.

Warm Springs Creek. The place to sing and be sung back to by the echo from mile-long Tapestry Wall. Tonight, a feast—the frozen steaks Tadito bought from Woody. Two fires, a small one for cooking, one to warm ourselves; natural rock benches to sit or lie on. Tad and I sing after dinner. His old Mexican crack (aye-yie-yie!) rings through the warm air, bringing memories of our early Tucson days, but this tops everything in *my* youth, and I suspect in his, too. Frank leans back against his bedroll, gazing into the fire with a look I've not seen before. Lines around his eyes and the tightness that often appears at the corners of his mouth are gone. I'd describe this as a look of utter peace. He's relaxed, his hands lie open beside him, palms up, and I'll be dinged—his boots are *off!*

The softness of the air, the strong violet-to-purple rim line, pasted on a flawless turquoise sky that almost rings with clarity; the campfire, the songs where they belong—in harmony with the river; the cold baths, the warmed rocks; all these sensations are what will sustain me for another year, get me through the garbage, the good times and mundane. These scenes are mine to keep—a gift like no other gift I've ever owned.

[Camp—mile 136, Warm Springs Creek] <END JOURNAL>

"We Three" (left to right: Tad Nichols, Katie Lee, Frank Wright), Lee's Ferry, 1955. Photo by Katie Lee.

Forgotten Canyon (mile 132), 1955. Photo by Tad Nichols.

Katie and Frank at Navajo Creek (mile 95.6), 1956. Photo by Tad Nichols.

Katie on Monte Chresto Island (mile 152.5), 1954. Photo by Frank Wright.

Inside Hidden Passage (mile 76.1), 1954. Photo by Tad Nichols.

Frank and Tad, "Stags at Bay," Halls Creek Bar (mile 118.7), 1955. Photo by Katie Lee.

Frank on cap above Hidden Passage (mile 76.3). Photo by Tad Nichols.

Icy pool in Iceburg Canyon, Katie and Frank standing in upper left corner (mile 101.6), 1955. Photo by Tad Nichols.

"The Pagan," Cattails Canyon (mile 54.3), 1957. Marty Koehler photo, courtesy of Katie Lee.

Gregory Butte from Spring Trail Canyon, looking upstream (mile 45.6), 1957.
Photo by Katie Lee.

TEN

Chameleon Light

Journal Note: Monday, September 26, 1955 (Third Day)

My bedroll is not where morning shade will find me. I'm down on the ledge near the water, where Syl slept last year, where she got an early scorching from the fireball. Now the sun comes up later, cooler, farther south, seems to come up even slower. But what makes the real difference, makes the canyon another place, is that it comes up *lower* ... and stays there. It has found the rim and warms me slowly from the bottom of my cocoon to the top. <END JOURNAL>

Good friends have private names for each other. Over the years Tad Nichols has acquired a nest of them from me—E.T., Tad-O, Tadpole, Professor, Tadito, for starters. He calls me pal and sweetie, or Kay. Frank is always Frank or J. Frank, or was until I saw his bootprints in soft mud that had reshaped them to a legendary size; now he's Bigfeets to me.

Last year Bigfeets gave me his special name. During a water fight he circled both my wrists in one big hand, index finger between them, plunked me down hard on the deck, and held me there, grinning—"What're you going to do now, Little Wrists? Better holler 'nuff!" I couldn't even budge, still I tried. "Holler 'nuff," he said again, gripping harder. "Oou-w-w-w," I squealed, "'nuff!"

Journal Note: September 26 (Continued)

Air hisses from the open valve on my mattress, and my pencil wiggles steadily over the journal, trying to record all of yesterday's happenings and feelings. Frank has gone up to the pool for spring water; E.T. squats beside the fire with a fork as long as his arm, circling smoke as he tends a frypan of sputtering bacon that's curling around his fork and flopping over the sides like Shirley Temple's curls. Coffee smells magnificent!!

Frank returns from the spring with the big canteen, puts it in the boat, then comes back and tosses out the bucket of clear water we spent some time getting last night.

"Hey-y-y! what'd you do that for? I haven't brushed my teeth yet, or filled my jug."

"Me either," chimes Tad.

Frank's got a funny look on his face. "I didn't think you'd want to drink it."

"Why not? We did—all of us. Tastes sweet as rain. Even makes the coffee smell better."

"Hmm-m-m, that's interesting. In the stream about five feet *above* where we got our water last night, I found this cute little feller," and from his jacket pocket he pulls a large, very dead, very wet packrat, holding it at eye level by its tail.

Tad belches his famous "Ra-a-atz!" I puff my cheeks in a simulated barf, take a sniff of the critter, decide he's a nice clean rat, take him by his ropy tail and toss him in the river, saying, "I doubt we'll get bubonic plague, and the coffee water has done boiled."

"I'm glad I don't drink coffee," says Frank, going for a plate of bacon and eggs. (As far as I know he doesn't even drink Mormon tea—that of the ephedra bush, which, thank you very much, tastes like green soap. Our fine coffee might taste like camel puddy to Frank, but he'd never say so.)

I pour myself a mugful and go sit between them on the ledge, feet dangling over the water as we eat and watch soft, yellow light slip across the brawny mile of Tapestry Wall. A movie in slow motion.

"How's the coffee?" asks E.T.

"Excellent. Have some."

"Yes-yes … mmm. I have to agree with you; it was a clean rat." He twists the hair on his crown between two long fingers—an ingrained mannerism he can't control—then tilts a greasy chin toward the wall and says, "Just look at that, the varnish; doesn't it remind you of fringe on a Spanish shawl?"

It does. Every strand is defined, as if lit from behind—in fact the whole canyon emerges in bright crystal clarity. Even our echoes chime back to us.

"But look, you guys, why does the wall seem so different now? Until this morning it was always kinda mudded together, hard to photograph, temperamental—and I know this will sound silly, but now it looks … well, sorta happy."

"Summertime light is too high and flat against it," says Tad. "You have to take it on a hazy day because direct light bleeds out the tapestry. In diffused light there's more definition. But you're right, sweetie, it's temperamental."

Bigfeets says, "I was here one afternoon when the sun had gone behind it and got a good shot from the reflected light off the rocks over east."

"Yeah, that might work," I say seriously. "But if we really want an *extra*ordinary photo, we're gonna have to move that wall."

We pass Olympia Bar. I know a bunch more about the peregrinations of all that placer mining junk than I did a year ago. They sure tore up the place; and, my god, the *noise* they must have made! Steam-driven paddle wheelers, propeller-driven launches, automobile engines, barges—ka-chunk-a-chunk-bang-clang-boom-blast all day long—amplified by the constant echo off these walls.

And now, so very quiet …

… like our steady flow with the current to our next stop—unforgettable Forgotten Canyon. Here, I first feel a kinship with the ancient ones and the embracing protection this Eden gave them. A wide plain stretches a mile or more up and down the Colorado in front of its entrance—a nice place to plant and grow things. It has a short sibling canyon beside it, where some pretty sorry Moki steps lead to the remains of a small cliff house. A huge pothole that retains water even in the dry time is close by and partly full, along with several smaller ones, nearly empty, all telling me how special this canyon was. Is. <END JOURNAL>

In my home I display only two photographs of the lost Glen—the one of Forgotten near its confluence that I stare into every morning, doing my exercises; the other deep inside Mystery Canyon. These two very different photos recall the light in those places. An indefinable light, unlike any other. Eliot Porter, in the Sierra Club Book, *The Place No One Knew* (a title that has always irritated me, with beautiful photos that utterly fail to capture the spirit of Glen Canyon) was able to portray the light better with his fine prose than with his microscopic camera techniques:

> *"A sudden shaft of sun … lights a strip of wall a dazzling yellow and is reflected to our eyes at water level from the thin curved edge where the pool laps the rock in gentle undulations, like golden threads reaching ahead to delineate for a moment the wavering separation of water from the stone." Or "… notice how the swirling surface of the green, opaque river converts light reflected from rocks and trees and sky into*

a moiré of interlacing lines and coils of color, or observe the festooned, evocative designs etched into the walls by water and lichens."

Journal Note: Still September 26

As for me, I can only explain how the light feels; its chameleon quality; the ambivalence it creates.

When a canyon has *everything,* from huge old cottonwoods, to stream bank willows, to monkey flowers and gilia and maidenhair fern, grass and moss, deep standing pools, slides, high waterfalls, sit-in potholes, crawl-in alcoves, cathedrals, Moki steps, ledges, ruins, wide places, narrow and twisty ones (where you must swim, wade, bridge, buttress, or chimney it; climb, cling, crawl through it, or backtrack and try to bench around the impasse), you can *never* tell what's coming up around the next bend. Will you walk into a blare of full sunlight, or a mere streak? Twist with the stream under a deep and dark overhang? Find yourself in mottled shade beneath a redbud? Or end up standing in a bowl of stone awash in light so indirect you've no idea where it's coming from?

Light sets the stage for canyon mood changes. Forever ongoing.

With his tripod, Tadpole stands in the shadow of the overhang near the place where I took the photograph that's on my bedroom wall. He is a soft shade of green—looks like a half-sprung frog crouched behind his camera—where there is no green at all. The green is on the ground, under the water, in the grass, and in the big cottonwood tree far to his left.

Leaving him and Frank, I walk upstream, round another bend, and suddenly I step into a stab of sunlight. A dozen feet beyond is a black hole (as far as I can tell), but in the streak that stretches up the sides of the U-shaped canyon bottom, the light cries out like a spotlight in front of a velvet curtain. It has changed my mood; if it wasn't here, I'd pass up this place altogether, but now the canyon asks if I wouldn't like to do my tennies-sticking-to-steep-stone act ... see how twenty feet one way or another will make a difference.

Farther along I enter a space of "quiet light" where no direct sunlight falls, yet is lambent—a liquid light that comes from all around and underfoot. Far out of sight overhead, it has ricocheted down and spread itself in ways that confuse the senses. It gets so weird in here sometimes I think I'm *hearing* the light, *smelling* the temperature and *feeling* the sound.

In this zone there is a presence ...

Only the sound of trickling water now, yet my ears ring with distant calls and soft footfalls, the hollow clunk of fired pots against stone, the scrape of *mano* (hand stone) on *metate*. I'm being led on a path to pre-history that makes me part of all that came before. I don't just know with my mind what it means; looking up, I *see* what it means. Once this stone dune was three hundred to five hundred feet high; trickles of water ran their gravitational course, making small egg-shaped hollows up there in the softer parts, which eons later became large pot-holes, which after more millennia became deep, convoluted, crevasses, which in turn some-times widened to two-arm-length passages—so I *know* what will endure, and am pleased to note it won't be me ... or you ... or any of us.

In this all-embracing light the stream reveals the sky, the sky fills the stream. A pool shows two moving crosses that scream, Aw-w-kk! Aw-w-kk! Their call ripples the pool's surface. The ravens rout me from my dream.

Coming from the quiet light, ahead I see a huge circular wall in full sunlight. It pulls me forward like a magnet, but I stop in the long shade before it, enjoying the play of low, autumn light against the great min-eral-painted curtain.

All Glen Canyon is a stage!

Somewhere behind me I hear the soft voices of Tad and Frank, blended with the talking stream, a canyon wren's down-the-flute song and the one-note Dr-r-r-r of a tiny frog. Suddenly I understand what it is I've missed up to now. Before, I've been here with many others, always chat-tering. Now, it filters into my consciousness that I must work my way *out* of commercial trips, full of the strangers I've brought here so they might help to save the place. Yet, it has taken only three days with friends who can sense when and where not to talk to know that the quiet commu-nion, the intimacy this canyon is offering me, will be lost if I go on let-ting strangers interfere with my purpose for coming here:

To learn what nature has to say.

We have a lengthy discussion over lunch at the foot of Forgotten's nar-rows—whether to climb the high-water Moki steps that stitch the canyon wall, eventually leading up, around and over to California bar; to cross the river and explore Smith Fork Canyon; or float on downriver. If we do everything I want to do, we won't get to Lee's Ferry in a month of Sundays—not that I want to.

Tad: "Those steps give me the willies."

Frank: "Miners made these—they're not so bad ... Moki ones are nearly gone."

Me: "I've never been up them. C'mon, Tadpole, you've done them be-fore. Lets go, it'll only take about fifteen minutes."

The two men look at each other with an "oh, yeah, sure" expression, knowing full well it will be an hour before we're back in the canyon bottom, but they humor me. After all, I'm just learning—I need all the help I can get.

Frank goes first, I follow, then Tad.

On these walls you're on your own—nobody stops to give you hand or foot assistance, and you'd better *start* with the correct footing or you're in deep doo-doo. It's okay to look as far as the guy behind you (if there is one) but keep your eyes *off* the ground wa-a-a-ay-y-y down there, or you could forget that you ain't no fly! All this I remind myself as I put one hand, then the other, in the step overhead that Frank's big foot has just vacated.

He turns and quietly says, "Leave a few steps between us in case I have to back down for some reason." (His gentle way of giving a lesson—he's done this hundreds of times, and there's no way he's going to back down, especially since these miner's Mokis are a breeze compared to the real thing).

I glance down at Tad just starting. He's not so dumb, or scared either; two cameras swinging from his shoulders, legs like a damn giraffe—could probably take them two at a time if he had to.

Up the wall, around *very* thin ledges, up more steep rises to the cap, until we're almost two hundred feet above a river flanked by deep green foliage sometimes so thick the mouth of a canyon won't be readily seen at river level. Upstream, we look over all of Sundog Bar, the mouth of Knowles Canyon and Smith Fork; downstream, two-mile-long California Bar and Hansen Canyon; and above everything, far to the north, rising dark blue into cobalt, we can see the tops of the Henry Mountains. Another world ... in just minutes ... twenty, to be exact. We take our photos and turn back.

Me: "Last guy up is first guy down."

Tad: "These steps give me the willies."

Me: "Willys-Knights, or Willies as in lots of guys named Willie?"

Frank: "Huh?"

Smith Fork is wide at the mouth and full of large cottonwoods. A clear, shallow stream carries a bit more water than Forgotten, and where the canyon narrows, cattails punctuate its flow. We burst the ripe ones open, laughing like little kids as they ooze from their stems and swirl like a dancer's veil in the air. They stick in our hair and tickle our noses, but we can't stop playing with them, because when they burst they form beautiful patterns, each one different.

A couple miles up it looks possible to walk out on top. I go up the Navajo as far as I dare. "Bigfeets, d'ya think we can get up just using these natural, eroded holes?"

"It probably could be done, but I don't think it's practical, Li'l Wrists." The drop is fifty or seventy-five feet, and there aren't many hand-holds. And it's getting ...

Late!

As the direct hit of sun leaves the wall and flares its parting shot against the spires, buttes, and mesas of the Colorado Plateau, our skins color to Wingate sandstone. The canyon's mood changes rapidly, turning our thoughts and our feet toward yet another light—our campfire.

Night settles cool in Glen Canyon in September. In the first weeks there's a noticeable brittleness in the air. Waters from up north are already chilled, and there's little chance they'll warm between the high walls, which now cast early shadows on the water. Nearby our camp in the quiet eddy, mist swirls and rises into the willows, as if the river's out on a cold night watching his breath vaporize. I call it "witches' breath" and stare at it for a long time. Tadito, the desert rat, sneezes—HORSE-shit!—and Bigfeets, when he thinks nobody's looking, stoically reaches for the small of his back and presses hard.

On a darkly varnished wall near the mouth of Smith Fork is an Anasazi story board. It pictures squiggles, dots and spirals, suns and snakes, animals and bugs; human and superhuman figures armed with bows and arrows, others with arrows through them; much game, many hunters; hands, a lot of feet and bird prints; heavy-hung Shaman figures with goofy headdresses, Kokopelli from the mythical (?) world, with his hump and his flute—and things the archaeologists, anthropologists, and other educated guessers will never figure out.

Our campfire near the petroglyph wall pulls the figures into strong relief, making them dance grotesquely in the flickering light. We lie facing them, propped on our bedrolls watching the square-shouldered gods move down through the centuries to join us. I point to one with my big toe.

"See that one there? Reminds me of Barry Goldwater."

"Which one?" asks Tad, "the guy with the large ... "

"No, sweetie, the one *without* the balls. He's been *down* this river and *still* he writes me stupid letters about how much more beneficial it will be to everyone when it's not here anymore."

Already having my suspicions, I decide now is the time to find out why Tad was late meeting us at the river. Turning from the dancing figures, I nail him with the firelight in my eyes. "What *were* you doing that kept you so long, E.T.?"

Frank feels something coming, gets up and heads for the kitchen box. "Cookies, anyone?"

"I'll have some," answers Tad, "might need to sweeten this exchange." He rolls over, facing me, props on an elbow, and sets his defenses: "I stayed for a meeting with some state officials so I could show them some slides of the canyon—give them some reasons not to build the dam."

"Did you tell them this time the slides were of Glen Canyon, the place they are intending to wipe off the map? Last time I went to one of your showings, you failed to mention that little item."

"Wasn't the time or place for it, sweetie."

"*Everyplace* is the time and place for it now, Tad, or we won't have the chance of a snowball in hell of stopping them. We can't let a single opportunity pass. I write the letters, I show your movie, I sing the songs, I write for newspapers and magazines. If there's a hearing I can get to, I go to protest their insane actions, their idiotic proposals, their greed—but there aren't enough of us to … "

"I know, and I've been around when you've had a go at some of the officials, even though I understand exactly why." He puffs slowly on his pipe, making little wheezing noises. "It doesn't help to get them angry."

"Damn it, why are you always defending these people, E.T.?"

"I'm not defending them, but I want you to see that the way you fight for our canyon doesn't always help."

"Yes, dear, I've heard that before—'get your facts down, your statistics up, and your emotions out.' What the hell's wrong with emotion? Without it we'd just be animals."

"Doesn't mix with the oil of politics, is what I infer."

"Neither does reason," offers Frank, opening the cookie tin and handing it around. "Katie's proposal of not building the dam high enough for water to enter the Rainbow Bridge National Monument *is* reasonable. It'd save a lot of beautiful country up here, too."

"Anyway," I persist, still wound up, "what's wrong with the way I fight for our river? I sure use more *reason* than the Wreckers when I'm at hearings ticking off reasons for keeping it. They've got their goddamn nerve telling me what it *should* be like when half of them *haven't ever seen this place!*"

Tad taps out his pipe on a nearby stone and says, "You aren't going to like this, but say it's left as is. All spring, summer, and fall, boats line the banks. How many beer cans would be sitting here beside us? Where would our freedom be to enjoy this solitude? How long before we'd have to find a new place to get away from all those we've helped lure here?"

"No!" I bark, "that kind of camper excludes himself; he's too lazy to get here. Now it's a river for *out*door people. When the Bu-Wreckers are done, it'll be a 'recreation area' for *in*door people. River people *earn* the thrill of seeing and being in a majestic place. It's the clods who need everything brought to them, packaged, arranged, and spoon-fed, who don't deserve a place like this. Make this ... this spiritual place a reservoir so they can see less faster? Insane! They'll dump their crap all over, squat and shit on the slickrock, climb out of their ski boats into their campers and drive away without the faintest notion of where they've been—just another playground with wall-to-wall water!

Tad plays devil's advocate. "Ah-ha, but it's *progress* to make Glen Canyon a reservoir. Your Bunglers of Resources don't know *why* it's progress, because the word has lost its meaning. What they really mean is it's *money*; in America the words are synonymous."

Still burning inside, I get up to put more wood on the fire. "Well, I *don't* want it to be a stinking puddle, and I have as much right to it as they do, more actually; I know and love it. My very soul is in this canyon, so ... I think I'll spend the rest of my days figuring a way to blow up their damn dam. Fucking politicians! O-oh, sorry Frank."

Tad pockets his pipe. *"Not* reasonable. *Highly* emotional, as I've said before."

He's right, of course. "Well, Tad-O, when every hidden pocket's been flooded, bulldozed, oil slicked, strip mined or made radioactive, where do we flee the techno-bureaucratic monster?"

"Not to worry, pal, by then our culture will have flown up its own ass, thereby obliterating itself. Have a cookie."

I sing for a long time, using Tad's shins for a backrest until he falls asleep and the fire fades to coals. I put away my guitar, get pj's and toothbrush from my duffel, and head for the boat while Frank rolls three warm rocks from the fire to the foot of each bedroll. His longhandles disappear into his sack as Tad awakens, wanders to the willows to watch the vapor rise from *his* stream, check Polaris, sniff the wind for any weather change, and return for a last stare at the coals. He doesn't have to look to see where I am.

"I smell your soap, pal ... things are back to river norm. You'd take a bath if there was ice floating out there!"

"You're right," I call to him. "Come on in, you're startin' t' get a little whiffy."

"In a pig's ass!"

"Something like that."

He snorts, rubs his thumb under his nose, says, "Goodnight, sweetie," and goes to his sack.

I pull myself up over *Tinny*'s stern and reach for my towel, rubbing hard to get the blood flowing while I exchange a few quiet words with my river friend and pull on my pajamas. For a minute I squat beside the coals warming my buns, then wiggle clean, warm, and glowing into my sack. A bath in that moving, living river is like slipping out of the womb all fresh and new. I glance to my right; Tad asleep again, Frank softly puffing with what I hope are sweet dreams. My worry and tension have floated on downstream; never felt so relaxed, so free. Tired, sleepy, can't close my eyes. ... I watch the dark shadow of the cliffs creep upstream, slowly erasing the moon's reflection on the water.

Later in the night—rocking, slipping, bed is shaking, shuffling me across it like a pea on a breadboard; hold on! No, no! Grip hard ... oh-h-h. ... I'm slipping over the edge ... slide ... spin-n-n-n. Fight! Sleep ... awake ... asleep. Awake! Where?

Ah-a-aah, water whispers. Realizing, at last, where I am, I sit up in the dark, feeling the night wrap around me like expensive silk. Must be past midnight—moon has sailed on and left a trail of stars in its wake; air is cool, smells of earth and mulch and silt. My two guys are sound asleep—Tad snores.

I know they didn't feel the earthquake. Neither did I, really; the dream is recurrent, a hangover from being in two major California earthquakes—one when I was six or seven, the other a couple of years ago. But that's only part of the reason for the dream. I've learned that it occurs when my subconscious registers a shakeup, a new direction that will affect, even change, my life. How long it takes to manifest in my conscious mind is always a question, but ...

It's a sign that *something* is in the wind.

[Camp—mile 132.0, Smith Fork] <END JOURNAL>

ELEVEN

~

Killing Loveliness

The beach where I awaken is flat and long, the sand rippled in patterns that only a river alive and well could fashion. It had to be a gentle and calm day when he played the sand into these little inch-apart corrugations, a river whose eddies swirled upstream in big scallops, changing the pattern here and there as the water dropped a foot or so. Tad had to shake me out of my sack before a higher sun removed the deep shadows between the ripples; left to me, I'd have waited 'til they were gone and missed nature's best effort. Part of the Professor's teaching is being there at right-light time.

Dutch oven biscuits! Ham 'n' eggs! Pineapple rings! Coffee!—with water from Forgotten Canyon; no rats sighted. We spend much of the morning on California Bar. From here down to Hall's Crossing (12 miles) was probably the largest concentration of placer mining in Glen Canyon. In the late 1800s, it is said, there were three or four dredges operating in the canyon at the same time and that their racket could be heard as far away as South Mountain! There's still much heavy machinery about—a buckled and broken narrow-gauge railway, ore carts and a steam boiler. The grave and cement headstone of the former owner, A. G. Turner, is still here, but the lead pipe fence around it has been knocked down, and pieces are missing. I'm real happy to see that the high walls of an incredible house, built of smooth river stones and very little mortar, still defy gravity by remaining stacked in what looks to be a most haphazard manner—guess no one's had the urge to pull it down ... yet. The rusty, iron forge still stands nearby, but next year I'll bet it's gone. Might take it myself the way things are disappearing around here; but no, I'd have to defer to E.T., who covets it far more than I. We both know Frank would disapprove. He says this claim, and all that's on it, belongs to the Gearhart's heirs and that they'll come to get it one day. Among other things missing is the 1846 Salt Lake City newspaper that was in an old steamer trunk in the tunnel. Someone had to take it so no one else could enjoy a look into the past.

Maybe the ghost of Ollie Prichard has returned.

In one of Slim Williams' tales he recalled this character Ollie, who used to work the Happy Jack back in the early days when it was a copper mine.

"Quite a hijacker he was, or more to the point, stinkin' crooked. He'd lift anything that was loose and some things that was tied down; once in a while things that was chained, bolted and locked down. Had a voice that ranged somewhere between the obnoxious and the everlasting, and there were persons out and about who would like to have put a hole in him that bled copiously from both ends."

"I guess you mean he was a thief, huh Slim?"

"I'd say he was more like a birth defect."

I understand why a lot of old relics are turning up missing. Everyone thinks this place is going to croak before too long, so the gleaners have begun to "save" what's left for their very own posterity. Bigfeets thinks it's polite to *ask*.

But Hallelujah! The treadle sewing machine in the tunnel is here intact. Mrs. Gearhart, did you sew patches on your minerman's pants? Make dresses for your girls, trousers for the boys? Wash their clothes in the river or in that oval copper boiler over there? Bet you had to boil 'em—miners are a dirty lot. It's dry in here, so all this stuff is pretty well preserved—pots and pans and milk cans, gallon jugs and dynamite boxes, piece of an old saddle and canvas bags. Oh-ho! ... so you got to ride up and down the bar and maybe swim the horse (mule?) across to visit whoever was there, or ride the barge. I see it half-buried in the sand, down there in a tangle of willow, tamarisk, and squawberry bushes.

~

Tad and I eat lunch with a dunk in the river. Nothing like sitting neck-deep in a cool, caressing river on a hot day with a sandwich in one hand and a cup of lemonade in the other. The sun may be lower in September, but it still has much authority. Now that I can do *what* I want *when* I want, without anyone even bothering to look my way, much less, make some sleazy remark about my birthday suit. I can do what comes *naturally.* Safe … is what I am, safe in the care of a Mormon Saint and an old buddy—all about as sexually attracted to one another as fish are to buffalo.

We cross to Hansen Creek on the right bank, where we have to walk through the willows and along the Kayenta ledge to enter its mouth. The most beautiful array of tapestry walls I've yet to see are in this canyon. Every bend shows another and each is a work of art. Yet, the canyons on this side of the river seem less intimate to me, wider as they meander up toward the Henrys. They get more sun, and possibly a stronger, more prevailing wind from the southwest, and their drainage is longer, with less pitch than those dropping sharply off the mesas on the other side, all of which makes them seem more *used*—full of history no doubt, but lacking the mystery that shrouds the left side. After two miles, a fault line crosses Hansen. I go up the left fissure, to turn and look down on my friends in the riverbed several hundred feet below. I think one could walk out on top here, but I'm not sure so I come back down. We snake on up the main canyon, stopping beneath a large hollowed-out dome. Bigfeets flakes out and takes a snooze. Tad goes up over a dune and into the Navajo where he finds, cut deeper by recent miners or explorers, some Moki steps leading to the cap. Upon returning, he says the canyon pinches out a couple more miles up, where it might be possible to walk out; but here, where I'm taking pictures of the changing colors on these wild tapestry walls, they are five to seven hundred feet high.

Without warning, it seems, the sun has pulled a shadow curtain up the tapestries, shifting our mood from snooze-and-lie-back to hurry-up-and-find-camp. As we walk back to the river, the warm air in our faces turns to a cool breeze at our backs, though I don't see how Tad can walk, he's so loaded down with rocks—even went back upstream to get a piece of chert he found while drinking. Pretty soon our boat will be underwater with *leaverites* (leave 'er right there); says he's going to tumble them when he gets home. I can't help laughing, because he'll leave 'em right where he dumps 'em for the next fifty years.

Tonight we camp on the left bank, still in sight of our last camp only three miles upstream. Now that's what I call progress. Our long hikes, the bliss of freedom, the excitement of discovery, the feel of the wind and water on our skins, the pure air and intensity of beauty all drain our strength for an early sack. Tad and I are there soon after dinner. Bigfeets takes off by himself, probably just to have a talk with the Colorado.

When he comes back, what seems like hours later, I wake up and he whispers over to me as he crawls into his sack that he's found another labyrinth. We'll go explore it in the morning. Even later, I wake to see fleeceback clouds completely covering the sky, a growing moon slipping out between as the herder drives them over the rim and on up river.

[Camp—mile 128.7] <END JOURNAL>

~

My journals tell me about things I've half forgotten, like various chores I was doing for other Rats, and a few historians, in the Glen—positioning names and places for them and taking photographs for verification. The most avid collector of river lore at that time, maybe the most avid ever, was Otis "Dock" Marston. (My two-inch-thick correspondence file written over the years will confirm this.) What was most important to me then, was the search for river folk songs to be used in a book or a record album, whatever came first. We had a kind of unwritten trade agreement—what he wanted to know about the river in exchange for what I wanted about the music. On our "We Three" trip I was taking photographs for him.

Dock had an uncanny knack for pissing people off. Didn't take me long to discover it was his *method* of digging for information (he wasn't subtle) that put people on what he called his "Mad-at-Dock" list. This list included Frank, Jim and Bob Rigg, Norm Nevills and his girls (Dock wanted Norm knocked off his pedestal), and a host of others who did not believe *everything* that happened on the river belonged in Dock's massive archives for the benefit of all river runners in the future. In other words, a good number of folks decided that *many* things were none of his damn business. And when he set out on a project, nine times out of ten it was one that couldn't help but cause contention, like getting it into his head that he could rate good oarsmen/boatmen on a scale of 1 to 10. How? By asking various passengers (and other boatmen) their opinion of a certain boatman in a certain rapid at a certain stage of water. Dynamite! Of course, the fur would fly. Or, having somehow *heard about* an "incident" (an upset/argument/discovery/accident/disagreement), would try to glean his information from different passengers on the trip rather than go to the leader of the expedition, whom (Dock already knew) might not want to tell him about it.

But I liked Dock because he was amusing and, in truth, as covetous, prejudiced, and protective of the river as the rest of us. He must have returned the sentiment, since I wasn't on the "Mad" list. I told him most of what he wanted to know, keeping what was none of his business under wraps. He never offended me, put me down, or took me for a ninny, even if he thought I was. I knew he was a rank chauvinist, but I could always give back what I got. Maybe he knew I was capable of putting a lash on the tongue that could leave a visible welt. Anyhow, I told him what I thought about his information-gathering methods, because he seemed not to understand how he tripped over his own roadblocks. He wrote, on September 22, 1955:

I am still taken aback by your comment on my real trouble which arises from gathering the records and traveling on the River at the same time. No one has ever brought out that point before.

Innocent as hell ... as if all he ever did was "gather the *records*." I wrote to him on October 7, 1955:

Seems to me, if a guy doesn't think you know anything about what he's telling you, a freer flow of conversation would seem evident ... I think the river is too big a place to become involved in petty arguments. I for one, would prefer to just hunt for my songs in the bubbles and forget the fights ... If your object in collecting this information is to discover how to make river travel as safe as possible for future runners, and not to involve people on a personal basis and criticize them for their mistakes, then I can't see why anybody should get sore.

... and from Dock on October 31, 1955:

Frank pointed out the cruelty angle in the delving for the simple truth. That is the first time anyone has brought that point up. I have discussed it with some and have considered getting a Ms written and then locking it up. But on the other side, there are numerous yarns now having currency which bear heavily on some of the River folk.

Yes, the "other side," the one he liked best. Dock most certainly *did* involve people on a personal basis; had a very strong opinion about how things should be done; had a most generous ego; didn't like to be one-upped; had his little jealousies; and I suspect he rather enjoyed his little game of pitting one against the other. Plus, he was highly critical.

Of course, if we'd known, cared, or bothered to check his marginal comments on what we sent him (even supposing he'd have let us), his "records" would have been much skimpier. Get this.

Journal of Katie Lee Made during the Traverse of the Grand Canyon from Bright Angel Creek to Temple Bar, July 1955, with Frank Wright's Oar-powered Section of Mexican Hat Expeditions (The Journal as copied is an edited and amended version of the notes kept during the trip on the water.)

This is what Dock underlined on page 4:

"Duane ... came in bow first, hit everything sideways, ended bow first and still came through with no water." (Dock's margin note: *"In other words bad boating but the rapid wasn't too tough."*)

"Willard ... cracked the bottom with a jolt that knocked him clear up off the seat. He put a hole in it dead center and another right stern." (Dock's margin note: *"Ros Johnson has rated him 'better than Garth.'"*)" (My note: *Garth is Dock's son, whom he rated 10 ... or maybe 9 out of modesty?*)

"Frank ... decided to run it" (not underlined; the rest is) "for the first time in his history of the river! ... Water to the gunnels ... Becky got knocked off and hung on 'til she could climb aboard." (Dock's margin note: *"Frank never has been able to handle this one."*) (My note: *She wasn't in Frank's boat, I was.*)

∼

Whoa there, Dock! Back up!

Marston wasn't running commercial trips in Grand Canyon—he took his family and his buddies, river-wise guys, very few oldies or non-swimmers. The cautious methods Frank was forced to use had absolutely nothing to do with being able to handle a rapid. At that time Frank was called "The Dean of Whitewater Oarsmen" in various magazine articles. Now it's my turn for critical analysis. Dock went to powerboats because he preferred speed and was not all that good at rowing through rapids, I was told by those who boated with him in his rowing days.

Marston wanted the impossible—the truth. The on-the-spot handwritten journals. Off-the-top-of-the-head statements and observations. He railed against Major Powell's journals, dressed up and fattened for publication; same for Dellenbaugh's, other River Rats', and mine—those I chose to send him, typed up, after the trips. (Ooooh my, how he would love this book, written *from* my journals—roll over in your grave, dear Dock!) He felt especially cheated when someone sent him an account wherein everything and everybody was just wonderful, from the mayonnaise to the mud. *Something* interesting must have happened;

why didn't the writer say so? Dock was supposed to be writing a book about the river all this time, but he enjoyed the gathering, the research, the interviews so much, he never got around to it. Besides, the material became titanic—so many boxes, wheelbarrows, and truckloads, that in the end there was no way he could organize it.

Not to worry. His prodigious collection, on nearly everything and everybody who dipped their fingers in the water, contributes more than any book he might have written. The Marston Collection rests there at the Huntington Library in Berkeley, California, for anyone with an inquiring mind, but I would admonish them that the truth evaded Dock a good percentage of the time, as it usually does those who seek it most avidly. For example:

"Frank never has been able to handle this one."

Frank Wright, in twenty years of river running on the Colorado, *never once* flipped a boat, lost a passenger overboard in a rapid, or injured anyone on his trips.

Journal Note: Wednesday, September 28, 1955
(We Three Trip, Fifth Day)

What an unbelievable sight!

As Tadito and I walk up to the little labyrinth Frank discovered last night, we stop dead in front of it and stare, thinking and muttering the same thing. How is it possible; this escalloped, furrowed, slice in the earth, not wide enough past the first ten feet to allow us to walk straight forward? The brilliant sun outside might well be eclipsed; not even a three-inch streak could reach the dry, pink sand floor. The scalloping rises fifty feet or more above us, then disappears in darkness. It's like looking up from the bottom of a primitive well, only far narrower. We squeeze into it a few yards then go down on hands and knees ... push-pull ... get stuck! Scrape more skin off our fingers, knees, shoulders and elbows. I'm first in line and can see a tantalizing fifty feet or more beyond, but can't even get my head through ... I look for a way to chimney up ... impossible. Can't turn around ... have to *back* out.

Why is it so narrow? Because floods rage down over bare slickrock. There are no boulders or tree stumps clasped between the walls overhead, no sticks or branches. Nothing falls in to divert the torrent of water that would, more quickly, gouge the rock and widen the fissure—only the very slow process of wind and sand on sandstone in the raging orgy of a storm.

Out into the light again, I look back at the shadowed entrance and see that this sensual side canyon's aperture resembles the intricate, smooth, pinkish folds of a *vulva.* <END JOURNAL>

No wonder Dick Sprang once wrote:

You call the river HE. I call Glen SHE. Grand is male. The San Juan was male. But Glen was goddess and bitch, saint and whore. She was Woman ... smiling in the sun, snarling in storms; a ball-cutter and murmuring caressing angel, always luring me, promising; casually or with wild passion giving just enough to entrap me forever; promising more than a man could survive if he permanently bedded her— thus pledging the best death of all ... I knew her carnal glory eight times. ... Glen, my lost love. She dressed in whore clothes, played a rinky-tink piano at noon, and at midnight, a mighty pipe organ brooding deep and black—muted echoing of desire beyond the slick-rocks. Hearing her under far-distant thunder you know why the slick-rocks were shaped the way they were, ground smooth by her killing loveliness ... She flicked her silk at me in backlighted cottonwoods from morning in Ticaboo to sundown in Moki. God, how I made love to her side canyons, glory holes beyond a man's fantasies of all lusts come true. But I never found satiation; she was too goddamn much the timeless Earth Goddess ... Yet the only peace I've ever known, I knew in Glen.

He or she ... the gender of places we love is personal.

Journal Note: September 28 (Continued)

The river is also an orderly Johnny Appleseed. In neat rows a foot apart, that no man-invented instrument could equal, it has sown a dozen rows of willow and tamarisk seedlings up the gently sloping bank downstream from our camp. They spring to life the minute the water recedes. Today the fuzzy greenery rises just above my ankles; come back tomorrow, weather holding, and they'll be up to my knee. The river's soil is that rich and ready to receive—ready to take away too. Our river rises much faster than he drops. Yet, always there is green somewhere on the banks, the bars, and most islands, to contrast with the corals, pinks, and lavenders of the surrounding walls.

We spot a wee side canyon about mile 126.5; oozy entrance, narrow and twisty ... only ... umm ... *full* of a green I ain't too fond of. Poison ivy! We hike up, easing around the itchy crop, to a tantalizing opening above a clear, cold pool. Can't get to it, through it, up it, or near it ... damn it. Doubt if anyone else will, either. <END JOURNAL>

~

Woody: "Indians used t'*eat* the stuff; that's how they got themselves immuned."

"Aw, no! Woody, you're so fulla shit, your eyes are brown. That'd kill them; they'd swell up and itch inside where they couldn't scratch."

"*Did*, I tell ya. Early in the spring, when the stuff is really potent, they'd take a little piece of the leaf, no bigger'n a pencil eraser, and swaller it."

"My mouth itches just thinkin' about that!"

"Couple days later, take another piece, little bit bigger this time ... swaller it."

"I suppose you got 'em eating a whole bush by the end of the week."

"Now listen, Miss Smartass, this here's a *fact*, told me by a Piute Indian. No, they didn't eat no whole bush, only about one leaf b'fore they'uz done; and then they could walk through the stuff all summer 'thout gettin' the itches."

"Well ... *I* heard that Indians just don't get it, period. Something to do with their genetic makeup—they're naturally immunized, doesn't affect them."

"Aw, that's crap. A'course they kin git it; they got skin, ain't they?"

Journal Note: Still September 28 (Afternoon)

Watch the ball in the roulette wheel, how it hugs the sides at high velocity, then drops to the bottom when it slows down.

That's us. We've dropped to the bottom in a tangled heap and are laughing so hard we can't get up. Moki Canyon has a short side piece about a mile up from its mouth, alveolated with bowls eight to ten feet deep, oval to round, sides not too steep to stick to *if* we move fast enough. We speed around the sides in a nearly horizontal position, both arms out for balance, and don't fall in until we run out of breath. I never thought Frank could move that fast, and I was *sure* Tadpole couldn't, yet here we are like six-year-olds, trying out our wings of freedom. Back in the prehistoric days, this canyon must have fairly buzzed with activity. Its great length, many springs, side canyons, and abundant ruins give testimony, and I get the sensation that we're not the first little kids that played around these water pockets when they were empty. But I'm hot and sweaty after all this zooming, and I know where there's a full one, clear and cool, just a little way—in sight even.

"You guys go on back and start lunch, huh? I'm gonna do what comes naturally in the cool, cool water up yonder," I say, thumbing the direction over my left shoulder.

Bigfeets' eyebrows raise and he starts to say something, but changes his mind and waves.

They head back to the boat.

When I reach the pothole, I'm glistening with sweat, my face burning hot, salt running into my mouth. Not wasting a moment, I flip off my tennies, undo my shirt, pull the scarf from my head, run down and jump in.

The clear, untouched pool accepts me into its emerald depths like a big drop of water. I am part of it … it is part of me … surely I was once a fish. I dive down again and again, feel the water-fingers softly caressing my hot face, tracing my underarms, my neck and breasts—nipples raised hard against the cold. Its roiling crisscrosses my back and bottom, moves between my legs and up through my toes like feathers, tickling. I bubble up from the depths, many degrees colder than the sun-warmed upper layer, yet with all my motion, no sand has stirred from the bottom. Looking down, treading slowly, the spectrum around my head flickers and waves in many shades of green, like an aurora. The pool lies half in, half out of the sun, and though the water is not going anywhere, it seems to move against me still, even as I lie immobile on its surface. I flip and turn, purring to the sensual caress. I have dipped into a private treasure and am wrapped in the arms of the True Gods.

Maybe ten, maybe fifteen minutes.

Cooled to a most pleasant temperature I swim back to the sunny side to climb out. Foot slips and I fall back in … try another place close by, but slip again. There are no handholds on the dry, smooth sandstone above me. The pool is not full to its sloping rim, so from above, the sides seemed to slope gently, yet from down here they are quite steep.

Far *too* steep!

I suck in a quick breath of panic. Frank and Tad have probably not even reached the boat, a mile away.

Cool it, girl! Get hold of yourself. There *has* to be a foothold somewhere. Anxiously, I swim around the sides, checking every spot, then notice that in so doing I've made slick those grips that might have been possible when dry, yet I go at them all again only to compound the problem.

I swim back to the place where I ran down and jumped in; it is no longer in the sun. My tennis shoes lie just out of reach, my scarf trailing over the nearest one.

"I'm not alone," I say aloud. "They'll come back for me when I don't show up for lunch."

Then with sheer stupid hope that Tad has stopped along the way to take more pictures, that they are still within earshot, I yell as loud as I can ...

"Fra-a-nk! Ta-a-ad! Big-fe-e-e-ets! E.T.! Come back!"

The sound echoes obediently from the vaulted wall six hundred feet above—then silence, stubborn and absolute.

You stupid, *stupid* little fool! You knew better than to get yourself into this fix. Dumb, incautious idiot!

How long? How long before they'll realize something's wrong? How long can I hold on? The sun is leaving the pool altogether and I am suddenly *very cold.* The few places where I can grip the slick wall are inadequate if I'm going to shiver ... and I'm starting to shiver now. There's a fingerhold I can stick to with much effort, but I must t-tread water m-most of the time ... legs so c-cold ... feel like they might cramp. Float on my back ... but I stirred up the cold from down deep ... no warm water ... on top ... anymore ... need to keep moving ... keep moving.

Bigfeets ... hurry! Tad ... please!

I tell myself I must not cry. But the only warmth in my whole body is spilling unrestrained from my eyes.

"Goddess and bitch ...

... carnal glory ...

... *killing loveliness.*" <END JOURNAL>

TWELVE

The Bond-fire

That's bullshit: "When we think we're about to drown, our whole life passes in front of us."

Must be *after* we've drowned, sucked that last breath of water into our lungs, that our subconscious punches "fast reverse" just before the bulb burns out.

Quién sabe? Quién hacer cosa?

My whole *future* was passing in front of me. All the things I had yet to accomplish were racing through my head, along with things I'd set up in the past that would surely help me in the future. I was some kinda rare fish, I knew that—probably the only folksinger in the business who didn't wear dirty sandals and a bird's nest in her hair.

I'd guested on TV shows up the kazoo, played benefits with Belafonte, dated a couple of columnists, been taken to the old Dill Pickle Club by Carl Sandburg for lunches, written articles for the travel section of the *Chicago Tribune* and *St. Louis Post-Dispatch,* lectured and showed Tad's San Juan/Glen Canyon film at women's clubs from the Great Lakes to Louisiana, and been interviewed like I was someone from outer space—which of course I was, to them. I had sung at well-known supper clubs and hotels that paid many more shekels than the coffeehouse circuit, like three weeks at the Chantilly Room of the Monclair Hotel in St. Louis, three at Mr. Kelley's in Chicago. There were fine reviews everywhere from the press, plus appearances on esteemed radio shows—*National Barn Dance* and Stud Terkel's popular WFMT show, *Midnight Special,* with Josh White.

All of the above in preparation for the months ahead. My agent had told me, my peers and friends confirmed, that I was ready to hit the big time—the Big Rotten Apple—New York! New York! Unless I made it in New York, they said, I hadn't really made it.

I could see it. The vision floated before my watery eyes. I *had* to play at the Blue Angel, the hottest nightclub in New York ... "*that's where I belong.*"

But first came pity.

Oh-o—oh-oh, poor me. ... I have loved and treasured your canyons beyond any other place on earth; I've trumpeted your magnificent beauty, mystery and wildness. How can you do this to me? All my hard work gone to pot ... pothole! Those wrangle-tangle days, the sadness (now I'll never be able to bring my son here), the hope, the pressure, the seeking to understand my worth—trying to find the real me, through you ...

THE VERY REASON I CAME HERE!

Too bad, cutie—the lurching walls call back to me—watch your step next time. Been here three years, heard all sorts of tales about my inviting-but-treacherous potholes, and think you're so "in step with the stone" you can walk straight up my walls, huh? Think again, stupid. Serves you right!

Does not! I trusted you (can ever a love be trusted?), you deceptive, tempting, teasing. ... You're like the Sirens; you made it *easy* to walk in, and now, you sonofabitch ...

Whoa, wait a minute ... walk in ... *walk* out? Maybe ... if I can ...

Then I get mad. Teeth-grinding furious. Totally pissed. I'll be damned if I am going to drown in your pot ...

I goddamn well will not!

Journal Note: Wednesday Afternoon, September 28, 1955 (Continued)

Half an hour later, when I hear them coming, I am sitting in the sun up from the pool, putting on my tennies.

The blue scarf spread beneath me nearly matches the color of my bod. I pull on shorts and halter, teeth chattering noisily, more now from nervous exhaustion than the cold. Bigfeets takes in the scene, cocks his head, and sucks in the corners of his mouth, deliberating. "Well, thank the Lord!" he says, a smile dissolving his puzzled look.

E.T.'s reaction is different. "What in bloody hell are you up to? You like to scared us to death. We thought ... "

"You lookin' for Indian ruins," I chatter, "that why you're up here?"

"When you didn't come for lunch ... "

Frank grips Tad's arm to silence him, looks at me, then at the pothole and asks simply, "How'd you manage to get out?"

"You'll never guess."

Tad kneels and touches my leg with the back of his hand. "My god, woman, you're an icicle! How long have you been in there?"

"Until about ten minutes ago."

"Why didn't you call?" asks Tad.

"Holy sh ... nuts, I *did* call. Every thirty seconds at first—takes a bunch of energy to holler, and I was getting thin on that."

"We were too far away to hear you by that time, anyway," says Frank, shaking his head.

Still chattering, my legs trembling, I hold out my hand for Frank to pull me to my feet. Tad begins to rub my back and arms vigorously. "We need to get your circulation going. You do her legs, Frank; she's the color of a blue heron."

He kneels on the slanting sandstone, takes on the rubbing task, and reminds me: "Thought I taught you about jumping into strange potholes last year."

Giving him a shamefaced look under dripping hair, I admit, "I thought you did too, Bigfeets. Obviously I failed to get the message, but after this one you don't have to worry."

"Tell us how you got out," Tad insists.

"You get in there and see if you can tell how I got out."

"I'll be damned ... you crwazy?"

"I'll clue you it doesn't help to get the sides wet."

"You didn't find any footholds?"

"Nary one."

Frank, whose mind works at solutions through observation, not deductive reasoning, begins to hone in on the solution. He notes the scarf lying at my feet. "Your scarf ... it had something to do with your escape, right?"

"You're getting warm ... me too. Thanks, guys, you can stop rubbing now, before I look like a pink flamingo."

"Where were your tennis shoes?" queries Frank.

"Way out of reach."

"How far?"

"Right here." Kneeling, I show them, some four feet above the pool's surface. Then I go after my shirt, which has almost blown into the water.

E.T. twiddles his cowlick and mutters. "The scarf. Mm-m, did you wrap it around you to get purchase on the rim?"

"What makes you think I had the scarf? I didn't. It was lying on top of my tennies ... one of them."

"Then why is it wet?"

"Okay. After screaming for you, and crying, and cussin' out this canyon and this pool like you wouldn't believe ... "

"I would," smirks Tad.

" ... the wind whipped its tail through here and blew one end of it closer, where I could just barely reach it."

"So you wrapped it around you to get purchase on the slope."

"I tried that, but it didn't work. First, with my hands just laying it across there, it slipped; then around my boobs trying to flutter kick and spring out. No way, slid back and scraped hell outta me poor knockers besides."

Frank, still on the observation track, asks, "How come only *one* of your shoes is wet?"

"Ah-ha!"

"Did it blow into the pool?"

"Nope."

Bigfeets picks up my scarf and stretches it out between his hands. It is over a yard long and wrinkled at one end.

"You tied a knot in this, didn't you?"

"Un-huh."

"Let's see." Tad takes the scarf from Frank, reties the knot, goes down to the pool, and wets it again. "Ah-ha!" he triumphantly concludes. "You flipped the knot at the shoes and somehow got one to you, put it on, and were able to get purchase and climb out! *Olé!*"

"No."

"Did you get *both* shoes?" asks Frank.

"Yup."

"Like Tad said?"

I nod.

"Did one fall in the water?"

"Wow! I'll say, and I almost lost it. I made about twenty passes with that scarf. The shoe would roll over and stop, roll again and turn vertical, then on the last fling it really came a-runnin'. Plop ... and down it went. I got it just before it sank past my toes."

While they try to imagine the rest of my scene, I unknot the scarf, tie it around my head and sigh, "Let's get out of here while we still have some of the afternoon left to explore. Besides, fellas, I'm hungry!"

We circle the pool and climb to the saddle of the bowl. E.T. stops and looks back. With long, slender fingers, he rubs his cheek and chin whiskers, now starting to itch with a five-day growth, and pulls his fighting caterpillar brows together in puzzlement. "How'd you get your shoes on and manage to keep one of them dry?"

I raise my eyebrows, blink, and say nothing.

"Okay then, how would *I* get my shoes on if I were in there and still keep one foot out of the water while ... "

"You wouldn't."

"Aw, c'mon, Kay. Are you going to tell us how you got out of there or not?"

"No. You have to use your noggin; might find yourself in the same fix someday and need to figure a way out. Hugh Cuttler told me he nearly drowned in one like this, and he's no dummy. You're a fart smeller—'scuse me [snicker], I mean a smart feller, so ... "

Frank interrupts with his ear-wiggle. "Maybe she didn't put the shoes on her *feet*."

"Right!" I shout.

"On your boobs?" he blinks.

"Ohferkrissake, E.T, be serious."

"On your *hands!*" Tad's caterpillars unlock. I nod and smile. "On your hands. Well, I'll be damned. And you must have the gotten purchase by kicking up out of the water with your hands *in your shoes* under you."

"You got it. Know what a flange is? We used to do it at the beach on parallel bars—rest your hip bones on your elbows, body and legs straight out. That's why I've got a skinned nose, or haven't you noticed? From the flange, I fell forward into the sandstone." I poke my nose under his and cross my eyes.

He smiles, says, "I'm sure glad it was no worse," gives me a pat and little hug.

"Ouch! My boobs."

"Oh ... uh ... sorry."

I have a last look at my prison—an emerald eye, quiet now, reflecting the sky, bright rainbow colors from the oil on my body twisting on its surface. An innocent and beautiful intaglio jewel, ten feet across, set in pink sandstone—no longer lethal, not even enticing now that it's out of the sun and I'm no longer hot and sweaty. There it will lie, unruffled except by passing wind and birds dipping to drink; sinking a bit each day as evaporation and seepage shorten its life, until only waterbugs and strange, primeval shrimp are left to lay their eggs in the mud and die with the pool, their progeny wiggling to life with the next filling.

I should still resent my captor, but I don't. A priceless canyon lesson has been learned for keeps. What I resent is my carelessness, not being more in tune with nature and her whimsical tricks. I need to sharpen those instincts dulled by civilization so that one glance will warn me: This is not a movie set, baby. This is the real thing. Watch it! <END JOURNAL>

~

Tales surrounding the Stanton Dredge are as imaginative and hard to believe as was its conception, size and construction. Conceived by Robert Brewster Stanton for his Hoskinini Mining Company, it was supposed to make millions for investors by dredging placer gold out of Glen Canyon. Just hauling the bugger piece by piece in freight wagons from the nearest railhead at Green River, over a road that had to be constructed from Hanksville, across the slickrock and down a dugway blasted out of Stanton Canyon to the river, must have been a real bitch. To look at what remains of the thing is a mind-blower! Here, at mile 121.5, it rests belly-up in the middle of the river where it fell off its barge after three months (some say six months, some a year).

If I hadn't seen an old photo of the Stanton Dredge—its two-story building with more than forty windows, sitting on a 36- by 105-foot barge weighing at least 180 tons and supporting 46 iron buckets on a mammoth, rolling chain—I'd never believe anyone could dream up such a crazy thing. But in early 1901 it puffed and clanked across the river like some belching, mechanical monster.

Now, the string of blue-red-rust-patinated buckets, each big enough to hold a person, lies half-buried in cracked mud, with tamarisk trees growing from the huge roller/separator. The trunk of a grand old cottonwood tree that was stuck atop the apparatus the last time I saw it has been snitched by Mr. River and carried to another resting place.

Naturally, the dredge was a bust. Cost: Over a $100,000—Return: Something like $70's worth of gold dust!

Ol' Robert Brewster Stanton had a whole bunch of wild ideas. One of the worst was to build a railroad beside the river, on its grade, all the way from Green River, Utah, or Grand Junction, Colorado—take your pick—through the Grand Canyon to ... I dunno ... to South America probably, if he could use someone else's money. Ever since my first trip down here, Jim, Frank, and assorted boatmen have been pointing out what are called the Stanton Stakes.

Art Green: "You don't eat 'em; they're survey stakes for his railroad dream. You'll see what's left of them at various places on the right bank where he was going to put it."

Frank Barrett (a miner at heart): "They could be Stanton's stakes, but were they for the rail line? He had the Hoksinini Dredge down there and staked a lot of claims to satisfy his shareholders."

Me: "You think they're claim stakes?"

Barrett: "Could be."

Woody Edgel: "I know where there's a couple of 'em makin' what's left of a clothesline."

A letter from Dock Marston to Frank:

May be of some help to your lectures to your dudes to tell them that Stanton proposed to run his rail line down the left bank of the Colorado until he passed below Lee's Ferry. With this in mind, it would hardly be kosher to accuse him of putting those stakes on the right bank for his rail line.

A letter from me to Dock:

Yeah, well, what he "proposed" and what he did were two different things! There are sheer high walls on the left bank there, Dock, and most other places on the left bank there are no stakes.

A letter from Dock to me:

Fire when ready, Katie! Please give your sources, as I am sure they differ from mine. I am sure the posts in Glen are not the Stanton Rail Survey. But I don't know what they are; could be from the USGS Survey, 1921. Please don't hold me too closely to account on this section. I know relatively little about Glen Canyon.

I always had the feeling, when Dock capitulated this way, that his tongue was having trouble gettin' through his cheek and the salt grains were thick enough to dance on. But I was wrong. He really wanted to "Dock-ument" what those stakes were and where they came from. He wanted the facts, man.

As for me, I don't really care. Stanton-Schmanton. What fascinates me are the shimmering colors in the walls rising above, the mile upon mile of rolling sandstone up there, and below, the laughing river that knows it all and doesn't care either.

The gold seekers ... were *they* enthralled? Did they ever really *see* this canyon? Was it just a long, hard, dirty diggin' job? If it wasn't, there's very little writing that rhapsodize the river or its canyons, yet I have to know those miners explored the ruins, the side canyons, and along the river corridor, if for no other reason than boredom with their digging jobs.

Journal Note: September 28 (Evening)

I'm in the stern, busily scribbling in my notebook, when I hear lotta water gushing over a whole lotta rocks.

Yipes! We're at Bullfrog. I slam down the notebook and jump in without even looking. Frank, at the oars, hollers, "Whoa!," pulls back and lets me swim ahead. I move in close to the wall to avoid scraping any rocks. The current is swifter, the water deeper here.

About a mile down they pick me up on the smelly right bank, near the splattered guano beneath the heron rookery. The birds are never here when we are—they always see us coming and take off. I pick my notebook up from the stern and, watching them, jot down the thought ...

> The heron's wings
>> On squeaky hinge
> Labor to lift his bulk in air.
>> On fractured sails he flies
> A bird who seems not ready
>> For the skies.

I also expect them to nosedive when they land, they look so top-heavy. But like a diva who *almost* trips over her train, they ruffle some feathers, do a kind of shimmy, wobble their necks and adjust their tiaras, then gaze back at their intruders with a cool, disdainful eye.

Our camp tonight, twenty minutes or so below Hall's Creek, is a mile long and neatly stacked with rows of driftwood left here by a well-organized river.

We know, without saying a word to each other, what we're going to do with it.

With sunlight still reflecting from cliffs across the way, turning our skins a soft Navajo bronze, we gather load on load of drift, drag it down a way from camp, stack it higher than our heads and leave it, then go about our tasks: get water, pump up mattresses, build a small cooking fire, set up the kitchen, and start preparing dinner, all with very little conversation.

It's not exactly tension strung between us; more like a quivering awareness, probably having to do with the scary thought that there might have been only *two* at this camp tonight, instead of We Three. Our nervous systems aren't yet free of static, and I feel I'm the one to blame.

Facing Bigfeets over the fire, I prop the spatula against a stone, stand and, without warning, push him backward into the woodpile. He shoots me a look of hurt surprise before he recognizes my devilish glee.

"There now!" I say. "The Wee People are at work here, and let's have no more of this silence. All evil thoughts out in the open!"

He comes after me with a big barbecue fork, chasing me around the fire. "I'm thinking some pretty evil thoughts, all right," he growls, "and you'll know what they are pretty darn quick."

E.T. backs away, shaggy brows dancing, and as I dash by, he sticks out his foot, sending me sprawling and laughing in the sand.

Frank pounces on my legs, pins me down and pricks my behind with the fork, saying, "Hmm-m, I think it's tender enough to serve, don't you, Tad?"

"Give it another poke and let me see."

"Ouch ... damn it, I have to sit on that!"

"You should have thought of that before you stashed me in the woodpile, little Miss Vixen."

"Yes yes," E.T. nods, "I think it's about ready. Maybe it should be tenderized a bit more before you salt and pepper it. Irish Bitch is tough, you know."

"Ah-ha! I think you're right." And with a few more whacks on my rump, he goes back to the fire to turn the ham steaks.

Mission accomplished, I massage my buns, pull a mock frown, and say, "Yer a coupla bullies, pickin' on a purr defenseless lass."

"Oh, sure," Tad says, "you're about as defenseless as a she mountain lion in heat."

"Who says I'm in heat!"

"Woody wants me to let him know when you are."

"Ohferkrissake!"

Shadows top the cliffs, and I go to change from shorts to jeans and heavy shirt. As I rummaged in my duffel for warmer clothes, I have to marvel that the three of us, from such disparate worlds, are here together, melded, as if we'd been this way all our lives.

The river, of course, is the catalyst. <END JOURNAL>

I know for a fact that if I had to spend more than a couple of days at Frank's house in Blanding—no matter how much I admire, love, and respect the man—I'd lose my marbles; as he would lose his if he had to spend the same time with me in some smoke-filled, booze-swilling supper club, however much he loved my singing.

And Tad? I'd be hard put to tolerate his slow, disciplined way of thinking, talking, and acting—proper and correct as it all may be. Whereas I, the jumping bean, would have him doing a lot more than twiddling his cowlick—he'd yank himself bald.

Though respectful of one, impatient with the other, I'd still have more in common with Tad than Bigfeets out there in the phony world. Here they're on near equal ground, with Frank a smidgen ahead. Yet, they complement each other; their knowledge of the southwest, the river's past and future, both practical and technical, come from opposite ends of the spectrum and fill my cup with a very rich brew.

Journal Note: September 28 (Evening)

Dinner is over. Dishes scoured with sand; washed in heated river water; garbage sacked and put in the boat, ready to dump midstream in the morning.

We go down and light the bondfire [sic—from my journal]. I like that. It should be spelled that way; that's what it does—draws and bonds those who gather round it. Some can stare into it for hours, hardly moving, using it as a release for their dreams, a trigger for their imagination. A camp without a fire is an *unnatural* thing—the night feels cold even when it's hot. Campfires appeal to what's left of the primitive in us, and after the first red, hot tongues have licked high, thrown their sparks to the wind, and settled into dancing blue flames, for me, that fire is a tranquilizer.

But not this one ... not tonight.

With the first scorching, leaping, blaze we war dance around it, hooting and hollering like maniacs, get our cameras and begin taking pictures. Then we throw sand on the fire, which turns the flames to blue and purple, making eerie masks of our faces. I roll up my jeans and step out into the water to take a reflection shot. Big mistake! Immediately, I sink to my buns in mud so gooey I can barely move in it—the jeans bog me down. My favorite thing has now become a liability, as I try to extricate myself from the quaking bog without turning into a chocolate drop.

~

I wander upstream to a place where rocks jut into the water, and I bathe in the cold river. I stand a long time before the fire before I crawl into my bedroll, surprised to hear Tad and Frank on the other side of the dying embers talking about the day.

I sigh and confide: "I've felt almost *too many* sensations today. Makes me marvel what a unique container we earthlings live in—the high/low, pleasure/pain we can tolerate and respond to."

Frank's hands are clasped behind his head, so I can see his face in the glow. "Well, I hope you don't sink too far when you go back to the nightclubs, Little Wrists, because you're one of those who feel very high highs, very low lows."

"You're one too, Bigfeets. If all this disappears in front of your eyes, it'll hurt you a lot."

Tad, lazily stuffing a pillow under his head, says, "Some people never feel enough to know what's high and what's low; have to go to a psychiatrist to find out."

"Sometimes I wish I could be like that. It'd save me bunches of trouble."

"You don't wish that. You wouldn't be here if you did."

"I said sometimes, E.T. What's different about today is that every sensation has registered so strongly, so completely filled my mind and body, that I'm satiated. That's new for me. I always want more, but I feel there are enough mental and physical sensations *right here* to keep me going forever. I think my river is trying to tell me that sensations are the *real food*, not just heady wine ... that I might be able to live here without needing the glitter and stuff from outside ... live here like Barrett and Woody and Slim."

Rising on his elbow, Tad replies, "Oh, no, Pal you wouldn't last six months. You've been part of the high concentrate; excitement-performance-creativity ... potent stuff in your field."

"Artists are like boats riding a wave of popularity; I think mine is moving to a place I don't want to go."

"Phooey," says Frank, "a talented person like you always finds a way. You'll think of something." He yawns, rolls over, and snuggles down in his bag.

Tad (to Frank, but *for* me) says, "Whatever it is, she'll have to have a response, an audience to make it worth the effort."

"Huh-uh; that's not what my river is telling me."

I listen to his voice intoning over the stones, and drift down into sleep ... smiling.

[Camp—mile 117.2] <END JOURNAL>

THIRTEEN

The Eye of the Beholder

Journal Note: Thursday, September 29, 1955
(We Three Trip, Sixth Day)

The sheer luxury of it!

Half asleep, I wiggle out of my pj's, unzip my sleeping bag, and roll like a pencil down the sand bank ... splat! The river punches a wide-awake "Ya-hooo!" out of me that echoes up and down Glen Canyon as I sink under the chilly, brown wavelets.

Through ears full of water I hear Tadito call, "There she goes!" Then, like a tiger freed from its cage, energy growing with every stroke, I push into midstream.

Gonna take you on, Mr. River!

Upstream against the current I swim, oblivious to everything but my thoughts and the soothing twist and curl of a river alive and well against my body. <END JOURNAL>

My thoughts: Just for a minute, they flash last winter—in contrast to *this* world, almost absurd. The gig in St. Louis, how beat I was; three shows a night, six nights a week, 9:00 P.M. to 1:00 A.M., never in bed before two or three in the morning, sleeping until two or three in the afternoon; finally, so run down I catch the flu, miss a night. Penicillin shot. Doctor's orders—stay in bed, drink much liquid. *No alcohol.* Fine, who needs it! But I had been drinking, with seemingly no ill effect, several shots of Jack Daniels every night at work—yet I hadn't tumbled to the outcome. After twenty-four hours in bed, flu or not, I couldn't stay down any longer and got up and went for a walk. It was winter. Snow out there. I bundled up and walked for two hours in Forest Park; ate a big meal, went to bed at 9:00. Up at 6:00 A.M., glowing with energy! Three nights later JD and I shook hands again, and again I couldn't drag myself from bed until late afternoon the next day—depleted, pooped. Get it, stupid? I said to me, that amber shit is where all your energy goes. From that day forth, no drinking on the job. Good thing too, 'cause I worked in lotta gin mills where I would never have to pay for it ... with money.

Journal Note: September 29 (Continued)

I have reached the island. No mud shallows here, just polished rocks and the exposed roots of willow and tamarisk. The river runs swifter than over by our camp, so I have to argue with him to get a foothold, pull myself up, and walk dripping wet and puffing onto the sand. Soft, silky sand, almost white—not a mark on it that hasn't been made by wind or river.

Hay-soos! It is so pure, so exquisite! I crawl through it like a lizard, flat on my belly, slide down its bunkers, wiggling and giggling; roll in it, pour handfuls of it over me until I'm completely dry, then burrow in its silkiness, cool on top, warmer a few inches down.

How have we come so far ... in the *wrong* direction?

Though my canyon world is serene but for a canyon wren's call and the *whish* of faster water in the narrow channel across the island, I can almost feel the drum and play of many bare feet; see them moving about this island, the compact naked bodies of the ancient ones we've decided to call savages simply because of that: naked bodies. Heaven forbid! How awful! How sinful, how crude and unholy.

We are the crude and unholy. Don't give me any stupid Adam and Eve fairy tales, invented by some uptight impotentate as a cover-up for his inadequacy. Anasazi males didn't run after their women all day with a hard-on because they were *naked*. Quite the opposite is my guess. He may have fashioned her a necklace of columbine or monkey flowers, entwined her toes with scarlet gilia, crowned her with jimsonweed, or tripped her and beat her to the ground—but cover her? Never. And if they needed a cold-weather covering, you can bet it warn't no puny leaf, fig or otherwise.

What are we hiding that is so menacing to us? Why do we give our children the leaf the minute we're sure they have something ripe enough to cover?

I push from beneath the sand and walk over the island, inspecting the intricate designs left by wind and water fingers.

On its high center there are hard rain spatters left by a quick shower before the river dropped. There's very little driftwood here; the river stacked it all over on our side. The brush is low, all bent in benediction to downstream gods. No lizard, snake, bug, or mouse trail marks the earth ... not yet. Do they know when to board or abandon ship? Do they feel it in the ground, hear it coming, raft out on a piece of drift, wait until the last branch bends to current, swim the rapid and make for shore? Or drown? Because, of course, this island isn't always here; neither are most of the others when heavy spring runoff scours them down. I've been on this same island when it was loaded with tracks, even deer. Now it's Mother Nature's slate, waiting for the first writer.

Oh-oh ... looks like that's me. Quite a scribbler, it seems. Tracks everywhere, and a complete *mess* where I did all that roll and tumble a while ago. But I didn't really disturb anything or anyone, just the sand. Still, I feel guilty about cluttering up the river's palette with my body marks, so I smooth them over, even knowing this afternoon's upstream wind will erase all evidence.

I smell bacon; slip in and float down to camp, hoping Tadito is doing the honors because one of the things we promised Bigfeets, insisted on furthermore, was that we do most of the cooking. This is his *vacation*. I planned the menu so we'd have something unlike the usual river fare; picked wild chives off the bars (put them in everything!), gathered watercress near springs, and pulled hearts of young cattails from the sidestreams. In a few minutes I'll scramble eggs with chives, cheddar cheese, and bacon chips, and we'll have *whole wheat* toast—an animal rarely seen in Utah. (Frank, poor man, suffered my river cuisine for two years before he confessed that chives—and onions—gave him heartburn.)

Floating quietly on almost no water, we enter the Kayenta ridge. From just above Lake Canyon to ten miles downstream into the Rincon, the bottom is sulcated bedrock that I can feel with my toes, trailing a foot out of the boat. We pass Two Deer Spring and Jacob's Pot—an alcove with a hole in the ceiling—and stop below a Moki cave, inaccessible except in very high water (maybe not even then). On the rock face, a faint row of stitches curves upward toward its mouth—once an ancient ladder, now too long eroded even to be called fingerholds. Below it, at our feet, we find a mess of footprints; not the first we've seen. They look to be about a week ahead of us—party of three or more; hard to tell. (Read about them in a Salt Lake paper, after getting back to Art Green's: In two rafts they *conquered* the wild, unconquerable Colorado! They went *upstream*—a journey hazardous beyond belief! Encountered dangerous rapids at Lake Canyon! Wonder what the dear lads would say if

I told them I couldn't even get my air mattress over the *rapids* without touching. Yet Frank, with a loaded boat, never scraped or bumped a stone.)

A short way up Lake is a waterfall—fifteen feet high, more or less, with enough pitch to scoot us downstream quite a way past the foot of the slide, and rough enough in spots to put a hole in the seat of my jeans, because of course we slide it more than once.

Long, curved, Kayenta ledges form cataracts where water tumbles, bubbles, spreads, then drops again—in some places, trailing a vibrant green, silky-haired moss. Because there's permanent water here, we find millions of little black water bugs that cling to every wet, rocky surface—even to us when we slide over them. The stream purrs softly through long stretches of reeds and cattails that stand tall and stiff in rippled sand. Cliff swallows dive past our ears, zoom and dip at the surface in what seems like some sort of game to see who'll snag a beak and fall in! We round a bend to be greeted by a exultation of frogs in chorus—every pitch and timbre, basso to soprano. And the canyon wren's taunting call is never out of hearing.

Lake Canyon's width supports stands of cottonwood and several large, sophisticated cliff houses. Centuries ago, ten miles above the canyon's mouth, the Anasazi lived beside an oasis—a lake formed by a dam of windblown sand and flash flood debris, and fed by seeps and springs. Breached by floods in 1915 and eroded now, its ancient bottom and broken bank reveal orange sands peppered with chips and arrowheads—tiny little bird points in every color of the rainbow—so waterfowl must have been plentiful. <END JOURNAL>

Dick Sprang: "Ever see the old buggy up Lake Canyon, way up, but way below the Hermit Lake area? Not wrecked, not gully-washed, but down in the canyon, beat up some, but sittin' there. Who, why, when?"

Journal Note: Still September 29

"You guys go on down to Schock Trail; I'll meet you there in about an hour."

I can tell Bigfeets isn't sure he likes this idea.

"Go on! I'm gonna ride my mattress, get some sun on me buns. How can I get in trouble? It's just a couple miles, and the water's knee-deep all the way."

"Okay," says Tad as he takes the oars, "we can have lunch on the bar. See you down there."

I stand where the river bubbles and sluices over the two-foot Kayenta ridge crossing the river, watching them ride away in their white water-bug, Tad dipping an oar now and then amid the brown scallops; feathering, backing, swirling through patterns that translate to channel, shoal, shallow, tongue, and sandbar.

I take everything off, roll my little wad of coverups into a ball, and belly-flop onto my mattress, steering it clumsily with flailing arms as the current immediately pulls me toward the hissing voice of a gravel bar. Meanwhile, downstream, *Tinny* glides serenely over the slap-slap waves, her crawling legs flashing in the sunlight. After many gravel-scraping push-ups, a blood streak slipping away, I wiggle free and float into slightly deeper, moving water.

I have a couple of miles to go on questionable three-mile-per-hour flow before I meet the guys at Schock's old trail, so I find the deepest channel and go for the easy route. Even so, my airy boat tends to spin out if I don't pay attention to the reading; not as easy this close to the surface as it is from a boatman's seat. Sometimes, legs dangling, sitting astride the mattress with the two ends poking up ridiculously front and back, my feet run along the sculpted bottom.

Gouged by stormborne boulders, grooved and hollowed, smoothed and polished by tons of sand and silt through millions of years, the bedrock defies description. If I hadn't seen the pattern exposed in a few side canyons, though much smaller in scale, I wouldn't have a clue what it looked like overall. But when a storm flushes a side stream's covering of sand and gravel down to bedrock, what you see is hard to believe. Gigantic fingers look to have combed through snarls in wavy sandstone without too much success, leaving strands bunched together here, splayed out there, or hopelessly balled up. If the drop is steep, the ladened water sculpts out goblins and knobby, fat figures that would fit well in Alice's Wonderland, for wherever a rock heavier and more compact than sandstone is wedged for any length of time, water-fingers will curl over, around, and underneath it until it drops or is forced on. Meanwhile the bedrock has been resculpted—another hollow in the bed, another sluice-way, ridge, arch, curve ... another ...

Now what's this?

A sensuous frequency ripples through me as my hand touches those silken curves, hollows, and convolutions on a body of stone, those erogenous zones so well known to lovers—places that, when free of clothing and released to passion, are most ardently pressed, kissed, tasted, and fondled.

He's naked!

No sand, no pebbles, only his sleek, unclothed body. I can almost see his flesh beneath the flowing veil. I pull my hand away and drop into the river on my knees. The mattress floats away. Leaning forward and reaching against the current, I feel for his muscular chest and limbs.

There!

The bulging muscle of an arm ... many arms ... and then a small, deep hole—his navel. I let the current move me backward to find a leg stretching downstream, another close beside it, and in between ... between ... my god, I don't believe this, but it's there! Heart racing, I stare into the water, waves curling against my upper arms and shoulders, then I drop quickly, face down. Holding to his arms, I suck in an underwater swimmer's breath, duck my head, and press my hips down against his erection.

An explosive, orgasmic roar fills my head, shakes me loose, rolls and tumbles me onto the shifting sands beside my eddied mattress. Coughing, still breathing heavily, and not quite believing what's just happened, I look back and say:

I've just lain with you, Big Boy. *What do you think of that?*

~

C.N. Sorensen	Peter Gregerson
The	May 25, 1894
May 18, 1894	
D. Dunshire	Bert & Lamont Manuill
Jan. 3, 1898	May 4, 1928
Ole & Soren Sorensen	W. Black 1927
May 28, 1928	

In a Moki ruin cave high above the river and off Schock's old trail to Iron Top Mesa are these names and dates on a big table rock in front of a kiva. The rock's edges are marked with tool-sharpening grooves from an age long before the Sorensens; and though the *manos* are gone, scraped and sunken parts in the big slab—which obviously fell from the ceiling even before the Old Ones came—were once *metates*.

"But," I ask Frank, "where is Schock? His name goes missing, yet the Sorensens seem to have stuck it out for thirty-four years."

"Well, he was probably ... "

"Nope ... changed my mind. Don't want to know who he was. It's enough that his name's not here—I'd rather guess what he was up to.

The trails we can still read aren't much more than a century old, right? Made by the miners for stock and machinery."

"This one sure was," says Tad. "Those steps up above are cut deep and wide, blasted in places."

"Those guys sure were mean to this place."

"There isn't much water up on Iron Top Mesa," offers Frank, "so they probably watered and kept some of their stock on this bar. It's large enough to feed a lot of cows and horses."

"What about people?" I ask.

"Yes yes, river-bottom soil, probably grow anything," Tad agrees. "Keep the stock out there on the island, the garden down here below on the bar."

"Ya-hoo! Roundup musta been fun when the river came up!"

"Little Wrists, I think they probably knew about when that was going to happen. Living outdoors all the time gives a person a chance to anticipate the weather."

"Surely they had something for shelter besides tents. Me now, I'da lived up here. These Mokis had it made—not a drop of rain can ..."

E.T.: "Helluva long way from your bath, pal. I can just see you hiking up this slickrock, thwee hundred feet above the river carrying a big jug of water on your head ... slim you down right smart!"

"Who's fat?" I laugh. "Anyhow, back then it was wetter, so alla you smart cats say." Tad goes to the rear of the cave. "Right here"—he points at the joining—"this dry seep could have been a flow. Navajo sandstone sitting on Kayenta, that's usually where the water comes out."

"Still does," says Frank, "especially this time of year."

We've ceased clicking shutters and sit close together looking out over the Glen. Low September sun still warms the rock, while in back of us the cave rests cool in shadow.

Our thoughts are in accord with the complete serenity before our eyes; sandy paws reach for the river through cuffs of green that are just beginning to show a yellow trim. Another long, thousand-foot, tapestry-streaked wall curves out of sight downstream. And the island! The island's nose is waved in pink-purplish sands, tesselated with polished rocks, and from there, over the whole center of the island, clear to the fringe of willows at river's edge, breasts of silken dunes tilt to the wind's caress.

"Look, you two, I know it's only midafternoon, but shouldn't we camp on the island tonight? Sky's clear, hardly any upstream wind, no smell of rain ... and golly, I love this place. My favorite bathing rock's down there; can see it from here."

Frank looks at his watch. "I think we can afford that ... "

I'm thinking: My god, he still wears that thing, a habit of years wrestling with time, always having to be on the spot to meet someone, or be met. No wonder my early journals record everything we did in minutes—Frank was always there to tell me how many.

But I say, "We're *here*, Bigfeets, light years away from the rat race and tick-tocks that keep us on the treadmill. I bet that you could tell the exact hour in this canyon with your eyes shut and never take another look at that watch."

"It's possible," he grins, "but I might need someone to tell me what day it is."

E.T. says, "I vote we camp here; okay by you Frank? We're about to lose our light over the wall soon, anyway."

I stand and stretch. "Maybe, Tad"—I cup my mouth and fake a loud whisper in his ear—"maybe you can even get Bigfeets to take off his underwear and roll in the sand like I did this morning. I'll go way downstream and commune with the frogs. What say?"

"Fat chance," Frank mutters.

"Try it," I plead, "You'll like it, Bigfeets. Makes you feel like a little kid again, like holding a pussycat. Honestly, it doesn't *hurt.*"

~

Old Sol is a rolling ball of fire along the high wall of Iron Top Mesa by the time we've descended to Schock Bar, rowed across the channel, and situated our camp on the island.

As we get our dinner, the Glen's extraordinary orange-velvet evening light spreads through the canyon, coloring us and our clothing like semiprecious stones under an infrared lamp, turning the brush and trees black.

My very own rock where I take my bath tonight is a perfect chair sitting a little way into the water, complete with soap dish hollow and an arm to drape my clothes over. Nearby, *Tinny* plays with her rope in the surge of a small cove. From my chair I can hear the river, prospecting among the rocks, picking those least secure, rolling them down ... one ... two ... three ... like a miser counting his priceless jewels.

Moonlight picks up the sun's afterglow as it fades on the water, bringing the dancing patterns back to life under night's subtle changes. A patch of red, reflected from our fire, is being juggled in the riffle. The daytime upstream winds have reversed and changed to a steady, downriver breeze, building little boondocks against the rocks and willow saplings and scooping out hollows behind them, where they twirl a moment before passing on.

The air cools. The wind softens.

I close my eyes on Paradise. The river, dropping a bit more of his floodtide, begins to chatter noisily with the stones.

[Camp—mile 110.6, Schock Island] <END JOURNAL>

~

Nils and Peter

Two men sit beside a cold fire pit at the outer lip of a prehistoric cave smoking silently—one a corncob pipe, the other a rolled cigarette with spit stains down the brown paper.

But no smoke curls into moonlight.

Their vacant eyes look down upon the island, where coals from our fire still glow, casting a pinkish light on the sand.

"Nils, vhat you s'pose t'em people coomin' down here on a Sunday picnic for?"

"Vhere vas you vhen the gorl vas talkin', Peter?—she say vhy. T'ey coomin' t' git away from a t'ing called t' rat race, un t' treadmill. I'm t'inkin' that means for t' same reason ve coomin'."

"Ah, ve vas here to vork and bring back t' gold—t'ey only coomin' fer coopla veeks, 'n t'ey don' take noothin' avay vit'um."

"Now, Peter, ve coomin' t' git away from t' rat race too, yah?"

"Speak fer yerself, not me—I voodn'ta left the ould country hadn'a been fer you."

"An' t'ey take vhat t'ey need avay vit 'em—some adventurin', peace and quiet, some beauties to remember, yah?"

"Ah, you crazy! Vhat kind adventurin' is vhat they do? T'ey got a boatload fulla fancy eatin' fer a month, t'ey got a little machine on t' back, get 'um up or down in no time, t'ey got no vater in t' river and no rapids no more. All t'ey do is valk a little vay and sleep on a soft bed at night!"

"Ya, vell now, maybe not t' same as vhen ve vas here, no. But t' peeples is gettin' softer 'n' richer, t'ey got more coomforts, don' need to vork so hard. To them is adventurin', to them is beautiful, is vild ... stirs soomthin' in the blood, like it vas den vit us, yah?"

"Ag'in you kin speak fer yerself, Nils Sorensen. I t'ought t'is place vas a hell of a hole—blisterin' days at the business end of a shoffel, vorking over sluices, separatin', haulin' rock, bringin' in the stock, feedin' t' horses—if that vas yore idea of t'Garden of Eden ... "

Nils pulls thoughtfully on the corncob pipe and looks dreamily out over the river—"An' I don' s'pose you remember the nights down on the bar in t' lean-to vit t' vater runnin' over the island, the moon shinin' down, makin' every-t'ing look like it vas paint in silver ... t' smell of t' river, the sound of t' vind in t' villow trees ... all you recall is t' pick and shoffel, yah?"

"Let me remind you, vile you vas leanin' on t' shoffel dreamin' out over the vater, or oop here diggin' fer ould pots and arrowheads, I vas down dere ex-ercisin' the vork tools and vishin' I vas back vhere the fjords iss deep and blue and t' vater iss cold!"

"Vell, too bad you vouldn't be livin' now to enjoy it. By their time, few more years, t'is vill be all one great big fjord."

Silence on the silence before Peter Gregerson answers. "Ya? How coom?"

"The goover'ment's puttin' in a fancy dam down by Lee's ould ferry. Gonna back vater up vay over Cass's place, an' the Dandy Crossin', and the Dirty Devil."

"Coover oop all this?"

"Ya. Effen t'is cave."

"By Gott! The goover'ment's no smarter now t'an they vas ven they dropped the price uff silver—t'en gold. Vhat a shtoopid t'ing t' do!"

"I vas t'inkin' you din't like t' place, Peter."

"Vell, by Gott, they yust shouldn't be drowndin' it. T'ere's plenty gold in here yet. Somebody could be make it rich!"

Nils raps the old pipe against his name on the tablerock. "Some coomin' fer gold, some coomin' fer peace, some fer t' new minerals and some ... fer love. In t' eye of t' beholder, Peter ... is all in t' eye of t' beholder. Yah."

FOURTEEN

The Bubble Trail

If I thought this river and this canyon, in summertime, brought me the peace and clarity I needed, I was unprepared for the additional gifts it handed out in fall; the color changes in walls and foliage, even in shadows—and in the sky. For instance, in midsummer—in compliance with the demands of a hot day—the morning skies are white when the sun crashes, with vengeance, over the canyon rim. Now, a cloudless sunrise blooms yellow into cornflower blue. The painted river runs red one day, brown the next, then tan, then back to its pale green, settling out. There is an *amplified* stillness; a crystal air that almost *rings* (one would expect fall haze anywhere else). Birds are migrating, and a seasonal modulation is evident in all riparian behavior.

Most fascinating of all, though, is the delicate light that alters the whole river corridor, bringing out features of the canyon I've never seen or even dreamed were there. Even the mouths of the canyons seem to have another shape, a more tantalizing call, and these are only the last days of September; imagine what the light is like come December or January. Another world again!

Journal Note: Friday, September 30, 1955
(We Three Trip, Seventh Day)

We've stopped for water this morning on the left bank at mile 101.6, just above the Rincon. I totally forget that I've been here before—a déjà vu feeling as we enter, but nothing fits. Each turn is unfamiliar until I see the spring two feet off the ground shooting out of bald rock, as if someone had left the faucet on.

Next the pool—sandy bottom, glassy, cold blue. There's no iceberg in it, but it looks as though a glacier had carved out the canyon and the twenty-foot drop-off into it. Tucked away from the sun under a huge overhang, I remember, it felt real nice last July. Now, my men being the sissies they are, we skirt it by tennie-sticking the steep, two-inch-thick Kayenta plates that have tilted, slipped, and frozen in time for our convenience—in step with the stone.

Intermittent seeps and stream (now dry) have left variegated ribbons in the middle of the bowl-like floor and down the walls—colored maroon in the center, edging into purples and violets outlined in chalk white. Again, that feeling of ice ... icicles. Like a toboggan run through an ice cave, the canyon twists and turns upward past the Kayenta blues and lavenders. Round a bend, the tube opens ...

Everything changes!

A grove of tall, slender cottonwoods that look like they've been carefully pruned from day one line the banks of a damp streambed. A few yards further on, the stream is running! Where does it go? Not over the bedrock toboggan run; that's dry. Down through the sandstone and out through the faucet?

Blow me down! That has to be it.

I rush ahead of the guys, along the sandy riverbed, through the grove, over the ledges, skirting pools or wading them—not so cold up here where sunlight reaches them. That crazy, tingling explorer syndrome has invaded my psyche; nothing else exists, only me and this canyon with Nature's perfection all around. There's no sign that anyone's been here before me but the beavers. Sedulous little critters must be on overtime; they've downed a lot of trees for their dams.

Hit by a bucket of ice water, I stop cold, bite my fists, and scream, "NO! You won't! You *can't* destroy this perfect place! You aren't just furry little chompers downing a few trees. Hell no! You want to wreck the whole place; leave no trace! Drop dead, you stinking bureaucrats! All of you!"

A shrill whistle returns me to the here-and-now. Tad. They want me back. We've fallen a bit behind our half-assed schedule and really must do some pressing on today.

Above the blue mirror I find E.T. waiting; Frank has gone on. A nagging voice calls up from the water, "Come on in ... come on in." Even though I'm just about the right temperature without getting wet, I hand Tad my clothes to take around, slide down the smooth ribbon, like last year ... woosh ...

Jeeeee-zus ... I'm sure I've cracked ice and gone under.

Iceberg Canyon was its name from then on. <END JOURNAL>

~

As the river and Glen's canyons revealed more and more secrets to me over the next seven years, my journals verify that several of the revelations were in or near Iceberg Canyon, and not always with just We Three in the company. Since we're at this spot on the river, I want to tell about them now.

Iceberg was just another unnamed canyon on the Glen Canyon maps. Slim Williams said it had been called Wilson *Canyon* after some guy who died about 1918 and had run stock up on Wilson (Grey) Mesa, and down Wilson *Creek* that runs into the San Juan.

"Who was he anyway? You said he ran stock."

Slim gave his wry, dry smile. "*Ran* ... as in pursued ... uh, liberated ... m-m-m, released ... "

"Oh-oh, I see. One a them *colorful* characters."

"There's a sign chipped in the rocks up on the rim trail above here. Ever see it?"

At this point I hadn't yet been up there, so my answer was, "No. What's it say?"

"KEEP YER GODDAM CATTLE OUT OF HERE! You oughta get up the right fork of that canyon you call Iceberg, Kate. About four miles from the river, there's a natural dam; big lake behind it, almost a quarter-mile long ... sometimes."

"How's that again? Lake? Way up there?"

"A beauty. We almost lost a guy one time, trying to get around it on the old Moki steps to a ruin that's hid, and just possibly untouched. It's not the only lake, either. There's a smaller one a mile below at the canyon's fork, probably built by Mokis to hold underground drainage from the big one ... "

September 1958, with Tad, Reet, and Doris

Oh, yes! That little one was ringed with cattails, willows wept over it, lily pads and swirls of lime-green algae floated on the reflected blue, and overall was the rustling paper sound of cottonwood leaves that filled all the space, *green*, up- and down-canyon, clear to the dark Wingate cliffs, just starting to show Navajo atop them.

The animal trail (that's all it was) was steep for a whole mile before we came to the rockfall that had dammed the canyon and formed the lake. Great chunks of both walls had cleaved off and fallen into the middle, filling it top to bottom, three hundred feet or more—no evidence that water ever flowed *over* the dam, and the canyon was too high up to collect enough runoff to top it. Had the earth rumbled here before the Basketmaker, Hohokam, Anasazi/Moki, during their time, or after it? Before, stupid. That's why the steps had been chipped in the stone—those guys had to get around the lake, too.

When we reached the top of the rockfall we couldn't have been more surprised. Immense!—a couple thousand feet long, three hundred feet across—an emerald set in pink stone, willows, and cottonwoods at both ends, its length reflecting Navajo sheerwalls. Tad and the others tried to negotiate the left side. Huh-uh; they benched out halfway up the lake.

I slipped in and swam across, but the water, immured between sandstone, looked too spooky too take on the length. After lunch I decided to try for the end, with a log in case I got tired. No bottom all the way to see or touch, and the upper end was pure defiance—waist-deep water wall-to-wall, the brush thicker with every step, trees sitting in water halfway up their trunks, and no way up the Navajo. Damn! So there it was, almost within my reach—one of the most thrilling sights I'd seen those six years on the river. The next trick was to get up there again, before the U. of U. or the Museum of Northern Arizona set their archaeologists loose on it; before the ruin was ravaged.

That was the first time.

September 1960, with Slim and Leo Walter

We were intent upon getting to that ruin above the lake, Slim and Leo praying that it wouldn't be full because they weren't about to try the "almost-lost-a-guy" steps again, and the very thought of the other alternative ... oh, shudder-shudder! Me, I couldn't have cared less. I was *ready* for the water. That steep, hot trail was a bitch!

I topped the dam first and gasped at the lake's beauty, doubled in reflection. Slim just stood waiting below, blue eyes looking up at me.

"Full huh? I was afraid of that. Next time"—and made as if to turn back.

"No ruin?" I teased. "Come on, we can swim it." His blond eyebrows disappeared under the rim of his hat. "What's the matter, can't you swim?"

"Sure, I kin swim, but I might get *wet*. I like the kind of trails I don't have to make bubbles on."

And lanky Leo, Slim's avid Moki-huntin' buddy, took one look at the distance from us to the far shore, made a U-turn, and said, "Be seein y'all at the lower lake." He was serious.

I thought maybe Slim didn't want to try swimming that far, so I suggested the log. We'd float part way.

He and Leo had done enough canyoneering and river-running with me to know my habit in the wilds and in no way begrudged me nature's blessing in the raw. I left my duds on the bank and slid into the lake, towing my Rollei in a waterproof case.

"Feels great," I shouted.

"Great! That stuff rots yer skin. It's for drinking, not for playing in." He stood there hugging himself, faking a shiver; quite an act.

"But the ruin, Slim." He'd only seen it through his binoculars when he was deer hunting, and I knew he was as turned on by virgin ruins as he was turned off by cold water.

"Yeah, the ruin," he groaned, "but did you ever consider ... I could dissolve in that stuff."

I was out there with no log, treading water, laughing so hard I nearly drowned myself, so I headed for the wall to find a fingerhold.

My theory, not entirely unfounded, is that men don't like cold water because it shrinks their manhood and makes tonsils out of their go-nads—especially don't like it when witnessed by the fair sex, whose only outward manifestation of cool temps is a couple of hardened nipples and a few goose pimples. I turned my back and waited to see if the big man was going to brave the unthinkable.

After much grumbling, I heard a big splash and some very fancy cussing. He grabbed his log, caught up with me, and we made it to the upper end about twenty minutes later.

Why we didn't bring our tennies, I'll never know, because we had to negotiate every possible kind of terrain—forest floor, sand, stick grass, cacti, *hot* sandstone and more water—on our bare feet, on our bare everything. Like little kids looking for treasure, we searched the canyons forks, looking for the cave that held the ruin he remembered seeing from above—and finally found it.

Too late.

The University of Utah had been there just two months before us and had dug a long trench from the middle out to the front. If we'd gotten there the year before, it would have been a virgin cave.

I'd never seen one like it. Flaked out by seeps, wind, temperature changes, and a once-upon-a-time stream, most likely, it hid beneath an overhang fifty feet deep, with an average seven-foot ceiling (now, that is). The actual floor was blanketed by eons of baby-powder silt so soft, cold, and deep, it felt like water flowing to my knees with every step—no way to tell how far it was to bedrock.

Never much of a pot hunter, I was content to just look and guess what lay beneath. Too much searching the ground would deny me the magic in these canyons, and Slim, who'd moved a few rocks around and done some digging in his day, said the place was most unusual—like no chips or pot shards; only corncobs, and plenty of them.

Part of the entrance was still covered, not with mortared stone like others in this area, but with woven reeds and grass. Not harmed, not stormed away, in a thousand years?

Then I heard the whispers of the Basketmakers in those reeds, telling me of peace and plenty, not strife and sorrow; of planting crops, and of harvests from the green haven down below us. Their spirits, not wishing to leave here yet, told me they had picked this perfect spot, not to hide … but to abide.

A sudden clatter and a dust plume from the end of the cave broke my link with the Old Ones. Slim stood among loose rock below the lip, rubbing his hind end.

"Never thought it would happen, but I just got my B.A. degree in archeology," he said.

"You what?"

"My bareassed degree. I found it with both hands; that makes me very intelligent. You've probably got one too, with a minor in corncobs." He pointed to those I'd collected and stashed on a nearby stone.

I shouldn't have laughed so hard—he might've been hurt—but there was no holding back. Laugh tears rolled and my stomach muscles ached while I tried to take pictures and gather my wits for our barefoot, bare-assed descent.

As Slim led the way down, he turned once more and said with a serious face and deep wigwam voice, "Remind Indian brave … at least wear socks."

That was the second time.

September 1961, Two Rookies and Me in a Shitty Hunk of Blubber

Remember? I said I'd go down this canyon with Frankenstein and King Kong if there was no other way? Well, this was the year—F. and K. K. in the form of two lashed-together, decked-over army surplus *rafts;* the first I'd ever set foot in!

I had two nice kids with *no* muscle; a loaned, inflated SCUD (I called it) that moved like a bogged hippo, and an ancient motor that barely worked at all. I not only looked that gift horse in the mouth; I rammed profanity down its throat all the way. To top it off, the river, bless his heart, picked that year to show me a thing or two by running at 30,000 cfs! One good "people thing" happened. At White Canyon, Slim, sensing my predicament, helped me put the SCUD together, gave me an extra motor, and said he and Leo would be coming down as far as the Rincon the next day in his aluminum canoe and would keep an eye out for us.

My journal is rife with weariness and bad happenings: Damned motor quit two miles above camp; goddamn SCUD barely moves with two of us on the oars. It deflated in the night. I spent half an hour blowing up her twenty compartments, then when the sun got high and we were finally loaded, she started popping her seams, and we had to go around and let the air out again. I wonder if this shit goes on every night! If I could stand to hear the name every day, we'd name the goddamn thing *Georgie*. At my Fluted Canyon, the motor broke again. Dean fixed it, then it stopped; starter wouldn't pull. First time in history I didn't swim Bullfrog; too worried. (Bright spot: Slim and Leo passed us, went ahead, and set up camp.) We sheared a pin two miles above camp, replaced it, and dropped the rest of the pins in the river. Arrived late, had to cook in the friggin' dark; Slim spilled the water and put the fire out! It started raining and blowing like hell! I spilled hot coffee on my hand! Ann dropped the bench with all the food on it! Everything was full of sand! No sooner got to bed than my air mattress sprung a leak. Slim helped me fix it and I was ready for sleep when it started to rain again; teased and sprinkled all night. Mattress went down again. The only good thing that happened was Slim standing over me in the morning with a nice hot cup of coffee.

And so it went, the whole trip. But the next night I saw something I'd never seen before on *any* river, and would not see again.

Iceberg Bar was too windy, muddy, and rocky for camp, so we crossed to the right bank, opposite the Upper Rincon. I heard it coming alright, but we were in the middle of dinner and stuff was scattered all over the beach. It roared up-canyon like twenty beating helicopters, lifting every sandbar into the air from the goddamn dam on up and throwing it at us. The only thing that didn't move was the Dutch oven. The kids snatched what they could and ran to their bedrolls. Slim grabbed his big tarp from the canoe, holding it open for me and Leo to crawl under. As I zipped by the fire, I grabbed the coffee pot and a cup and we sat under the tarp drinking coffee, getting wetter and wetter as it seeped through.

Slim was not a happy camper. "Goddamn turtle-flippin' wind!" he growled. A half-hour later, it quit. I was so beat, I could hardly make it to my sack, where I flaked ... and died!

Slim said the sound of the canoe banging against the bar woke him. He grabbed his flash and beamed it out to the boats. Jesus! He leaped out in his shorts and pulled the canoe up as far as he could, but even if he woke everybody up to help, he knew the SCUD would just have to lie there and take it. He figured I was real fagged, or I'd have heard the boats shifting around. He didn't want to wake me, but he knew I'd want to see what was happening out there, so he came over and whispered in my ear.

"Kate, wake up a minute and look at the river."

"Hmmmm?"

"Want you to see the river—it won't be like this in the morning."

I sat up, looking out into pitch dark. "What? Whassamatter? Boat in trouble? Oh, god!"

"No, but the river's up. I moved the canoe, and I think the raft will be okay there in the eddy."

He gave me the flashlight. "Turn it out there and tell me if you see any water."

I flicked it on and stared, shocked. Jeezus Christamighty!

"Ever seen that before?"

"Never. How in hell will we get downriver tomorrow?"

"It'll be gone in about an hour, be way ahead of you. That's why I woke you up, thought you'd want to see it."

"Holymoses! I can't see any water at all!"

Two hundred feet across, bank to bank, and as far up and down as the flash could penetrate, was a solid, racing log jam. It heaved and writhed—a prehistoric amphibian, beating and sloshing the banks, obliterating the natural sounds of the river with an ominous hissing and growling. Now and then a tree trunk would catch on a submerged rock, flip up, and crash into another part of the jam like a sea monster rearing out of the deep. Logs clanged against the end of the canoe, sounding like far-off voodoo drums.

I don't know how long I stood there watching that awesome sight, shivering, feeling the earth vibrate under my bare feet and up through my spine, tingling. I grabbed my solar plexus, breathed in rhythm with the surge and rush of the river's violent force.

Power! Power! Go … go, Life Force, I prayed. One day you'll do it, Big Boy, and *this is how!*

Journal Note: 1955—Back to We Three at the Rincon

The old Glen Canyon made a move here at mile 100 long before we bipeds were invented. Looks like the whole place got the shakes and just up-ended, dumping layer on layer of strata headfirst into the river and tipping what was once beneath high in the air above it—Kayenta, Wingate, Chinle, Shinarump, Moenkopi, and Cedar Mesa. A river that once hooked a U around the Rincon now passes smoothly by it, beginning the longest straight stretch in the Glen. Four miles floating through a Wingate passageway with hanging canyons that tease us on the right; and on our left, a massive straightwall of deep maroon, here and there burnished with a gunmetal blue. Mean-lookin' rock, this. Sharp edged, room-sized chunks, hard to hike on. Hot, too. Never mind; we'll do it tomorrow, up Bowns Canyon, an arm of Navajo Creek—a canyon that's not hanging, one we can get into.

Tonight we're camping on the bar.

E.T. is showing me how to take moonlight pictures. Just after the sun goes down and the moon comes over the rim, that's when we have to do it. He sets up his tripod, and using the timer, we get several of the three of us sitting by the fire, me in the middle singing and playing the guitar, moon behind us shining on the water. Oh-h-hh ... what a night!

After our dinner we start up the creek looking for a clean pothole for my bath; a few yards, and we're gum-balled! In the moonlight we see catfish wiggling up a six-inch-wide, two-inch-deep channel—some coming up, others going home. We run them upstream with sticks—catch them in our hands. Sliding through the mud, we fall in the creek, trip over each other, step on the fish, and laugh until we're hoarse. Finally, we manage to get five fish into a water bucket for breakfast.

I give up on the clean pothole and go down by the boat for my bath, weather still perfect, river somewhere between refreshing and stimulating. There's silver paint all over the rocks and walls, and a shimmering path of it leads upstream to the glowing disk in the sky. In the shrill moonlight I see that every place I had clothing I am an even tan. Sliding into the river, over his pavement of smooth stones, I twist and wiggle between them like the fish to scrape off the sweet-smelling mud.

"River, talk to me. You have to help me through the year."

He sputters over a small drop, sucks in a breath, and goofs off in the turn beyond the bar.

I wait. Nothing. Then I throw a rock in the millrace he's created. It hits, bounces, and ...

"There is a tavern in the town ... bllllibbllle ... in the town.

"Ah-h-hhh. That's better!" You see, by now I've learned how to ask questions and get answers. "I know there's a damn tavern in a town, yer honor, the question is what to do about it?"

We talk as long as I can stay awake.

"Yessir! I will ... I will recall *this night,* when I'm out there among 'em and I find things are at their very worst. Then you'll send me your music on a sheet of silver moonlight—you'll send this night of beauty, peace, and joy with two wonderful friends, and the memory of this pure happiness will pull me through.

"Thank you ... and goodnight."

[Camp—mile 95.6, Navajo Bar] <small>END JOURNAL</small>

FIFTEEN

Subtle Currents

Journal Note: Saturday, October 1, 1955
(We Three Trip, Eighth Day)

Each new discovery surpasses the last. It seems the tougher these canyons are to penetrate, the more beauty they hide. I leave a part of me in the arms of Bowns Canyon; leave blood and tears in exchange for what I've seen and will remember all my life.

Over, under, and around Wingate boulders, through water in tunnels of tumbled rock, past rabbit brush, datura, and stunted cottonwood, we make our way to the base of the Kayenta. Ah-hhh, bedrock at last!

As we round a bend and come over a small rise, I feel like I've been hit in the middle of my everything. I grab for Frank's arm and say, "Wait a minute, Bigfeets, I don't think I can take much more of this. It's *too* beautiful!" Suddenly I'm crying. He nods, takes my hand, and squeezes hard. When I look at him, there are tears in his eyes as well.

I ask myself, *what's here* that triggers an emotion so overwhelming it brings tears? It's not like theater, where our emotions are aroused by what we hear, and we cry over words and evolving situations. This is *rock*—inert—water, air, aromas, silence, light, and shadowplay. Words would mock this scene.

Our tears have come unexpectedly because we're thankful to the point of overflowing. We've just been handed a spectacular gift—rare, flawless, stunning to the senses—and the privilege has touched our hearts in a wash humility and reverence. I am humbled and bow my head before these generous Canyon Gods, glad to be one who can shed tears.

Floyd Dominy would probably stop here and take a piss.

We put a lot of film through our cameras trying to capture what to us is the essence of Glen Canyon, but it won't fit the frame. E.T. knows this before we do and is walking ahead, ready to try something else.

There's a pool; I swim it, they skirt it. There's another; do the same. They insist I go on and call back if there's more worth seeing. Worth seeing! Are they so intent on taking photos that they're missing the point? I'm snap-snap-snapping too, but on the run.

Leaving them, I move up-canyon slowly, trailing the fingers of one hand along the wall. The Kayenta stairsteps up gradually, falling into spiral-ribbed patterns. Each turn throws me off balance, saying, one more turn ... one more. Each pool heightens the mystery, conceals something deep down I wish I could see. I'm moving faster now ... another bend ... can't stop even long enough to call them. Well, tough titty, they're the ones who cut me loose!

Ooooh, lookie ... a mauve waterfall, now dry. Insurmountable? *Quién sabe?* I start the ascent, thirty or forty feet to the top with a mirror pool below reflecting the entire canyon. This is tricky—one slip and *I'm* the waterfall. I hear voices as I reach the spillway but rush on anyway, completely mesmerized by a canyon that has quick-changed itself into a narrow and untracked sandy floor with borders of soft pink Navajo sandstone that reach up and lean open like wings unfolding.

Frank calls: "Katie, where are you? Are you hurt?" I turn to see him rushing toward me.

"Me, hurt? No, why?"

He lets go a sigh and points to my leg. "You left quite a trail. Maybe we should put a stop to that flow before it runs over the fall." Blood runs from my knee, down my leg, and sinks into the sand.

"Omygosh, didn't even know it, Frank. I'll clean it off on the way down. Please take my camera. I'm going to swim every pool, shallow, deep, wide, or narrow, all the way back to the river."

He grins and shakes his head. "Tad's right; you must be part fish, part ice cube—but where'd you get such a warm heart?"

I smile and hug him. "I thought you'd never ask."

～

For half an hour I've been squatting on my heels in a crack, on nearly vertical slickrock, a hundred feet above the river, waiting for my guys. I've learned a helluva lot about walking slickrock or I'd be frozen with fright. A while ago I could see Tad high above me, just an ant on salmon rock against an azure sky. Frank is way beyond in the never-never, looking for a J. W. Black inscription, which *I'm* supposed to be hunting, for Dock Marston. Should be somewhere near the mouth of the Escalante, a hundred feet above the river, he said. <END JOURNAL>

[It so happened that "J.W. Black—FEB. 2 1896" was *six hundred* feet above the river, through an arch, over a flat, in a cave hidden by brush, written in five-inch charcoal letters, seven feet above the floor.]

Journal Note: October 1 (Continued)

For once, I've given up the climb, but now I'm worried. Where are they? This stuff may *look* like the bald tummy of a giant teddy bear, but anyone can fall off of it, and for seasoned slickrock climbers they've been gone too long.

My mind wanders.

What would I do if they didn't come back? Supposing broken bones, how could I get them out? All the worst scenarios flash by. I look down at the boat. Providing I can get the motor on and started, I'll head quickly for Forbidding Bar, where Art comes up in the *Tseh Na-ni-ah-go Atin*. But this is October; likely nobody's there ... and if not, when? Will I panic? Will I be cool?

Maybe I could handle it, because I've noted when something *really serious* happens, I don't even swear.

Shit-o-dear! There they are, comin' down the wall.

A jet rips the sound barrier as I take the oars.

Then a cr-aa-ack!-rumble-boommm! and a plume of dust rises from the rim of a hundred-foot bench a quarter mile upstream.

"You know," says Tad, "I sure don't want to be in Labby when one of those things flies over."

"A canyon two feet wide, six hundred feet deep—neither do I!" says Frank.

"Sandstone sandwich, with very little meat," is my conclusion.

~

"Oh, look. There's a Not-a-Stanton Survey Stake ... heh-heh." I point to the right bank—"And see what else? A couple hundred yards on down, caught in the rocks on the point, that great big stack of driftwood. Shall we stop and burn it?"

Bigfeets: "Let's get out and see if it's practical. We don't want to set fire to anything on the bank."

Tad: "Dan Davis has asked us to burn the really big ones. If you think it's safe, Frank, I'd say this qualifies."

Me: "Good. I need some fire shots for my slide show."

Tad: "Don't stay too close, pal. Those rocks are going to get hot and shoot all over like shrapnel."

We take our pictures and leave when the fire's mostly burned out, a rock or two still popping. In the boat I ready up for what's around the bend— *"then the San Juan flows right on to meet his blood relation"*—and jump out behind the boat.

Surprise! Surprise!

The Old San Juan is two shallow streams on both sides of a half-mile long island full of bird prints and poop. A couple of years ago, where I felt the mighty Colorado pushing the S. J. against the wall and dancing me around in circles, sandbars now spank *Tinny*'s bottom, and mine. We beach the boat and walk up the *middle* of the San Juan river. Looking at us now, I have to smile, as opposed to a week ago—the ease with which we ramble, picking up whatever interests us, looking, maybe exclaiming, and throwing it down again. We've had to put a limit on Tad; no more rocks! He and I are brown as bark. Bigfeets is barefoot and down to swim trunks (tennies replaced boots after the first day). Nobody tells us what to do, or when, and we have not seen another living soul.

I yell, "Hey, my dears—maybe it's gone dry up at Mexican Hat under the bridge? Gold! Gold!" Coming alongside Tad, I add, "By the way Tadito, Art might not be bullshitting me after all. Dick Sprang told me the name of that old prospector who struck it rich when this 'ere river went dry. His name was James Douglas; 1909 it was, and he waited until *1929* (I always heard it was *ten* years) before he jumped off the bridge. He even left a note."

We walk back to *Tinny*, where I dig out my journal, hand it to Tad, and tell him to read aloud while I take the oars to Hidden Passage.

"When this you see
My old body in the river will be
There is no one in the world
To blame for this
Only me."

He rubs his double-jointed thumb back and forth under a wrinkled-up nose, in a typical E.T. mode of rumination.

"Poor guy; he wasn't much of a poet, either."

~

Hidden Passage Bar. E.T.'s favorite camp.

Nature's benches, ledges, bunks and tables; swallows streaking, canyon wrens calling, frogs barfing, and beavers slapping. Not a gnat, not a fly or mosquito. (No pesky bugs at all in the Glen until the last two years before the dam). Many parties camp here, but by the time we arrive in October, a river swollen by late summer rains has rinsed it clean of all but the little mice that Tad feeds with our scraps—those he doesn't eat. He's our dispose-all, yet he'll exit the trip just as lean as he entered; never gains a pound. I will always remember him standing in his typical outdoor pose, balanced on one foot, the other cocked up on his knee like a stork, plate in hand, silhouetted against the river.

The sky put on its yellow slicker at sunset. We're familiar with what that means—weather moving in. But not right away. The moon is so intense, so fierce tonight, I swear I can feel its heat. We set up our tripods, open the shutters, and take time exposures to capture the Glen's utter change of character beneath its gossamer scrim. The light is liquid, pouring into dark fissures, pulling out the detail, softening the contrast, and transforming male strength to feminine seductiveness. On our film, moon and stars will trace their paths across the deep blue; the river, wide and unbroken, will be a sheet of molten silver. <END JOURNAL>

~

[Something else happened here at Hidden Passage that is forever burned into my memory. A year later (1956), we were again here in October, but with a greater sense of urgency. On April 11th of that year, the Upper Colorado River Project Act was passed, spelling out the doom.]

We'd talked about hiking Hidden Passage in moonlight even before our trip began. The mysterious quality that seemed to pervade in daytime was intensified under moonglow, making it both exciting and eerie, sending an aquamarine light into the canyon's narrow depths.

For reasons unexplained, we spoke in whispers as we walked beside a stream that seemed to flow stronger and gurgle louder than it had in times past. We waded between high sloping banks of maidenhair fern that had turned to bright turquoise—they bobbed under a seep and shivered in a light breeze. We skirted gentle sluices, stooping to feel them run through our fingers, awed by the patient force of moving water that ultimately wins. Dilation darkened our eyes, amazement heightened our whispers. As our intimacy with the canyon grew, all that we said and did threaded past in slow motion. E.T.'s long, precise stride seemed to bounce, dreamlike, each step without a sound. Frank, beside him, glided as if on skis. For once, I was lagging behind, wrapped in a timeless aura—not at all certain that I hadn't been standing right there a thousand, two thousand, ten thousand years ago.

The thought must have occurred to us all at the same time—that we were passing through a subterranean fairyland in a sparkling blue sea—but only Tad voiced it—"Feels like we're walking under water"—before he realized he shouldn't have.

I lost it completely; went to my knees crying hysterically, screaming obscenities at the politicians and bureaucracies that had orchestrated the drowning of Eden.

"I hope they die! All of them! Horrible, slow, agonizing deaths, like they're going to do to my canyons!"

～

Journal Note: October 1 (Evening)

I take my bedroll to a ledge, where I can dangle one arm over the side into the current, and am on my way to dreamland when something takes a nip at my finger, startling me upright with a yelp. E.T. is asleep and snoring, and Frank, having come from a bath and shave, is just crawling in.

"You'd better move, Little Wrists. Those weren't beaver you heard; it's sandbanks falling in. River's rising."

But I don't move. Not for a while.

I roll onto my stomach and put my hand back in the river, this time catching and letting go small pieces of drift as they sprint past my fingers. There's a new melody now under the slight overhang where I lie, which means Frank is correct. The river's found a new hole to poke his fingers into—or an old hole he started a few centuries ago and is still working on. Before, when I drifted off, he was in the key of F-major; now it's a throaty E-minor. Strips of angel-hair clouds ride west to east on a high wind over the monoliths; an upstream eddy and the downstream current argue in a whirlpool until they disappear beneath the surface. On and on the river goes, never stopping, taking part of the rock with him, down ... down to the sea ... ?

Life is a river ...

... a stream of consciousness that flows through our existence, bringing valuables from our upstream past: primordial memory, instinct, mystical wisdom. And the river is continuous, inseparable from any part of itself, an extension. We could learn the art of living from the river; learn to flow from source, through understanding, into the sea of wisdom. But it's not easy to read the subtle currents where we float in the constant present, with the future hiding just around the bend. More often than not, we breast back upstream against the flow. This river journey is showing me how to read the current to my downstream future, teaching me not to fight my destiny, not hang by my hope strings, but to guide myself to the next beach until the water rises again.

I *can* swim.

~

It would be impossible to guess how many lives *this river* has changed. Most river folk I know have expressed the phenomenon one way or another. Our canyon-cutting Colorado is known to have put many a disarrayed life back together. Others he roughs up in his rapids when they most need the jolt. Many, especially those who've come to know the Glen, look inward, lie back, discover (and then become) who they really are.

Take Bigfeets. Since day one a smile has not left his face. I've never seen such deep contentment, such a change in one already so gentle, reassuring, and kind. Talk about "not seeing the forest for the trees;" Frank couldn't see the *river* for the passengers. He's told me he keeps doing it for the *people* he's gotten to know, respect, and learn from—those he writes to, who come back many times and are now his friends—not the river. Not the *river?* At first I'm in shock, then I realize it's no wonder. Each year since 1948, when he made his first boat trip with Norm Nevills, he has rowed every scheduled trip but one, averaging six trips per season on the San Juan, three to five from Hite, and one in Grand Canyon. Sandwiched in between all that, he once rowed from Green River, Wyoming, and again from Green River, Utah, to Lee's Ferry.

The river is the *job* he's never had time to enjoy.

Until now.

I dare him to tell me it's just me and Tad, just our amazement and reverence rubbing off on him, or that he's seeing it through *our* eyes only. Balderdash! He's *feeling* it for the first time, and look what it's done for him!

I've learned that Bigfeets is a very private person, revealing little of his inner self. Whenever there's a direct hit, ambiguity reigns supreme. I think it's because he's protecting a very tender and loving soul. Like me at my job, the walls he's built are high and strong, the gate most always closed.

And now ... "the walls come tumblin' da-yown."

Take Tadito. Talk about *time*—he might as well *be* time, he has so much of it. *Mañana,* Buanna. Africa, Egypt, the Galápagos, you name it. Been there, done that—made films of erupting volcanoes for *National Geographic;* had photographs in major color mags everywhere; made nature films to hell 'n' gone. He and Mary Jane have been all over the world. Me, I ain't been around the block … yet. Still, like me, he says *this* is the spot. Glen Canyon, this river, has it all. We talked about it before dinner tonight.

"Why, Tad-O. What makes it so special?"

He stretches his arms up high, palms up, and almost whispers, "The light, sweetie, look at the *light*. Crwist! It drives me cr-ayz-ee!"

"That all?"

"No, of course not."

"What then?"

"Oh, well, mmm … you know. The canyons … each one full of surprises; the colors, the air, stone textures, the river, peaceful and quiet; not like the Grand, not like an assignment either, more like a vacation."

"C'mon your whole life's a vacation. You can do better than that. Why does this place make you *feel* different? Or does it?"

"Oh, yes yes … yes yes." He stops and looks upriver for a long time, then shaking his head, says, "I don't know, Kay; I rweally can't tell you … why. Maybe it's the silence, the secrets it holds, the ruins, maybe because its so … clean … hardly touched."

"You're the one who said I must *see* this. You actually got me here. Why?"

"I knew you'd love it; it's your kind of place."

"How'd you know?"

"Chrwist, pal, every time we'd try to reach you, your mother'd say, 'She's up at Sabino Canyon, or Tanque Verde Falls, or Bear Canyon.' Wherever water moved, there you were. You told me you'd never run a river. I thought this would be the perfect place.

"You were right. It is! Thanks, Tad-O."

"And this trip, just the three of us, is the best of all. Don't you agree?"

"Far and away, I say. The *best*."

"Just to see Frank so relaxed, and having a grweat time, no worries. Bet he's taken five rolls of film already. The poor guy never had a chance to do that before."

Take me: I fight for time to get here, work for money to make the time. These two friends know that out there in the artificial world, where my job is, I keep the *natural* world in my peripheral vision; hold my longing for it inside until it's possible to touch the Earth once again.

This place is my life jacket. It's that simple.

The first river experience was so stunning, it wouldn't fit in the scope of my imagination. But soon afterward, that imagination, which had been dragging its feet for a long time, literally soared. I got creative as all hell—started writing, had new ideas for plays, songs, poems, Cabaret Theatre shows, new chording for the guitar, the works.

I told E.T. this is one of the reasons Glen Canyon is so special to me.

"Yes yes. You exprwest it perfectly! That's exactly what happens with my photographs ... something ... composition ... I get a new perspective when I'm here. Nowhere else is there such a variety of forms and textures. From the smallest to the largest, the shapes are incwredible."

"Everything here seems to be lit from within, huh Professor?"

"That's a great way to put it, sweetie."

"Heh-heh. I got it from you, Tadito."

~

Sometimes the river talks to me in my sleep.

I dream here more than other places, perhaps because there's nothing to clog the pathway to the subconscious. Tonight I'm offered one of my repeat dreams—one that's both exciting and scary, and one that takes very little analysis.

I'm running down a sidewalk, taking big strides, each one longer and easier than the last—really covering ground. Next I'm out in the open, alongside a dirt road with telephone poles beside it. With each step I rise higher in the air, like a bouncing ball. Over every obstacle I go in a kind of slow motion, noting every minute thing—shadows, brush, stones— where my feet touch down.

I begin to wonder—can I leap high enough to go above the telephone wires? Something tells me that I can, but *I have to know I can before I attempt it,* or I won't be able to do it.

I set my mind to leap above, even beyond the wires and out over the field. On the next leap I *assure myself that I can fly,* that I can float above the ground.

I do it! ... go for a long time ... a long way.

Sometimes the dream will take a different form.

If there's the *slightest doubt* that I might not make it to the heights, I'll bounce up and down two or three times, preparing to soar, but will come right down; it just won't happen. I may bounce higher than my head, but I can't soar. Other times, when I'm way, way up there, so far I can barely make things out below, I begin to worry that I'll drop down too quickly and be hurt when I hit the ground. I seem to know that I can't *stay* up there forever, so I try to figure how to come down easy. If I start to fall too fast, I lose my breath, and I can feel the pain in my feet and legs before I even hit the ground.

That's when I wake up.

Tonight my dream lets me fly high above the world, over every sort of terrain. I float down smoothly, somewhere near a mountain I can easily descend to wherever I'm going …

… to *wherever* I am going.

[Camp—mile 76.2, Hidden Passage Bar] <small>END JOURNAL</small>

∼

SIXTEEN

Earthstone Drums and a Crystal Wave

Journal Note: Sunday, October 2, 1955 (We Three Trip, Day 9, Mile 75.8) Music Temple

> I'm gonna live this life I sing about, down in my soul.
>   Oh yes, in my soul.
> I'm gonna fight for the right, and the shun the wro-o-ng.
>   Shun the wrong
> Down in the streets, or in my home—
> When I got company, when I'm alone—
> I'm gonna li-i-ive the life I sing about, down in my soul.
>
>   Every day, everywhere
>   On this busy thoroughfare,
>   Lotta folks scorn me,
>   Look down upon me,
>   I know they don' like me, but I don't care.
>
> You can't sing one thing, and try to live another—
> Be a saint in your church, and a Devil undercover.
> You got t' li-i-ive the life you sing about, down in your soul.
>   Oh, yes, in your soul.

I lean the guitar against the bank of maidenhair fern and look overhead at the twisting umbilical above the pool in Music Temple. My last chord on invisible wings spirals up … and up … on up … from this womb. Here is where I *listen* beyond the words. Many times I've sung the message, but after today I'm going to start tracking the reality—down in my soul.

∼

We have a rotten job ahead.

Not wanting to distress the music, diminish the delight it has become to sing here, or deny Frank the pleasure of hearing one of his now-favored songs, I have gone directly to the fern bank without even looking at the desecration on the rock shelf across from the pool.

Sometime between June 4—when Frank and I were last here—and today, October 2, some bipeds have *chiseled* their witless monikers into the sandstone beside the historic names of Hillers, Dellenbaugh, Bishop, and C. Powell, then have had the temerity to sign the register as well! Someone else, as pissed off as we, has written across their signatures in heavy block letters: SHOULD BE CONDEMNED TO HELL FOR WRITING NAMES IN MUSIC TEMPLE.

Woody told us about this act of vandalism before we left Hite, so we have the tools with us to obliterate their graffiti. It takes us the best part of an hour ... but the Temple feels clean again when we leave.

A mile and a half downriver, I'll be damned is there isn't another effrontery! What's going on here? Six feet above the talus slope, in aluminum spray paint, on a wall that's stood unmarked for millennia, is the hairdresser's message:

JOHANNOUS

SAFFARY

HITE - GUS LARRY

I'd like to dress his hair—with a scalping knife! The Prussian who introduced himself to me a year ago at Forbidding Bar, and who can't spell. We can neither scrape nor chip off the paint without further marring the surface, so in a bucket we mix mud to the right consistency and plaster it over. Next year we'll see if the mud or the paint wins. My bets are on Colly Raddy's good gumbo.

It is really hard for me to accept the fact that there are people brainless enough to besmirch this place with more than their footprints and a campfire that's easily erased by high water, but of course I know as well as E.T. that the increasing travel in the Glen will always carry some scum downriver. Thus, we've elected to restore and put the offences out of sight, so as not to tempt the "monkey-see, monkey-do" mentality. Anybody wants to call that arrogant, go ahead. Those who know and love the river thank us.

Klondike Bar is our next goal, but as usual we become sidetracked.

At mile 71.4 on the left bank, the Plan & Profile maps show Oak Creek, but downstream, at mile 71.2, is another canyon *not* named on the map. Most intriguing. We doubt that it's a fork of Oak Creek and decide to climb to the top of the boulder-strewn peak, downstream of the drainage from Navajo Mountain, to see where it goes.

The cone we stand on gives us a 360-degree view—Navajo Mountain, Rainbow Plateau, Cummings Mesa, Kaiparowits Plateau, downriver, upriver, across to Twilight Canyon—the world of the Glen above our heads and at our feet, all its secrets, surprises and mysteries hidden in the creases. What has grabbed my attention is the odd way this canyon wishbones into the Colorado. It obviously trundles down from high on the flank of Navajo Mountain, hidden in folds we still aren't high enough to see. Yet, within fifty feet of the big river it hits a buttress, hangs a right, and flows along beside it for a mile or more *in the opposite direction,* then hangs another right, heading back up toward the mountain for half a mile. At last it hears the call and takes a sharp hook left for its final three-quarter-mile run to the Colorado, forming a wishbone shape where we stand overlooking the pulled-apart halves. Way in the southern distance, where the mountain snuggles into its foothills, is a lone Navajo hogan. We can't see the depth of the wishbone, so we roll a large boulder from the lip into its jaws. It strikes no walls and gives a count of eight seconds before hitting bottom.

For years Frank and Tad have wanted a panoramic shot, a full-circle view of the Glen. Here it is. I snap a few frames while they set up their tripods and begin an hour's work.

Down off the cone, I hike the buttress (in some places only thirty feet wide) that separates a river, running west, from a stream, running east. From the cone it appeared fragile, a single elephant's trunk in a herd of pachyderm. Now it seems more like the Great Wall of China.

I remove my tennies. The sandstone is warm and beautifully layered in thin ridges of orange and buff, rose and mauve, tilted so they butt into each other at odd angles. Crossbedding, it's called—something the wind and water did eons ago, leaving the story here to be told in stone. Wandering alone up here on the ridge, under the slap of my bare feet, the tone in the stone changes! A set of drums lies concealed beneath a bulge or bubble, a thin layer not yet broken through by wind or weather. Fascinated, I stoop and tap these places with my hands. Each sends back a different note! Completely entranced, I sit for a long time, laugh aloud, and play a melodic rhythm on my earth-stone drums.

Who would believe there is *music* in sandstone?

I hear a sound like dice rattling in a leather cup and look up to see two ravens sitting on a stone outcrop, kr-uk-k-kling about my presence.

What's up, guys? My drumming call you in? They seem disturbed by this strange activity on their shitting ground. Yes, they do do doo-doo here. I've stepped on it now and then—good clean stuff. I hear something else. The clean, clear air has brought me a whistle—Tad's. Almost half a mile away, the two ants up on the cone are wiggling in the heat waves. Time to go.

We slip-slide down off our peak to the streambed, where it flows shallow and several feet wide, over sand and gravel. By now it is hotter'n hell! We're parched, so we sprawl with our arms and heads in the cool, cool water and drink 'til we're nearly foundered. Sated, with tennies in hand, we make for the boat—but I lag back, still thirsty, dropping down to drink now and again.

I have the feeling I'm being followed.

Don't see anything, but hear an odd sound, a kind of whispering gurgle. Prone and drinking, at eye level with the surface, I see a tiny crystal clear wave, an inch or more high, *on top* of the normal flow, and moving faster than the water beneath it. A kind of miniature flash flood? But there's been no rain up on the mountain, and if there had been, it would be plenty muddy. This wave pushes no debris before it. I wait 'til it hits my nose then scramble up and run downstream.

"Hey! Tad, Frank. Wait up. Come back! Something crazy is happening here!"

Well, we play with the wave, chase it, let it get ahead, try to stop it or divert it. We wait for it, walk beside it, even through it. But the wave stays put, just moves with the drop in the stream's bed, and follows us the half mile to the boat.

We jabber back and forth, trying to figure out the reason for it.

E.T. theorizes that in the heat of day, sun evaporates water from the river and the small canyons. By early afternoon the deep side canyons are left in shade—they've cooled, evaporation ceases, flow increases.

"But Tad, why the visible and steady headwater, like its coming from *one place?*"

"You mean a spring."

"Maybe. Maybe a whole bunch of springs. But *all* of this creek is spring water," I remind him, "not just the wave."

Bigfeets says, "Rock expands when it heats. We've seen that often enough."

Tad: "So when the weather's hot, that would narrow the crevasses through which springs flow."

"Yeah! And when they cool, the openings widen, allowing for more and quicker release, because it's been held back all day—thus headwater?"

"Well ... I don't know," says Tad. "Too many variables; I'll have to think about it. We already know most of these sidestreams flow stronger at night, but this wave ... hmmm ... never saw that before."

"I've got another idea," says Frank. "Some Navajo's sheep fell in a big pothole and raised the stream level all of a sudden."

"That's it, Bigfeets! Probably just as logical as some scientist's explanation. What're they called, hydro ... "

"Educated guessers," offers Tad.

"Or one o' them Wreck-the-nation Bureau hired gun-ologists, who know that water flows one way only—toward money!"

But in my heart, *I know* what it is. It's Mother Nature ... *breathing*.
<END JOURNAL>

Again, while we're here at Wishbone (Dock says the Navajos call it Blackwater), I want to relate some things that happened later in the vicinity.

October 6, 1956 (Mile 71.2)

We hiked past the flowing water, up the dry hot-potato-rocks bottom, three to nine feet wide most of the way. My friend Hugh Cutler had told me there was a rockfall that couldn't be gotten over about 3 miles up from the river, and Bigfeets verified that because he'd come upon it earlier that summer. When he and Tad reached the rockfall, I was sitting smugly above it, swinging my legs over the edge, singing. The waterhole below had dried up, so I was able to chimney up between the boulder and the canyon wall.

The floor narrowed, and walls rose to two hundred feet. It became the inside of a rock tumbler, each turn revealing more bizarre shapes— larger-than-life elephant's feet with their toes spread out, buttresses jutting from the walls, where we'd hide, then jump out to spook each other.

Hugh also told me there were Moki steps up a fault that crossed the canyon just before it forked. The steps led to the cap between Wishbone and Forbidding Canyons, where he'd found a cairn that cached a jar with a couple of calling cards in it left there by John Wetherill, the guide and trading post owner who'd taken both Teddy Roosevelt and Zane Grey to Rainbow Bridge around 1913. Hugh advised me to get the other card before the cairn was discovered by someone else.

We got to the fault and mounted the steps, hiked all over between the two canyons, but never found the cairn.

~

An earlier trip found me up there with Kent Frost (a boatman for Frank and the owner, with his wife Fern, of a Jeep tour business out of Monticello, Utah; they'd pushed the first trails into the Needles area.) It was a hotter'n hell day in June, so we dipped into every pothole along the way. Again we looked for the cairn—hiked a good six sweaty miles—but either someone had already found it, or I'd misinterpreted Hugh's directions.

In the process, we stumbled on another Glen Canyon mystery.

Near the top of the cap, at a spot where it was all but flat, we came upon a rectangular pool approximately three feet deep, perhaps seventy-five feet long by thirty feet wide, so perfect it could have been chipped or drilled out with tools—but there were no such marks in evidence, either primitive or modern. It was near to the brim with clear, *cold* water. Was it nature's work, or was it man's?

We entered cautiously, sharing the pool with descendants of the ancient trilobite, which wiggled for the bottom like inch-long accordions. I scooped one up and held it squirming in my palm for Kent.

"Take a look at what once ruled the earth, and let that be a lesson to you, Kent!"

"You can eat 'em," he grinned, "if you're starving."

We felt along the straight sides and bottom, thinking the pool might be spring fed, but no. Kent—who has Jeeped, hiked, walked, floated, crawled, hung, climbed, swung, waded, or swum about every crevasse in southeastern Utah—couldn't guess what made the pool, or what made the water (always in the sun) so cold! From up there we could see every crease on Navajo Mountain—from the tall pines on top to the slickrock thighs between the canyons, where they poked out from under a ruffled skirt of juniper and piñon—yet none of the drainage came to the pool. We decided it was nature's rain-fed shrimp hatchery and bird bath, put there to cool us off on this hot day.

"Kent, we'll be overdue for lunch if we don't get a move on."

"We'll take a shortcut," he said. "Follow me."

We started down a fault line bordering Forbidding Canyon. As usual I was gawking at everything around me, checking out the potholes. Some had bushes growing beside them, one had reeds in it, another a *tree* beside it, even way up here on this bald rock. I lagged a bit behind Kent, and when I looked up, I saw only his head disappearing over the lip of a downgrade.

Watching only my feet now, I took about ten steps down the wall and suddenly *knew* there was no place for step number eleven. Kent was thirty feet below, tennies sticking on what only the wildest imagination would call a ledge, with more freefall below him.

I clutched. Sweat broke out all over my body, my legs trembled, my stomach lurched. I started to lean *backward*, which would have pushed my feet right out from under me.

Then, softly and calmly, Kent's voice broke through:

"Don't lean back, Katie. You're not in any trouble. Stand up straight and point your toes down. Look to your left; see that nice little ridge? Put'chr little foot right there."

I took a big gulp of air, swallowed cotton, and tried to sit down. (Squatting, sitting, prone on my back or stomach, I would have been a cascade to oblivion.)

"Ohh-h no-o-o"—he almost sang it—"don't sit down; lean out."

"L-l-lean out! You crazy? You gonna catch me? I *can't lean out!"*

"Oh, yeah, sure you can. Look at your feet, not at me, and lean *over your shoes.* It's easy."

Easy, my sweet ass! "I'm turning around, Kent. I'm not coming down that way!"

I tried to shift my weight and reverse. Holymoley … worse. No place to go, and I thought I'd mastered slickrock hiking. By then, I was a running sweat machine, shaking all over, on the verge of panic—afraid even to breathe—frozen to the rock!

Then Kent's quiet slow drawl. "See, you're not slippin'. I'd come up there and get you, Katie, but I know you can get down here on your own."

Somehow, I gained control and muddled through. *Did* lean slightly forward, put my little foot in the no-ridge to my left, and found the imperceptible ridges in the crossbedding of forgiving sandstone. By the time I reached Kent, I was laughing—amazed at the security I felt by just shifting my weight, leaning out, which literally pushed my feet into the rock.

On an adrenaline high I finished the descent.

We made it in time for lunch.

*Journal Note: October 2, 1955 (We Three Trip,
Cathedral Canyon, Afternoon of Day 9)*

We've had to use the little motor on *Tinny* to make up the time to get
here—neither Tad nor Frank have been inside the canyon, and I've insisted they *must* see it, even though there's almost no sun and it might
be cool.

First, through a hundred yards of knee-deep mud—abandon shoes—
to Cathedral #1. At its end is the first pool crossing. We've taken our
cameras and Tad's air mattress to float them. It leaks; abandon air mattress and Tad's camera. Bigfeets stares at the twenty-foot fern-banked
black hole we must swim, grimaces, and slides in. Five strokes get him
up, over, and out on the rock. When he can breath again he gasps, "Ye
Gods! That's cold!"

E.T. tests the surface with his toes, shudders, and moans, "Katie, I
simply cannot dip my tool in that cool pool!" But he does, riding
halfway out of the water in three mammoth strokes, making a bow wave
so big he doesn't even get his back wet until he claws at the rock and
slides back in before Frank can lend a hand. "Mother of Chrwist! I'll
never be the same!" is his shivering comment. Then me, swimming with
my camera—no fuss, no muss—except I'm laughing so hard I have trouble getting out the far end. <END JOURNAL>

[Perhaps my reader should know that a friend once said to me, "Anyone
ever tell you, you've got a sadistic sense of humor? You'd make a perfect
torture chamber director. Anyone's discomfort short of death and
bloody murder sends you into hysterical laughter."]

Journal Note: October 2 (Continued)

Another cathedral—another bottomless pool with a struggle over the
boulder at its end—and *I* abandon camera. Even without it, all my
breath and strength are needed just to swim. Between each narrow we
seek the few streaks of sun to stand in for their little warmth.

The third long, serpentine swim—so narrow our elbows hit the
sides—ultimately gets E.T. He says, "I never felt so alone and spooked
in my life. I look ahead and you're gone; look back and Frank hasn't
started yet; and there I am in the middle of that dark, narrow trwench,
freezing cold!"

E.T.'s got the blue shivers. Frank is taking it, but he's also starting to
turn a little blue, and I … I'm beginning to wonder. How can I be so
mean to these men who are so good to me?

We stand in a wee streak of sun for a long time, then pick our way to the fourth narrows. They can't see but a few feet ahead, but I remember it's a lo-o-ong one, longer than the last. The joking has ceased—not funny to them anymore, let alone fun—and we have it all to go back through. As torture director I pull the plug, and we turn back. Tad keeps crying that his manhood will never return to normal. Frank, who hasn't gone barefoot since he was a kid, is sore and probably as cold as both Tad and I put together, but with his typical stoicism, he never says a word. Me? I've been warmer.

So ... the experience I wanted them to have, like mine last year, I goofed up. They missed the spirit of that incredible canyon altogether because of so much physical discomfort—all to please inconsiderate me, rather than do what we came here for—to enjoy ourselves. <END JOURNAL>

[Many moons later, Frank told me that when he came out of the canyon he had no feeling in his legs or feet! Canyon lesson: Do not take even *strong* men swimming into long narrows except during hot, midsummer days. Unlike women, they ain't got much subcutaneous fat.]

Journal Note: Still October 2

Old Mr. River has come up about five inches and taken on his usual blush. We note the drift and feel the increased current as we float down to mile 64.5, below Klondike Bar, where we find warm sand glistening in the sun. We can't wait to lie in it and cover ourselves over.

After we get the blood circulating again, we elect to stay, even though the sun is well above the canyon rim. It is wonderful to camp early, and Bigfeets appreciates it more than anyone; too many trips he's had to cook by flashlight and firelight, too many times groped for a bedding place in the dark. He and I gather wood and start dinner.

I look around for E.T. but can see only his footprints trailing off downriver; wonder where he's gone.

The river, having risen between the slender young tamarisk saplings, is gurgling with the anticipation of uprooting them before morning. In this mood his voice is teasing, taunting as he pushes, then pulls, backs off as if forgetting about it, then rushes in to grab more soil from beneath them. They lean out, stumble and fall in, then suddenly flip violently back up like a released spring, tassels spraying water high in the air. They stand, shuddering a few moments, waiting for the next surge to bend them again, repeating the same crazy dance over and over, until the river finally gulps them down for good.

By the time steam rises from our yummy pot of stew, Tad has returned with news of a bizarre find just a few yards down the beach and on top of the first sandstone bench, but he won't tell us what it is—says he'll take us there tomorrow morning. I try my damnedest to get a clue, but he's tighter than an old maid's purse at a peep show.

"Tomorrow," he repeats. "You can't believe it 'til you see it with your own eyes; maybe not even then."

The western sky now rivals the blaze of our campfire. It folds over, turns reds to blues; purples usurp pinks and violets, and under all rolls a plume of indigo with a gold-fringed opening through which Jesus rays pierce the bastions of Cummings Mesa.

Even though it is still quite warm, hot buckets of water for our baths and hot rocks at the foot of each bedroll feel mighty nice after those freezing, serpentine pools across the way. I've sung every night except one, way back there somewhere, but tonight we're all kinda strung out, and before the last light fades into starlight, we're all snugly bedded down, and the only one singing is the river.

Tadito and Bigfeets are snoring. but I can't sleep.

I'm thinking about love—not of some*one* but of some*place*. As my intimacy with this canyon grows every day, it wraps around me like a lover's arms. There will be odd moments during the day when I'm alone with the canyon, the river, in the pools, or on the cap, that I feel a sudden warmth, and so help me, a caress—something, a presence—that wordlessly offers me ... what? Peace? A sanction in return for my love?

Which brings me to ask myself: Have I truly ever loved anyone? Deeply, unselfishly, without reservation, unceasingly, through thick and thin, 'til death do us part? All that jazz. I've often told myself that I have, but no. Only the love for a friend is like that—a friend you don't have to deal with on a daily basis. I've cared for someone, been in and out of passion, amorous relations, and sexulations, but *love* as I understand it—that "forever" business—huh-uh. I'm more like the river, flowing on, finding new beaches to build or tear down, seeking the high ground, and yup—wallowing in the low. The creative personality comes hard by love. Held too tightly, asked to eddy out and stay, or pulled into a lover's wayward current, it feels the tug of downstream life, slips over the bar, and is gone.

Again, the clouds have moved on. I thought surely we'd have a storm by now, or at least a few drops of rain, but no—it stays perfect, day after glorious day.

I watch a late moon's light slide in a slow silver wave across the pebbled beach to my bedroll, past the fire pit, across the sparkling sand to the guy's beds, and slowly over the top of the bench where Tad's new mystery lies, waiting for tomorrow. Oh, if this could only last. But if it did, like other beautiful things, would it fade into the ordinary with too much repetition? How could *this place* ever be monotonous?

I could ask Bigfeets if I really wanted an answer.

[Camp—mile 64.4, Balanced Rock Bar] <END JOURNAL>

PART THREE

~

The Wild Secret Heart

∼

SEVENTEEN

The Hour Glass

We're now in what, for me, is the Wild Secret Heart of Glen Canyon. From mile 76 downriver to mile 56, through a dozen gentle meanders, the River God billets fifteen of his most enticing offspring. Above those side canyons, the Nature Goddess has left enough curiosities and works of art—on *both* sides of the river—to boggle the mind. From Navajo Point (elevation 7,212 feet) on the upthrust Kaiparowits Plateau, to the Colorado River at our sandy bar (3,223 feet), the land is pure drama; it staircases down through every color, shape, and form of rock imaginable.

Journal Note: October 3, 1955 (We Three Trip, Day 10, Balanced Rocks Bar—Mile 64.4)

Dawn rises feverish over east and throws a scattering of pink sequins on a river twisting below cliffs of midnight blue. *Ah, mi amor!* The sight is like a caress!

I just want to lie here and listen to the special stillness in this canyon. It has a quality analogous to pure air—I can breath it in, feel it filtering through my pores. Like Good Medicine, it clears the cobwebs from my brain. By stillness I don't mean silence, because no matter where we are along the river's edge, and at times many feet above it, we can always hear his voice. By listening I've come to know his moods. This morning he's got a throat full of cold chocolate—sounds like he's gargling for a late evening performance. Could even be a light show.

In the cold shadow of the cliff I see Tad, first up, has built the fire so Frank won't do it. I'm truly grateful to him—still ashamed of myself for being the cause of that icy swim yesterday. I sure don't want Bigfeets becoming unwell on my account.

Crawling lazily and late from my sack, I go wedge between them where they stand warming their buns, faces turned upstream to a sun that only moments ago bloomed over Cummings Mesa and spread across our camp. "Wow!" I whisper, "I could spend two years in this stretch and not begin to see even half of it."

Tad: "We'll be lucky if we make two miles today, especially after I show you what I found yesterday. How many more canyons and how many ... "

"Twenty-five ... and only five days."

"Jesus! We'll never make it," he says, twiddling his cowlick.

Frank puts an arm around my shoulder. "If I could get you *out* of one canyon in time to get you *into* another, we could snoop in most of them, Little Wrists."

"Trouble is," Tad reminds him, "she doesn't want to *snoop*. She wants to explore to the end of every one."

"You're right, sweetie, I just can't help it. Guess I'll have to curtail my craving for those deep and narrow twisties, or take them by myself."

"Nope," says Frank, "that's strictly against the rules. We left you alone once too often already, and we do have a *few* more years to explore, hopefully." He wrinkles his nose at me.

"Always looking out for me, aren't you, Bigfeets? Wonder when I'll get the knack of worrying about you before I freeze your buns off?"

After breakfast we get ourselves ready for Tad's bizarre discovery. While I stash our "goodies" in the kitchen box, away from the little critters, the two of them go ahead with camera equipment hanging all over them. I'm glad to have only one camera, because the climb to the bench turns out to be a steep tennie-sticker. [You must remember that tennies in those days, mostly called sneakers, had no tread—merely a roughed-up flat bottom.] On inclines like this, I often marvel how the Old Ones must have navigated these tortuous slopes—probably as if they were nothing, being built lower to the ground than we are and with bare feet almost like suction cups.

When I come up behind the guys on the slickrock bench, I find them bottoms up, elbows akimbo, fingers splayed out like two big frogs, studying something on the ground with Darwinian scrutiny. The sight is so absurd that I can't quit laughing. I almost drop my camera and fall into a deep canyon that twists west of the bench. Eventually, they explain they're trying to fathom how this page from nature's joke book came about.

Centuries ago, or maybe even in the last century, head-sized boulders gravitated from the Kaiparowits and came to rest on the softer Navajo. When old Mama Nature couldn't wash them away or blow them off with her monkeyshine winds, she cleared away everything beneath them, leaving perfectly balanced, dark, polished rocks on pink pyramid legs the size of a dime at their vertex. They have weathered into shapes that resemble a herd of drunken turtles, some with two legs, some with three, a few with only one—average height, two to five inches.

Between us, we probably take fifty slides, very carefully. Some are so close together that in stooping to shoot one, we might accidentally knock over another. We manage not to destroy anything and *swear* to tell absolutely *no one* where they are. Not likely they'll be found unless we leak it, because the ascent to this bench is indeed tricky and doesn't look like it really goes anywhere. [Several years later, we found that many of the little turtles *had* been knocked off their perches. No one to blame but ourselves. Over time, we told one or two special friends, who told a couple more, who also ... until the inevitable.]

~

Back in camp we find one of the Glen's unique pink rattlers emerging from the willows, seeking to warm itself in the sun. In the event it might want to nap in our skillet, E.T. elects to remove it. It's a young'un, still cold and not aggressive. He finds a stick, pins it to the ground, then pinches it with thumb and forefinger just behind the head and takes it to the end of the bar, where he tosses it up on the warm rocks—the customary method for removal among those of us who aren't into killing rattlesnakes. [Incidentally, they don't really crawl in bed with you to get warm. In all my years in Glen I was never bitten by any kind of creepcrawly, and we all slept on the ground, in the open.] We leave our stuff in camp and go no miles at all, really—just across the river to an interesting canyon entrance that's been staring back at us since we climbed to the Balanced Rocks.

From high overhead on the V-shaped, seeping walls to the sweet trickle of a stream at our feet, we inch upward over cataracts of maidenhair fern, trying not to step on too much of it or pull it from the walls. The fern lessens and it widens into narrow graceful curves that cuddle bank after bank of columbine, red monkey flowers, and gilia. A half mile and it ends at a clear pool of the *cold* stuff. A conchiform, in soft hues of pink and violet, spirals above and beyond it—a teasing, mysterious aperture that drives me nuts because it looks so *easy* and is just out of reach. I swim the pool to the sandbar to see how deeply anyone beneath me would sink if they held my feet against the wall while I tried to reach the ledge. Guess who isn't interested? Can't say I blame them, but ohmygod, I do want up there. Next time! (My maps are full of these two words, with not nearly enough of them crossed off.)

Tad remarks that the first part of this canyon is a glen full of fern, so I put it in my first journal as Fern Glen. <END JOURNAL>

A Year Later (The Next We Three Trip, October 8–9, 1956)

Frank: "What'll we do about those steps we want to chip at the end of the Fern Glen?"

Me: "Let's go chip them now, but not go up them, then we come back, make camp here on Balanced Rock Bar and in the morning go see how far we get beyond the bottleneck. Make sense?"

Tad and Frank looked at each other and shrugged. Tad said for them both, "It does if we don't have to swim anything."

Me: "No pools in there."

Tad: "There's one where we have to chip." He hugged himself and shuddered.

Me: "It's only crotch high, Tadito, probably only to your knees.

Tad: "Okay, let's go."

The first step would not be a toehold, but a drilled one where we put a stick that could be removed, making the upper steps look unreachable. The pool lay rippleless in a bowl of sand. Innocent. But looking up, where I had so longed to go last year, I could feel the rage of stormborne water that sometimes poured through that convoluted mystery! Taking turns, we stood hip deep in the pool, drilling the first hole. Bigfeets pushed in a stout stick and, standing on it, moved the ferns aside to begin the first real step. To his surprise there was a natural hole there already. We chipped six shallow steps, one tiny fingerhold, and went back to the boat for dinner.

The walk up next morning was chilly, so we wore jackets and pants, changing to shorts at the pool. Frank waded in to place the two sticks; I climbed to the top of the steps and waited for my guys. Walls like rippling blue-grey veils seemed to move with us as we spiraled upward through that slender passage, touching both sides with arms outstretched. Our muted voices reverberated, and our footfalls beat a drumlike ring on the sand.

Fifty yards ... and it ended.

We leaned against a stone teepee one hundred feet tall, its smoke hole revealing pink walls five hundred more above that. No sound but our breathing. Had a human stood here before? Prehistoric peoples' intimacy with the canyons made it possible. Still, there were no other steps up the wall and no way in except to fall from above.

"I think we're the first," I breathed. "What a gift!"

Standing in the twilight bottom of that bowl of stone flooded the senses. Touching the velvet walls gave me a sensation of being in the timeless womb of the Earth Mother. I whispered my thought:

"This is the first holy place I have ever been."

Halfway back we noticed a deep, worn-to-velvet sluiceway. Eyeing its track upward we saw a beautiful little arch, a skylight to the outer gorge, where the water actually comes from. Millions of years ago it was just a pothole. When we walked up a talus slope to take pictures, we could see where the canyon's old watercourse ran before it broke through. Lying on our backs, we marked the eons of time, felt the earth turn, walked down our *renamed* canyon, Little Arch, very satisfied with our venture.

Journal Note: October 3, 1955 (Continued)

And still we haven't gotten back into Driftwood beyond its "stopper" where Jim disappeared, letting me and my Hollywood friends wait below, wondering what he'd find. I still remember his shit-eatin' grin when he said, "Just more of the same," which I knew bloody well it wasn't. I make a puny attempt to coax E.T. and Frank back upstream to have a go at it, but they say ...

"Next time!" <END JOURNAL>

~

... and that time was October of 1956, the following year.

My journal says, "I cannot begin to tell this story; even the photographs we take don't tell it. You must feel the textures with your own bare feet and fingers, steep in the sun's heat after a cold slap from the pools, watch the tattered blue ribbon of sky diminish between the walls ... shrinking ... thinning ... gone!"

Each canyon's smell, its colors and sounds, its solitude, width, or depth; all these things elicit mood swings bordering on the schizophrenic. Their personalities don't alter much through the ages, only with time as we perceive it—in weeks, hours, minutes; yes, even seconds.

For example, take a livid purple/orange, smooth, shaded wall. Take your eyes away while the shade moves two inches, then look up to see that same wall changed to rose/peach, with a series of Teton-like abrasions etched across its surface under a sun now straight above it. Look again ten minutes later and the Tetons will be gone.

Or check the mood changes of something as inert as a rippled mud bank or quaking bog. Early morning finds it blue as glacial ice—I even shiver as I walk by—*uncomfortable*. Back for lunch, it flashes gold and brown beneath the sun—warm and slurpy on bare feet—*inviting*. After siesta, all is velvet green, topped by four frogs fornicating, also green in the re-reflected light. I hunker down to watch—*fascinating*. Back in late afternoon, it is deepest orange and red, dotted with tints of indigo; hard here, soft there, crests cold, troughs warm—*tricky*.

Driftwood ...

There is a challenge in *every* canyon to gain its end or know the pain of defeat, but I knew in my soul that what this canyon coveted was even more magnificent than the treasures I'd already seen. From above, on the Klondike Trail, I had looked into its serpentine depths, seated with rows of knobby-headed gods in capes. The opposing walls of the canyon actually curved around and over the top of each standing monolith, forming cowls streaked with rain marks. But the canyon's floor was something else again.

We helped each other up a crumbling fissure to the base of the steep and dark talus cone. Built of blowing sand, droppings from the ceiling, and untouched by rain, the only marks it bore were diagonal prints from Jim's traverse two years before. *No one* had been there since.

On that quiet day with the merest breeze, I leaned into a wall and felt, even heard, the power of a raging storm battering the stone, honing it down to the graceful curves of its recalcitrant nature. High above us in the fluting, an immense tree trunk was wedged, where it would stay until the wrath of some future deluge broke it away. I read these marks of violence along the walls in nicks and gouges, some recent, some long smoothed over by that same hand in a more compassionate mood.

We reached a small valley touched with golden leaves standing against the tumbled rock in a fault line. The blue river of sky opened to a lake, and an eyelet arch high in the rim made a tiny reef off its shore. A delightful cascade glittered at the bottom of the picture. Over the sound of whispery water floated a canyon wren's arpeggio.

I heard a soft whirring in my ears and felt I was evaporating from this space, leaving it for another ... far, far away. I dropped the reflection of myself and passed into another dimension ...

Thought dissolved and was replaced by sensation. I breathed the sandstone, saw it as my flesh, tasted it, felt it move through my veins, a red-orange life-giving energy. The tiny window on the rim became *my* eye … rocks called a greeting … the stream moved in circles around me, sang and threw up misty veils. My body disappeared, and I became an iridescent bubble on the water's surface, floating down, kissing the stones as I passed. Dropping over a cataract, I burst, then formed again beside other bubbles. Everything in the canyon sang to me, touched me, loved me. I returned it all—the touches, the love, the songs.

I became the canyon.

A frond of maidenhair fern, drawn softly across my cheek and over my eyes, popped the iridescent bubble.

Tad.

"Hey, pal! Let's find the end of this beauty while I still have some vestige of me manhood left unfrozen—and get back in time to eat lunch for a change, what say?"

Never allow reality to form a patina over your dreams, or it becomes impossible to reenter the picture and capture the magic once again.

Journal Note: Still October 3

It is noon of our tenth day when we cross back to camp from Fern Glen/ Little Arch. We have lunch. The guys flake out and take a snooze. I take my journal, walk down to the end of this perfect bar to write and catch some rays.

The shore is bright, the sand deep and silky, the colors delicate pink, pearl, sparkling gold and silver; clean—so clean and smooth, not salty and sticky like ocean sand. It actually whistles as I scuff through it barefooted; full of silicon, unusual in the Glen. Near the water it has formed a rippled rib cage for the river.

I lie face down on the silkiness to catch forty winks, but like a viper striking, I recall Frank's words from this morning:

" … *we have a FEW more years to explore.* … "

I look at the river—live, moving, so loved—then watch the far bank move upstream. While the river sands still, I write:

> RECIPROCITY
> I have heard the raven's caw
> Seen the ferret struggle in the eagle's maw,
> Walked in canyon narrows where the sandstone jaw
> Cut as though it were ice
> And it was nice!

I have heard the drumlike ring of feet on clay,
A winding boulder-crusted floor has led my way
To mute impasse where choking crevasse lay
Like tumbled dice
But it was nice!

Naked in the sun and wind
(There are those who say I've sinned)
With rushing waters I've been pinned
To earth, neat and concise.
And that was nice!

Once on the river's sandy paw
I built my fire, stared in awe
At Mother Nature's tender claw
Yet cruel device.
And said, "She's nice!"

Last night I dreamed on this same beach
Of foreign men who came to teach
Her how to cut her river's breach
With crude advice.
And they weren't nice!

They said, "We'll dam your canyon's art,
Drown it out, rip it apart."
So I stabbed them through the heart
Once! Twice! Thrice!
And it was nice!

I hear Tad's whistle. Time to bury these thoughts—turn pure hatred to pure love—to hug the bosom I lie upon, the bosom that soothes and feeds, yet cares not for me, nor for anyone. Time to cover up the bod. Time to move on.

We pack our gear, load the boat, and don't take three pulls on the oars before we see the mouth of the canyon I nearly fell into when we were up looking at the Balanced Rocks—but we can't stop. Another "next time!" So I put it in my journal as *Balanced Rocks Canyon* even before we explored it.

Walls along the river are not so high now. The Navajo is thinning as we go downstream, and above it we can see bits of the Carmel, even some Entrada. At mile 61 we pull *Tinny* onto the right bank, cross the sand, and walk where we've never walked before.

"Now, why would anyone want to get up on the cap from *here?*" E.T. scratches his whiskers and stands back from the wall, staring at a knotted, weathered rope, secured (maybe) somewhere out of sight. It dangles beside a makeshift ladder and a series of poorly chipped steps—not Moki, more recent.

"Dunno," I say. "Other places on this side of the river give easier access to that bench. We just left one at Balanced Rocks."

What Frank says sounds likely: "This could be an old miner's trail off the Klondike; a shortcut, or an alternate in high water, like the one at California Bar."

I give the rope a couple of pulls then hang my weight on it. There's a slight pop as a strand breaks, spirals down and smacks me on the arm. Little pebbles slide down the crevasse.

"Oops! Guess not, fellers. Not *me* anyhow."

"I'll say not you," Frank agrees. "Not anybody else, either, if they're smart."

The poor ladder's no better, Tad observes. "We'll pass up this climb and try the canyon floor instead, huh?"

I scan the bench, muttering sadly. "A dangling rope to another mystery; wish we'd found it before it got so rotten. I'll be dreaming about why it's here for weeks."

"If it makes you feel better, I heard that someone did go up it, but they didn't find anything," says Bigfeets.

"C'mon," Tad urges, "there are three forks to this canyon. We're bound to find something more interesting than a dangling rope and a broken-down ladder."

We choose the left fork, which trenches deep into the Kayenta. The bottom squirms, rises, and narrows with every few yards, until we're forced to backtrack and mount a prominent ridge many feet above.

This canyon has the pox! Honeycomb holes perforate the lower walls. Even the usually smooth Navajo above is infected with pimples and gouges. The ephemeral stream sinuates below, looking innocent, flashing blue here, orange there, silver around the next bend, and decorating each damp, sandy bend with sprigs of green. A redbud, stunted by the stream's frequent tantrums, defiantly grows out of solid stone, or so it seems.

Rising sheer, another two hundred feet above our ridge, a wall topped with a row of sandstone bogeymen confronts a line of clouds moving intently from the west. As we watch, the lowering sun breaks through them, igniting the whole wall! For a few moments everything turns warm and rosy in the blaze, but sunlight leaves the wall as quickly as it came, returning our canyon to its bruised, purplish hues.

We look at each other, nod, and without a word turn back.

M-m-mm ... what's in there?!

A shadowy drainage teases us into entering between fluted walls that immediately close in, turning canyon to cave, mild air to cold, and light to gradual eclipse.

"We could be in Alaska," I whisper. "This is like a hike through an ice tunnel!"

Tad shudders and we inch father along to a kind of platform.

Ooooh—spooky in here. I turn, look overhead; all black rock.

At my back and unknown to me, E.T. has picked up a hawk's feather, which he draws across the back of my neck and croaks ...

"Bats!"

I duck, spin, fling up my arm, and sock him smack in the midriff.

"Ha ... ooo ... ff!" He starts to laugh, but with the breath knocked from him he can only squat, sputter, and cough.

"Oh, Tadito, I'm sorry; it was just reflex. I didn't know you were there; can't imagine why I reacted so violently. Actually, I like bats."

"Phoo-k-uh! ... s'what I thought!" is all he can gasp.

~

Out of the canyon we've called Dangling Rope, we see that clouds are making a goose down quilt for the sky. Sounds are muffled, air is close, and the shine is off of Mr. River, revealing his true character. He seems subdued but is not; he is waiting.

We aren't. Quickly, we *motor* three miles down, to camp on Wild-horse Bar, knowing it's the only place to be for now—a secure mooring, a long, untracked beach, and most important, a few shallow overhangs for our sleeping bags behind the willow and tamarisk, now fading to gold.

"I think she's going to bust," says Tad, dropping a load of driftwood near the fire and sneezing his famous sneeze: "Whooo-Izzzz-sheee? Sometimes the sneeze is "HORSE-shit!" He keeps us amused by putting words to his various effusions. When he burps, its "Nerrtz!" for a short one, "Raa-a-aats!" for a long one. When he hiccoughs he's a frog: Orrrk! I tell him he needs a word for his nether sound, like maybe, BOOM! or KRA-A-ACK!"

He rubs an arched thumb under his nose and says, "I think *that* one speaks for itself, especially when I get an echo."

"But look, sweetie," I remind him," aren't you proud? We made almost *six* miles today and explored two new canyons."

Frank says, "I don't trust you, Little-Miss-Wrists. You'll probably want to take us back three or four miles for those we didn't see."

No Bigfeets, we *have* to go on. Anyhow, we can hike the cap tomorrow if it isn't raining, or even if it is. I don't want to be in a canyon when it rains, and I hate being in the boat."

E.T. says, "I've always wanted to check out Wildhorse Mesa. There must be some wonderful vistas from way ... Ooo-lala! Look at that!"

At our backs, the sky has put on war paint, making us run around like tourists at a powwow, snapping pictures and almost burning our dinner before some heavy, blue and gassy looking cumulus burp over the rim and obscure the whole show.

~

This storm does not roar up the canyon as they generally do, but drops straight down with soft rain and muffled thunder.

My overhang is about two feet high and mostly dry, but if I forget where I am and suddenly sit up, I'll have a neat gash on my forehead. I've spent the first hour discouraging the mice from making a nest in my hair. Between fits of sleep, some of the ceiling flakes off and drops down my neck. Just as well; the runoff has found a way between me and the wall. I reach up and make a channel for it to drain out and away from me.

It turns cold. Thunder shakes the ground. The river, one hundred feet away, makes the sounds of a sloppy eater. Yet in spite of all, I feel snug against the Earth in this little womb of rock and sand. Finally, I turn tummy down, pull the bag over my head, and slip into dreams.

They come in weird abstract pictures—whole days are grains of sand slipping down the narrow neck of an hourglass. When I try to turn it over, I find it bolted down, only a few grains remaining in the top crystal.

Toward morning I hear the coyotes singing.

[Camp—mile 58, Wildhorse Bar] <END JOURNAL>

EIGHTEEN

Shamans and Fools

Journal Note: October 4, 1955 (We Three Trip,
Day 11, Wildhorse Bar—Miles 58–56.5)

The rising sun can't quite get up. Seems like he's squashed under layers of heavy purple and orange blankets, but a half-hour past the rim, he kicks off the covers and sends his rays down on three soggy River Rats.

To say the least, our camp is damp, and that moistens our spirits a bit. However, smart campers that we are, we've stashed driftwood under the overhangs, and a warming fire is under way. I come alive with my first cup of coffee, E.T. half-alive, and Bigfeets is somewhere in-between, salivating over a griddle of bacon and eggs. We elect to spend the morning up on Wildhorse Mesa, not sure what the cloud man is up to yet. A wind has come up that didn't seem to be with the storm last night, and it comes from the south. Over east the cloud displays are going wild. Long swords of inky blue knife through a lather of cumulus, as if shot by some obscure archer beyond the rim. Tops of the cumulus, torn by a jet stream, leave gray hair streaking out behind, yet sun lights the face of each billow.

"Bigfeets, d'ya reckon the storm could turn around and come back on us?" (For many years Frank and Dora have run the weather station in Blanding. With his natural modesty, he'll say he can't tell any more than the next guy. Nonetheless, I take his word above all others).

"Possibly, but it looks to be going on north from here, to the Henrys; not much activity over Navajo Mountain."

On that note, we throw tarps over our gear, rock them down, tie our ponchos around our waists, and climb a low ledge near our camp, only to find many winding labyrinths that refuse us passage to the mesa. A few feet in, they end in seventy-five-foot flutings to a cobalt sky, so we switchback the steep dunestone, careful of protruding stratification that tends to crumble beneath our feet after last night's rain.

The adrenaline of anticipation is a signal that the world of the Glen is about to change one more time. First of all, the freedom of the cap is exhilarating—still mysterious and tantalizing, but in far different ways than in the canyons below. Looking down into those secret pockets where I've been, I discover new facets, and those I can *never* get into set my curiosity ablaze!

From up here (like Dick Sprang), I note the feminine aspect more than the masculine. Those with an eye for it can look upon voluptuous cleavage, lovely rounded bottoms, bare tummies and manly chests, all of fleshlike stone, lolling against the earth and each other. There never was, or will be, a landscape as erotic as Glen Canyon's. Eye of the beholder. Well ... I understand why they don't call it the Titty State, but Beehive? *No* imagination!

The river, busily stripping and carrying away earth and rock, wanders turgid and red between the cliff's rumpled skirts, their hems trimmed with lacy yellow rabbitbrush. Islands and gravel bars seen from here are as readable as lines in the palm of a hand. Head line. Heart line. Life line.

Fate line?

We hike on, up and up, past the bare rock to a far-flung sand and gravel mesa that tilts gently to the next stone ridges a mile away. We cross hard, flat pans filled with Navajo marbles—thousands of perfectly round extrusions spread evenly over the surface and graded in size as they wash down from pan to pan, the smallest at the bottom.

From here we can no longer see the river canyon, only the sloping mesa lying clean and untouched, each scrubby bush a respectful distance from its neighbor. No prints but animal's and our own; no sound save a whistle of wind and an occasional cranky raven riding thermals. More billows of stone (Carmel) roll above us on the skyline, and we seem to be afloat halfway between earth and sky. Wind lifts my arms like wings, and its rush puts me in motion though I stand still.

"Hey! Where are the wild horses?" I ask when we stop to catch our breath.

"The name's quixotic would be my guess." E.T. turns over a rock to see what might be living or hiding there. "D'you know where it comes from, Frank?"

"I think someone out of Escalante ran cattle below the Kaiparowits; horses got loose ... "

"Here? I fling my arms to the horizons. How'n hell would they get here? Like Pegasus? Look at those crenelated bastions!"

"Golly, you sure are using big words." Frank wrinkles his nose at me.

"Why not? They're big cliffs! About the only way down them is to fall." I smile at him. "*Hell* is not a big word, Bigfeets."

His weather prediction has proven out. Even the wind is warm, so before going down we rest in the shade of a stunted juniper. I lie back near the trunk and touch cold steel.

"Yipes! What's this?"

Beneath the tree is a rusted, steel-jawed trap. Sprung, thank god, or I could be minus an arm! I pull the wicked-looking thing out and dangle it by its chain.

"Frank's probably right," Tad decides. "Horses, cowboys, cows … and coyotes."

"I'm taking it down with me," I state decisively. "Coyotes are my friends." <END JOURNAL>

~

There are many places, on both left and right banks throughout the Glen, where I've hiked to the cap over the years. Most, but not all, are recorded in my journals and are vivid in my memory because of the treacherous routes to get there. However, in this case, the route was insignificant to the experience. I do recall that I had gone up a dry fork of either Annie's Canyon (mile 107.8) or Lost Eden (mile 118.0), both on the right bank.

Clearly, I was losing it; didn't mention it to anyone, or they'd have thought so too. Don't remember what trip. Do remember I was alone, it was hot as hell, and I was nude as a marble, lying in a cradle of slickrock.

At first I thought I was dreaming, but I do not sleep or even catnap at midday, so whatever reverie I was floating in produced a sound. I sat up, turned my head this way and that, listening. I looked in the sky for a jet. Nothing. No matter which way I turned, I heard a sound I'd never heard before. It hummed … just humm-m-m-med. I put one ear to the stone—no change. Stood up and moved slowly in a circle—still no change. There was *no* wind; like I said, hot—sun like a blowtorch. It couldn't have been breezes sifting through perforations in the strata. Anyhow, the rock was dense and smooth there. There were a few little titty mounds nearby; I went and sat between them, sweating. Still heard it. Did I feel a vibration through my bare feet? To this day, I'm not sure, but the sound kept on—same intensity, same key. The closest I can come to describing it is a low bagpipe drone from far, far away. (I flashed on a time I'd backpacked the Escalante alone. After the third day of not seeing any-one or hearing another voice, other than my own talking to me, I got a ringing—not a hum—in my ears. It would *not* go away. I shook my head, tried to pop my ears by holding my nose and blowing. It kept on ringing. I was afraid to put my hands over my ears for fear I'd still hear it; finally did, and it rang *inside* my head, all day into night. Kee-rist! I wondered, how am I gonna get to sleep?)

Sitting there amid the *humming*, certain that it was all in my head, I at last put my hands over my ears.

The humming *stopped*.

Then I figured I must be getting sunstroke and better get the hell out of there. After climbing down, maybe fifty feet or so, the hum became fainter, and shortly after, there was no more at all.

But I wasn't crazy.

Letter from Dick Sprang, 1995:

It was a tricky one, but once out on top, you're in a dream world [Above Smith Fork between mile 132 and 133]. *Strange kind of slickrock and a bunch of large petrified lizards all walking toward the river. If you're very quiet you can hear the slickrock hum, just like it does—or did—down on top of the big domes at the mouth of Halls* [mile 118.3]. *Funny, never heard the hum east of the river. Always west.*

Right, Dick. Right bank, all three places. I once thought I heard it on the cap above Music Temple, but it wasn't the same sound, and it didn't keep going. There it *could* have been wind in the rock, because the stone is more porous. I wonder: Do they merely *hum* now because they can no longer fly with the wind? Whereas, when they were moving sand giants, their voice was more like breakers booming, or gongs sounding beneath them. I've heard that sound too. Well ... as yet, no hydrologist has ex-plained for me the Enigma of the Crystal Wave of Water, and no geolo-gist the Conundrum of the Hum in Stone; doubt if I'd accept their the-ories anyhow. I just believe Mother Nature speaks in obscure ways to those who care to listen.

Journal Note: Afternoon, Day 11

The mouth of the canyon opposite upper Wildhorse Bar is stuffed with tamarisk and pea vines so dense we almost give up. Inside, a whole other story. But our time is closing in, and Tad manifests this by hurrying up the meandering stream ahead of us to see as much as possible.

A flat sand and gravel floor, wide enough for brilliant sun to light each bend; open enough for redbuds (arrayed beneath a great arched proscenium) to spread their oriental filminess against a deep orange wall streaked with desert varnish. Red monkey flowers, columbine, gilia, a kind of stock orchid, and penstemon grow at the foot of the wall. Tiny lavender moths light on plants, walls, our noses—some unfortunates on water. Trapped! And the whole canyon rings with the canyon wren's songs! Must be home base. We don't seem to bother them—the inquisitive, perky little tail-up things fan us with their wings, never quite sitting on us, never stopping their *bel canto*. Wow! To hear a canyon wren's song smack-dab in my ear! Little pink lizards the exact color of the walls streak upward, stop just out of reach, and do push-ups. Why do they do that? Are they out of breath? Cooling their tummies? Exercising? Preparing to crap? Jacking off? If it's the latter, they're very sexy reptiles. They do it a lot.

Like many other canyons, this half-mile beauty ends at a deep sand-rimmed pool. Above it a twisting purple-pink grotto trickles clear water, all surrounded by forty-foot banks of maindenhair fern—shimmering emeralds, more alive, even more delicate, than those in Little Arch. The pool holds bouquets of watercress, sweet but tangy—we browse on it. I try so hard to get up into the grotto—Frank's help, his shoulders, a branch ... can't get a fingerhold. E.T. won't help; calls, "Come on, pal!"

He's right. We must leave. Back to the boat!

What sets this canyon we named Grotto apart from others? The time of day? Weather? The yellow brightness, canyon wren music, and flowers, all at the same time? Water whispering secrets from above the grotto? The *smell* of the water in the rock (not at all like water in the river or in mud)?

Yes. All of those things.

A mere mile downstream ... Whoa! Stop ... we must ... *we can't!* The hourglass spills too fast for us, no matter how strategically we plan. The itch to see inside is so profound as we pass that I almost jump out of the boat so they will have to come back for me. But I will float past the entrance by then, and they won't fall for it anyway. Damn! [A year passed before we explored that canyon. Afterward we named it (or Tad did) when we found him tightly huddled into himself, soaking up the only spot of sun near its mouth, and chattering ... "Brr-rrr ... this place is like a ... DUNGEON!"]

The entrance was a missing tooth in the wall. Dark, very narrow, *no* growth inside, a flat mud-sand-gravel floor. Almost immediately above our heads, the walls began to rise, overhang, and flute into each other, dimming the light and cutting off the sky. The smell was sweet mud inhalant. Air currents circulated, warm ... cool ... warm ... cold. Walls that *looked* slick with water were dust dry; no seeps, no moss, just sculpted stone, glistening in the refracted light. Our cries of astonishment resounded like clappers in a bell, and a clicked shutter could be heard around two bends. The few places where a tiny slice of sunlight struck the fluting or the floor, I fancied some poor soul shackled to the wall and almost heard the clank of chains as he moved to gaze up at the only source of shredded light.

Ritual bled from the walls. In that sepulcher, color spoke—blue, blood red, aubergine, violet, gold, rusty orange—all were deeply bruised. I had no doubt that shamans, medicine men, witch doctors, had once used this chamber to their great advantage—for sorcery, to gorgonize their subjects. There were dark hollows where, from above, a victim could be leapt upon or terrorized by some thrown object, and the entire vault was a ventriloquist.

This meager mile of fascination ceased at a rend in the rock that was wet and slick as a dolphin, and not even body width. Still, it was hauntingly beautiful in its otherworldly way, and singular. No other canyon emitted the aura of Dungeon. [One springtide we were able to *row* up into the catacombs, but could not swim or walk from there—it was wall-to-wall omnivorous mud! When the river dropped, the maw was choked with silt banks that formed an opaque lagoon, where penetration meant a chilly mattress ride of a couple hundred feet before meeting solid ground. Simply, it was a bitch to get into until the summer storms flushed its interstices.]

~

At Rock Creek (mile 55) we meet the boatman's nemesis—ye olde upstream wind. Fresh and constant, it marcels the muddy river through a straight four-mile corridor to our intended camp at the mouth of West Canyon Creek. I've been rowing since Grotto, but when this blowhard hits us, I ship the oars and start *Tinny*'s little outboard. The hourglass, you know; darn thing never stops, and we have more dirty work to obliterate this afternoon.

DISTING—whatever the hell that is—now *was*. Someone else has erased KILROY WAS HERE that marred the same wall last year. Across the river is FOR RENT, in white lead paint, letters a foot high against a smooth, deep maroon wall. Frank manages to sand it out with more chunks of maroon sandstone. It occurs to us that we're going to have a job keeping up with the dipshits who do this sort of thing. I know why they do it, but I also know there is no cure until the moron arrives at a state of consciousness, which more often than not fails to happen in a whole lifetime.

We're but a mile from tonight's home—waves slapping like snares against *Tinny*'s sides—when we see an inviting bite in the Glen's left wall. The bite is fronted by high, glistening sandbanks and panoplied with dancing tamarisk saplings. Frank finds a drainage cut in the bank and pops in. For the nonce, we're out of the wind, but sand whirls around us as we walk toward the protection of the walls. Though low, the sun stays warm on our backs while it flirts with the open lips of the side canyon.

A cool, short labyrinth. The delicate pink stone at the entrance looks soft and easy to imprint, like real dunes of real sand, but once inside we are caught between pillars of eternity—rippled, silver-grey walls that we can touch with both hands in some places. A dry, boulder-strewn floor that averages five feet wide has a bit of water in a few catchments, and beneath a rise to some inviting narrows lie two serious pools. Above and beyond this enchanting niche rise towering sun-drenched cliffs that reflect a perfect light for pictures, and we shoot-shoot-shoot until the sun falls to rimside. With its collapse, there comes a soft and plaintive call from above the pools, one I know by heart but have not heard before inside the canyons.

Coo-loou Coo-coo-coo. The mourning, or rain, dove.

What a home it has! One of its very own colors. There's an answer from somewhere far away, then a startled clap and the panting of wings. I look up. Then, down through the erotic sinuosity, feathers float, rise, twirl … then drift to the floor. Only then do I notice many more, so blended with the stones that I'd missed them on the way in.

DOVE CANYON.

West Canyon Creek enters from the left at a sharp right turn of the river. Just below its mouth is a high, solid bank with some vegetation up the sides and on the long, flat top. Its been here a while, acting as a buttress for a leaning, two-hundred-foot wall where nature has painted a delicate curtain in soft rose and lavender—or orange and ochre, depending on the brush of the day. We haul our gear up the slope to find, quite unexpectedly, an inscription Dock has asked me to be on the lookout for:

J Wetherill 7-2-21. (The same Trader John whose calling card we've searched for above Forbidding, and who did some of the first anthropological digging in the vicinity of Navajo Mountain around the turn of the century.)

Turns out the entire wall is a gallery of petroglyphs unlike any others we've seen, and probably older. They're very faint and impossible to detect from the river.

E.T., running his fingers along the vague indentations, says, "I'm tempted to chalk this guy over so I can see what he really looks like ... but I don't have any chalk."

"And wouldn't if you did have," I tell him.

"This near to the closing of the d ... uh ... our trip, I might."

"And be like those shitheads we just erased? I doubt it."

"It's the only one I've seen with hairy gonads."

"Gonads? That's a woman's pudenda, silly."

"Oh, really! Then what's that little curl of a thing flopped over the top of it?"

"Ingress for male, egress for child, Professor. You certainly never saw a phallus drawn *that* small—they outsized those things considerable in this culture; any culture, now that I think of it."

Bigfeets, looking over our shoulders, says, "You both can feel free to talk English. I know what most of those words mean."

"Well, Frank," asks Tad, "what do you think all this is up above here? These sharp triangular lines, this bulge, only one arm with fingers; no head it would seem."

"Kinda looks like half man, half woman. Heck, I don't know. You both can figure it out while I go get some firewood."

"Mmm-mm, yes yes; it is a bit androgynous, now that he ... the bulge on this side, maybe symbolic of birth, and the jointed legs spread out and down."

"Real comfy!" I say.

"Those big-shouldered people down the wall, locked in rather bizarre embrace, they don't look too much at ease either ... uuh ... "

"Maybe we've found the Moki *Kama Sutra*—Shiva, the destroyer; Brahma, the creator; Vishnu, the preserver, all rolled into one. Wall's full of weirdoes, looks to me."

"Where'd you get all this information, pal?" Tad-O gives me his high-brows look of surprise.

Loftily, I reply, "It's not information, old buddy, it's knowledge—ancient symbolism. You forget I studied Jung."

"Malinowski says the aborigine made love in a squatting position, like this ... uh ... critter here, bent legs and all."

"Im-phucking-possible! What a crazy hypothesis. Who was he? Some sort of voyeur hiding in the bushes after the ice age?

"He was a famous turn-of-the-century anthropologist." Visualizing it, Tad chuckles, "It would be rather difficult, wouldn't it?"

"Feelthy peectures," I conclude. "C'mon, let's cook."

... The wind has done what it's supposed to do—died.

I bake a cake in the Dutch oven. Two very pungent odors mingle on the up-and-down-draft: wild mud and domestic baking. I can taste them both. Bigfeets has snagged a catfish. It lies atop the grate, cleaned, floured, and heavily chived [poor Frank hadn't told me about his belly rumbles yet].

The velvet air is cool and fragrant with river musk. While we watch, a shadowy tide moves up the great prow of the Grand Bench and washes over its fiery orange top deck. Slowly it will sink beneath violet waves, into twilight, down to darkness—then, after midnight, the hulk will rise again, like a ghost ship, its outline shimmering beneath a waning moon.

But now the evening sky is intensely blue. A penumbra forms along the top of the escarpment. The blue deepens, then a touch of green; it deepens, bleeds upward, and condenses into the vibrant miracle of gem turquoise, a color unique to deserts and seen only where deserts are.

Suddenly, I understand why the Indians so love the stone.

The wall behind us dances with shadows as we walk back and forth between it and the fire doing clean-up chores and unrolling our beds. I play and sing for a long, long time tonight with Tadito's *carcajadas* punctuating the Mexican choruses. Bigfeets lies on his roll, bare feet to the fire, listening like no one else listens to my songs.

Two more nights, two and a half days ... Lee's Ferry. The end.

~

Stars rock up and down on the waves. They light up my life in this quiet inlet where I lie, holding to a rock, letting the river caress and soothe my tired-sad-happy body. Always did have this kinship with moving water—the water multiform—both sacred and sensual. But falling in love with the River God is not the same as falling in love with a man for a sexual journey.

What say, Mr. River? What have you taught me?

I know that I need this place—this sanctuary—like I need my skin to collect myself, to construct my future, to observe and fortify my soul. I need your counsel, your space and beauty, to help me dump the detritus. No matter that you possess me through worship of you.

Look at you out there—eddying, resting, going around, or over, or under whatever's in your way; wearing it down or taking it with you, bending, twisting, floating it—must be what we call compromise. Well, I can do that, if necessary, for a little while, until things go *my* way. Whenever I change my creative route, the journey gets rough. In showbiz it drives agents and managers wacky—got to have a label, be a label, wear a label, or they can't "sell" you. Tough titty! I don't wanna be like everybody else.

You've taught me to be myself, and not someone else's idea of me.

Another thing I've learned: My gods and goddesses are *here*, not under some man-constructed dome ... doom! I believe in the sun, moon, stars—things that keep their course—things I can see and feel. My *life* is up to *me*, therefore I must make time for communion, for exchange with Nature, the Earth, and Yer Honor—Glen Canyon; be you mother, whore, bitch, queen, lover, saint or shaman, you restoreth my soul.

> *Eddy ... with me now ...*
> *Do not breast the current.*
> *The rising tide of stormy consciousness*
> *Will lift you once again ... Downstream.*

~

I'm dreaming. I'm *not* dreaming. Something heavy is sitting on my back! I rock to shake it off, feel it move to my bottom and sit there. I bump up to push it off, then cry out! But there's no sound. The thing presses down until I'm almost out of breath. Struggling, I get to my knees and peer over my shoulder.

Nothing.

I sit up, breathing rapidly. No movement anywhere. Both men sleep soundly. The ghost ship has risen in dark outline before a moon already gone to portside, yet I can see the river moving under deep blue, and hear him ... always and forever, I hear him.

What was that on my back?

[Camp—mile 50.9, West Canyon] <END JOURNAL>

NINETEEN

~

A Night with Thor

Journal Note: October 5, 1955—(We Three Trip,
Day 12—West Canyon Creek, Mile 50.9)

"Don't come that way! NO! DON'T COME THAT WAY!" I scream.
"I'm alright now." My heroes ... ungh!

They stop a hundred feet away and watch this mud-coated thing
crawl from the shade into full sun, roll over, and wheeze, "Holy shit!"

It takes them a few seconds to switch off the panic button, then E.T.
offers a tentative "Oink-oink?" and Frank puts a hand over his mouth,
trying to suppress his laughter.

"Oink yourself, smart-ass."

I've come ahead of them this morning to check the best route into
West Creek. Everyone knows Tad's favorite canyon is notorious for the
quaking bog at its entrance, so I enter cautiously, close to the wall. Just
when I think I've got it made, I plunge in over my knees and start going
down. I have to lean forward, slog and crawl my way to solid ground.

"You guys better try the other side, and bring my jeans and sneakers,
please—there on the bank behind you."

They manage to stay topside until they reach me, but when they see
my appalling condition, they don't know whether to start laughing again
or get serious.

Bigfeets asks, "How far did you sink?"

"Past my hips. Gad, I've never been in so *deep*. It was scary."

Tad offers me a hand. "Are you still with shorts? I can't see under all
that muck."

I stand and feel. Yipes! Muddy bog sucked off me shorts, but left me
drawers. Fantastic! Now *I* start laughing; the whole picture is too ludi-
crous.

Bigfeets shakes his head and says to Tad, "Every time we leave her
alone, see what happens?"

"Yes yes, she's a dirty mess," he nods, scratching his tacky beard. "What will she ever do without us?"

I think about that too, but don't say so out loud.

This time they go ahead while I stop at a small alcove to rinse myself and my clothes—a sunny spot to dry and reflect on what someone told to me about "quickmud" in the Glen's canyons. Said it was a myth, there wasn't any; always bedrock, never more than three feet down. I wonder if the dude is still above ground.

West Canyon—wide, long, winding fifteen or twenty miles up to Rainbow Plateau; full of sunshine, cottonwoods, grassy banks, and a constant flow, which is why Tad likes it so much. Frank, too, I'm sure—no long trenches to swim, no deep potholes to negotiate, and no quaking bogs past the entrance.

About four miles up, the Navajo graze and water their sheep in the creek's bed—they herd them down off the cap via unique trails built on the slickrock. Only the bottom part of this one remains, slanting upward in switchbacks. Every six feet or so, holes picked in the sandstone keep large rocks in place that act as buttresses for small tree trunks laid against them. Across these at right angles, more trees and branches are laid. Rock and gravel fill in the spaces, making a four-foot-wide stock trail. Where it gives out, we make our own way.

Old Man Wind has again become sassy. Vexed. Strong enough to topple an unwary climber into space. When Tad opens his mouth to say "Pushy bastard!" the wind puffs out his cheeks and sends a streak of saliva to his ear. As we climb higher it accelerates to near-gale proportions, snapping our clothing and making us crouch to maintain our balance.

Nevertheless, the cap is a photographer's dream—miles and miles of it. Both guys take off packing tripods, shirts flying, looking like two mammoth dragonflies that can't find a place to light. I head westward into the gale and before long find myself in the studio of a mad ceramist! Massive bowls, sculpted by windy fingers, are flung upside down in heaps, melted against each other and baked in the kiln of the sun. I roam around and between them, but progress is difficult. Tired of being pushed and shoved, I try removing my clothes, only to discover the same erosion process at work on my body. I lie face down to cut the sandblasting, but there's little change. It stings enough to hurt, then tickles, then scratches.

My thoughts dance and swirl with these sensations ...

... If they take my river away from me, this is how I'd like to meet my gods and goddesses, up here in this vast, rolling sea of clean stone—dried, shriveled, pecked cleaner still by ravens, my bones dropped into fluted chambers, chewed and strewn by coyotes across the Rainbow Plateau to wander with the wind and water—back to Mother Earth. Nice.

But for now, get dressed before I bleed!

We converge where we parted and stand quietly, looking at the strange moonscape beauty below and all around us, so tuned to each other's moods and preferences that we no longer need talk. We're down to looks and sign language—a squeeze on the arm, a pat on the back, a smile, a hug, a sigh, a tear. I know now, this is the *only* way to go to ground, to attend the magic here. One, two friends; never more. For almost a week, when Frank comes to where I might be resting or writing, he merely places his shadow across my face or the page, and I know he's there to suggest something or, more often, just to give me his reluctant kind of smile that says we have to get on with it. I'll nod, get up, and we'll go. Tad might poke a leg of his tripod in my tummy hole or at my bum, which means he's back, or now's the time. I may ask him if he got some good ones, or just rise and say nothing.

It isn't as turbulent down in the canyon bottom when we start back for lunch. I run ahead, just because I feel like running without the wind bashing me around. At a sunlit pool beneath an overhang, I'm stopped for the hundredth time by light reflecting on a sandstone backdrop—a rhythmic dance, choreographed by wind playing with water.

Bigfeets and Tad join me to watch the show. It's ... a twirling sequined skirt? Mermaids surfacing? Gold snakes in a chorus line? A Ferris wheel after dark? Not merely ripples taking light from the sun.

"No," says Frank, "it's music on the walls."

"*If Music be the food of life, play on. Take heed therefore how ye hear.*" Shakespeare?

Once out from the mucky mouth of West Canyon, we all need a rinsing. While we're at it, we clean *Tinny's* sides, scoop out the sand accumulated in her innards, and spruce up her decks. She's been a good little ship, light, comfortable, and maneuverable. While they get lunch I try to list all the wildlife we've seen on the river and up on the cap. Forget the millions of birds, other than the very few I know or take note of: quail, water ouzel, kingfisher, canyon wren, phainopepla, cliff swallow, western tanager, cardinal, snowy egret, blue heron, Canadian honker, duck, great horned owl, screech owl, redtail and other hawks, peregrine falcon, uncountable LBBs (little brown birds), and ravens-ravens-ravens! There have been deer, beavers, ringtail cats, pack rats, field mice, coyotes, bob-cats, lizards, chuckawallas, frogs, toads, raccoons, skunks, rabbits, chip-munks, snakes (rattle, water, grass, and gopher) catfish, chubs, minnows, pollywogs, little green turtles, a desert tortoise, those primordial-looking shrimp, bees, wasps, ants, moths, bats, and black widows. There are cen-tipedes and scorpions here, but I've never seen them. This little bit by one who is much more attentive to wall patterns, light changes, erotic sinu-ousities (and *feeling* them) than to things that wiggle, flit, and dig; who is interested in sensing what lives inside things that are inert, seeking their hidden life and energy, looking past their outward appearance. And find-ing what? Secrets. Healing. Roots. Food for the soul.

Frank and E.T. are taking a siesta, but my thoughts are going through a riffle. Staring at the river, I think: Is Tad right? Will I forever need the stimulation of performing? Will I eventually grow tired of the river? But that's not the point. The point is to *have the place;* to know it's here when I need it; to regroup and take a fresh outlook to the *other* reality—the one where I make the bucks to get here so I can forget the place where I make the bucks. <END JOURNAL>

Journal Note: Afternoon, Day 12

At mile 44.5 we're offended, once again, by the scat of another ani-mal—this one two-legged. He's left his shit—POST NO BILLS—on the clean, straight wall at the top of a talus slope seventy-five feet above the water, for all to see. We spend an hour mudding it out. (We later dis-cover there are two of them; the same whose names Jim, I, and the Hol-lywoodites erased that day in Loper's cave, where all the *historic* river runners names are preserved.)

Entering the left bank is Face Canyon (mile 44.3), similar in some ways to West Canyon Creek because it runs a constant stream. We enter it carrying our tennies. Even Frank's tender soles have toughened a bit, while mine conform to the contours as if they've never been shod.

Sun slants along one wall just before its disappearance and stays long enough to catch my eye and hold it. Above the high-water mark, like healed sutures, is the faint pattern of Moki steps. We check the opposite wall for the route out; not here, but a bit farther on there are more, even fainter, that curve over a hump thirty feet above, to a small ledge. Above there the lofty Navajo reaches another two hundred feet into blue heaven. Unlike those in Labyrinth, these can't be flash flood exits; they had to be for a crossing!

The more I see of these long-gone ladders, the more I think the Mokis did most of their traveling up top. Because of the river's muddy or brushy banks, its constant current (and maybe even rapids then), it would take a traveler longer to get from his canyon to her canyon; they, too, had to deal with time, light and dark, rain and sun. Why, in all the rock art we've seen, is there no indication of anything that looks like a boat or a raft?

More wonders to spark our imaginations!

We're just making ready to move on up the canyon when we hear a slight whishing sound, and once again we see the Crystal Wave on top of the regular flow, moving very slowly toward us. We observe that we're on the same side of the river (the drainage again from Navajo Mountain), and whatever solar heat was here is now gone, as it was in Wishbone a few days ago. This flow is slower than the other one—the canyon is wider. By the time we skip over it, round another bend or two, and start back, we catch up and pass the wave on our way to the boat, still wondering. Why?

The day has grown whiskers. Not to worry, we're only four miles from camp.

In the little cove at Kane Creek we beach and sit a spell, rocking in the eddy, just watching the river—more beautiful as the sun drops behind us than I have ever seen it. Both walls ablaze in red-gold, making a red-gold and *green* serpent of the river—a serpent with scales that ripple in the current as he twists upstream for two miles before rounding a bend. Majesty!

Forcing ourselves to action, we carry the first load up to find ... "Ohhh sh ... nuts, Bigfeets. Boy Sprouts have been here before us. This bar is a dirty mess!"

We move up to the rock shelves; they, too, are full of litter. "My lord, how can people be so inconsiderate of others? Who are these pigs? Where are the scout masters? And what kind of dum-dums are they, to let their brats leave a mess like this?"

"Kinda hard to keep one's faith in human nature, isn't it?" says E.T. "Not just Sprouts, either." He holds up a beer bottle.

"Is it because they don't know how to camp on this river?" I ask Frank. "Don't they understand the old Colorado takes *everything* and leaves *nothing?* Or don't they give a damn?"

"Probably some of both, Katie. But you shouldn't worry about it, or try to take it on yourself. Don't let it spoil pleasure."

I smile at him. "Don't worry. I won't go that far."

"Just forget it now, pal," says Tad. "We'll clean up tomorrow before we go. I'm hungry; let's cook."

They're both right. I need to keep bettering *myself*, which should take up all my time, instead of worrying about the clods. Still, it hurts to see the complete thoughtlessness of others, like it probably hurt someone else to see *me* that way, when I was ... when I still am.

Mr. River is performing his famous ventriloquist act, like he does at hundreds of places in the Glen and Grand. Here at Kane Cove, he slurps, gurgles, then rushes out around a rock face, very businesslike. Facing the water, we hear nothing—the sound comes from behind us, up against the wall, one hundred feet away. Norm Nevills used to drive his passengers dippy by telling them, "Yeah, there's another stream entering the Colorado over there. Flows right out of the wall; go look at it."

This is such a beautiful bar ... I mean *was*. Rock terraces as flat as the river; sitting places, almost like real chairs; and wide, long shelves for our bedrooms tonight. Tad builds up the fire for the evening concert.

I make the hot chocolate; Frank brings me the guitar.

I don't know why it's always women who're supposed to look better by candlelight and firelight. A lot of men do, too. Tad's shaggy brows seem to dance in the flickering flame, and the beard adds a touch of piquancy to his laid-back character. Frank, who shaves almost every day, looks like a mischievous schoolboy with big ears and upturned nose. I sing all his favorites, knowing we've only one more night to enjoy this freedom—the last for a year to be ourselves, to have the love and companionship of friends who sift the chaff and keep the whole grain.

Do I see tears in Frank's eyes?

Our thoughts and feelings burn deep and unspoken, but I know it's been the most wonderful twelve days of my life. I'm sure there will be more, yet underneath is the feeling that it can't quite be duplicated. Well, maybe so, but it *could* be even better. I hold hard to that thought as I listen with genuine fondness to Tadito's snoring. Not that he doesn't like my singing; he just fades easily, then tomorrow morning he'll come put his arm around my shoulders and apologize.

I go downstream, to the low end of the bench, to take my bath. The aura of peace, happiness, and love is so strong, now I begin to tear up. How can *anything*, any reality, be this perfect? What have we done to ourselves that we can only find it in rare moments and in rare places? Why can't the *real* world speak to us, like this one does to me tonight? Because we've covered our Earth with too many bipeds, that's why. The Mother should have arranged fertility for us like she does for some fish—*only ten minutes a year*, and that ten hit-or-miss. What can possibly touch masses glued to the tarmac all their lives? To the money table? To the *system?* Nothing.

Above my bed tonight, many falling stars short circuit and go out against a black velvet void—those that don't fall on the water. I'm on a low shelf where I can almost touch the river—his lullaby so lovely, I listen a long time before my eyes get heavy. It's quite late when the moon peals across the water, and it occurs to me that like the men beside the fire tonight, the river under moonlight is more handsome, softened, vulnerable …

Oh god, yes! *Now he's vulnerable!*

That's why there is salt water at Kane Creek tonight.

[Camp—mile 40.5] <END JOURNAL>

Journal Note: October 6, 1955
(We Three Trip, Morning, Day 13)

We clean up the bar, sluice down the lower ledges with buckets of water, burn the paper, put the orange peelings in a can with some sand and bend the lid down inside, pick up the pop and beer bottles, fill them with water, and dump the whole mess into the deepest part of the river.

Dawdling, procrastinating, we move slowly under emotional molasses, afraid of tomorrow, not wanting to get any closer to it than we have to. We aren't planning to do Labby today, but we do need some sprucing up. Circle Pool, in the spur near the entrance, is the answer; probably the last place we can rinse mud from our duds and I can wash my hair. It has turned into a fright wig under two weeks of sun, wind, and my river's silty shampoo.

Clean as whistles, we board *Tinny*, who now sports a pair of drying shorts on the shank of each oar.

Mile 33.2—Cottonwood Creek on our old Plan & Profiles (renamed Gunsight Canyon on the new quads).

The canyon's bottom lip pouts into the river at a concave turn, so it's easy to imagine how much water flushes in when the cfs's are high. Because a sudden cold wind has risen, we don jackets before braving the thirty-foot narrow entrance. We're prepared for more of the same, but (surprise!) just inside it opens to a huge, nearly round, flat, floor with a few trees near the upper end of the circle, then it narrows again and continues on. High on our right is a grand alcove. At the top of the arch, two hundred feet above us, where the canyon walls nearly come together, a ribbon of sky sends pale, blue light down through the contortion.

An eerie whisper of passed centuries pervades, their history written on the walls by flood marks a hundred feet above our heads. We climb up to find that ruffled pages of packed mud (each sheaf a different consistency and color, yet solid as rock) have left a storybook of past flows. Another twenty-five feet of very tricky slickrock climbing, and we reach the floor of the alcove, which is deep, wide, and dry, despite marks of an ancient seep. Much debris has fallen, but beneath it there are signs of a ruin—not a great winter home, but marvelous in summer. Cool, protected, hidden, but far enough above the mudbank? <END JOURNAL>

[Major Powell established the U.S. Geological Survey, and in the 1870s they began recording water flows on the Colorado River. Here are some random, pre-dam highs from the USGS *Water Supply Bulletin:*
July 8, 1884—300,000 cfs
June 19, 1921—200,000 cfs
July 2, 1927—127,000 cfs
June 12–13, 1952—122,000 cfs
June 8, 1957—123,280 cfs

What were the flows ten centuries ago? Do these pages of mud one hundred feet above the canyon floor tell of 300,000 cfs; 600,000 cfs? A much higher riverbed? Backup from a choked sidestream? Or the Colorado when molten lava flowed into Grand Canyon, damming it (at Lava Falls) and the Little Colorado (at Grand Falls) as well?]

Journal Note: Day 13 (Continued)

I seem to have fallen into another of The Glen's famous time warps—a little removed, kind of dizzy ...
... I'm here ten centuries ago, watching the water steadily rise up the wall, inching toward the floor of my home, listening to the angry, roiling river. I feel the wind poke me in the back, hear the far-off rumble of thunder, and see the soft light quickly turn ominous ...
"Hey! C'mon down from there—the weather's done a flip!"
Tad, a mere speck silhouetted below at the canyon's entrance, tripod slung over one shoulder, is gesturing wildly. "Looks like a storm coming; let's find camp. *Andale!*" <END JOURNAL>

～

More than once in my ten glorious years there, I've watched the soft rain's gentle penetration of sandstone—a thing almost sensual judging by the sighs of bliss, the murmurs and sucking sounds it offers in response. Watched too, the other mood—the passionate power of Thor's wild sex with the Glen. One night in particular illuminates my memory screen—a fervent, orgiastic night of lightning, thunder, lashing winds, and torrents of rain.

With a prelude of faraway timpani, lightning began behind dense clouds, like the flickering of an ailing florescent tube. Within minutes, beneath dark and roiling cumulus, the flicker turned to pulsing veins seeking the earth—and finally, to candent arteries that cut through and night and danced over the canyon, all accompanied by deafening cracks of thunder.

But twenty-five feet above the river, the cave was dry and firelight played upon the walls—a picture window to the pageantry outside. A sudden blast of wind brought with it a spray that sent sparks from the fire in a swirling dance toward the ceiling, then back into the storm, where they spit and went out. In a rare moment of blackness, there came a booming crash. The earth shook and an ominous roar was added to the cacophony. Everyone tensed and I moved to the brink cautiously to see what the next flashes would reveal.

On our right an airborne river of frothing water dove from the top of a three-hundred-foot sheerwall and plunged unobstructed to the sand, hitting more than fifty feet from the cliff's base. Within minutes the beach was washed away, exposing boulders the size of cars. One split the descending geyser and sent water flying in two directions like the wings of a gigantic moth. Spray blew back up the fall to again be gathered in the plunge—split, sprayed, and returned upward in one continuous cycle.

Of course they all thought I was crazy, but I had to get into it—join the orgy, feel the passion, not just see it. Impossible to get beneath the fall—now and then rocks came shooting over the rim—but I could dash through and under a spraying wing until I choked on the spume and had to dash out again. I worked my way back against the slightly undercut wall, where the beach was still intact and where missiles wouldn't find me. The ground vibrated; the wall wheezed and shook. From beneath, through a series of flashes—my adrenaline whipped to a froth—I watched the torrent shoot, tumble, and tear the ground apart in a fit of madness!

Great Zeus, what wild, raw power! Nature on a rampage—the miracle of angry, violent water!

No, not really a miracle. The mere scratching of an itch. A turning of the earth. Only the fact that I could witness it made it so—for me.

Journal Note: October 6, 1955
(We Three Trip—The Last Night)

Frank lies on his back atop his bedroll, staring at the eroded ceiling. I sit Yoga fashion, cheek against the curve of my guitar, ear over the sound-hole, strumming softly. E.T. is at the back wall talking to the furry ones, coaxing them to eat from his hand.

"I don't think they like cheese," he says.

"Heck they don't," corrects Frank. "They ate half a pound of it when we were here last, uninvited!"

"That was at Hidden Passage Bar, where everyone camps. These little fellows don't seem to know what it is."

"Leave it there a few minutes. I'll bet they find out."

"Come here, little mouse. Eat this—it's good for you."

I stop strumming. "How d'you know it's good for them? With all the preservatives in it, it'll probably embalm them."

"Can't let them starve. They're plenty hungry, because they just ate all our dinner scraps."

"Then they're *full*, dum-dum."

"Ouch! That's my finger!"

I turn around. "Hey, did you get them to come *that* close?"

"Yes yes, but they're very nervous. Keep playing; that seems to soothe them."

"I hope they know when it's bedtime. I don't dig them making a nest in my hair."

"Play, woman! Try again, mousie; the nice lady will sing for you."

Through This World

I have roamed this world for pleasure
    By starry night, by dawn and by day
Just to find my fondest treasure
    A rolling river, carving its way.

No more distant shores will find me
I'm so weary of the foam.
Broken dreams are all behind me,
Colly Raddy is callin' me home.

Through this world I cannot wander
    Over ocean's deep and wide
I'll just go and hire a Boatman
    To row me down the silvery tide.

Bigfeets brings cups of hot chocolate with marshmallows floating on top. We sit beside the fire, contented. Crystal beads of water drop into rain puddles, making the sound of a xylophone, sweetly up and down the scale.

"'Member the legend of the curse of the Medicine Man on Posey and his people?" I ask them.

"Sure," says Frank, who as a boy remembers *seeing* Posey. "It's not a very old legend."

"I thought about it tonight. It could happen, you know."

"I suppose it could," he muses. "When the winds come up the canyon, even when they're only playing, it sounds like a siren going off."

Tad takes a slurp of hot chocolate. "Chingado! Hot! What's supposed to've made the Medicine Man lay a curse on Posey's people? I've heard it so many ways, I forget. His Piute name was So-ah-ju-ee, wasn't it?"

Me: "I heard that he cursed them with a storm so terrifying, it would blow out the sun and his people'd die from lack of warmth and light. The river would rise, drown everyone—right, Bigfeets?"

"But *why* the curse?" repeats Tad, taking a more cautious sip of his chocolate.

Frank says, "There was a sick baby in the tribe, and they called the Medicine Man in to cure it. When it died they threatened to kill him, and he said if they did, the curse would avenge his death."

"And Posey, So-ah-ju-ee, killed the Medicine Man, the shaman?" I ask.

"He and some others. Arth Chaffin told me one time he had a Piute working for him at the ferry, and once, when a big blow came up, the Indian was scared to death—kept repeating, "Mebbe so him right ... mebbe so him right!"

Tadito smiles. "Mebbe so him right, huh?"

"It's too late for Posey," I say. "He died of lead poisoning after his last raid on Blanding. But, oh boy, I'd like to see a storm that would blow out every dam on this river, and a few more besides."

Frank brings warm rocks to the foot of each bedroll. Bats flick in and out of the overhang and down toward the river, to dip the surface for insects or a drink. An occasional breeze brings spray from the trickling water, and mice squeak in the rocks at the back wall. Somewhere, far across the water, a great horned owl begins his nightly inquisitions.

We fall asleep with watersong in our ears.

[Camp—mile 26.2] <END JOURNAL>

TWENTY

Down the Tongue

Journal Note: October 7, 1955—"We Three,"
Day 14 (Takeout)

The xylophone notes of dripping water have been replaced by the sound of Mr. River seriously on his way somewhere. Ah, yes, last evening's little drenching has upped the cfs, giving us just the excuse we wanted for not putting the outboard on *Tinny*'s rear end. Now we need not listen to its alien sound on our last day in paradise.

Twenty-six miles ... to that other world.

Slowly, slowly—like a boat in the calm water above a rapid, we prepare ourselves for the tongue and rapids of the civilized world (barbaric would be more accurate) after two weeks of the quicksilvery stuff. Freedom. We have been very lucky; haven't seen one soul or one boat since we left Hite, only a few footprints in the mud, and the Wonder Lady. Nature.

Antelope Canyon slides by. The sun has made our day nice and toasty—the air, after the rain, too pure and clear to find words for. Wright Bar, with the longest panel of petroglyphs in the Glen, stops us for some photos, then Wahweap and Sentinel Rock. Now, mile 15—the place of real dread, should it come to pass. I refuse to look, to tarnish this day. The goddamn damsite! I think God *would* damn it; there are better ways. *Please*, let some guiding hand lead them elsewhere!

I look at all of us now, tan as little children of the sun. I'd say men and women, but we don't seem as cunning or calculating as adults. Bigfeets at the tiller—eyes squinting, shirt off, feet bare, his pants rolled up. Tad's lanky frame draped across the bedrolls, center, reading a journal of some of the other trips. Myself, stretched full length across the bow on my air mattress, collecting enough sun on my back to last through Chicago's or New York's cold, icy winter—this to remember when the whalebone digs at my hips and the makeup begins to itch under the spotlight.

I watch the formations subtly change as we glide by Ferry Swale. At the last bend before Lee's Ferry, Tad and I dress for the world-at-large. To me it's like pulling the clothes of sweat and labor over a gossamer gown. They don't feel cumbersome, exactly; they just feel unnecessary.

Our We Three trip has left nothing to be desired—except maybe a lifetime of the same. <END JOURNAL>

~

[I skip here to the last day of the '56 and '57 We Three trips. There were no more. After them, I introduced only six other souls to the magic of Glen Canyon before its death in January of 1963.]

Journal Note: The Following Year—October 14, 1956 (We Three's Second Trip, Nearing Mile 15)

Down below is the horrendous scar on the wall—the machinery and crap that it takes to stop the flow of centuries. At Sentinel Rock the bloody business of the dam's beginning is evident. They've got white lead paint all over the walls, have had for several miles upstream (for coffer dams, I suppose) and below the site itself. This being Saturday, the men are all up at Art Green's lapping up the booze. That'll make Art happy. He doesn't give a shit about this river, only the money he can make from it. He's happy as hell to have a marina (Wahweap) and a big puddle to play in instead! A big gaudy sign—an infringement on our rights, since this part of the Colorado is navigable—blares:

WARNING: No travel beyond this point to Lee's Ferry. Blasting on Canyon walls is dangerous to boat travel.

(To myself, quietly, says I: "Fuck you, Junior—try and stop us.") The Wreck-the-nation Bureau has provided no exit road; Colorado river guides have the constitutional right to proceed. Sadly, some are ignorant of the fact and believe the Wrecker's press releases, such as "Today the Department of Interior curtailed boat travel on the Colorado River between ... ," etc. (Thanks a lot, Mr. Seaton!) If we had the time, I'd cover the whole thing over with mud, like the other graffiti—futile, but I'd do it anyway.

Frank goes up Wahweap a way to see if they've brought a road down to the river. There's one there, but pretty sorry as roads go, and it's for the dam builders (they want *us* to exit twenty-five miles upstream at Kane Creek). A mile farther on, a cable crosses the top of the canyon. Bold white numbers are splattered over the desert varnish, a flyspeck trail of them down both walls where the abutments will eventually go. Dotting the shore are strange boats, flags, survey equipment, tools, and hieroglyphics peculiar to those who drill diversion tunnels into *sandstone* (heh-heh!) to fool the river into escape tunnels while they surreptitiously build a plug in his path. Little men crawl down the walls from the top via rope chairs, all silent and busy, marking it for charges. Tomorrow! President Eisenhower presses a button in Washington, and the first explosion rips away a millennium of the river's patient, enduring caress.

We don't talk much the last few miles, but we *know* a lot, and we're happy inside. We've had a rare experience, and dam or no goddamn dam, they can't take that away from us. We have been what I've discovered very few human beings can be. We've been *free*—utterly, completely *free*—for two weeks, totally independent of anyone but ourselves. Nobody has said a cross word or had a moment's misunderstanding. We've laughed and lived to the fullest here in Glen Canyon, on the luscious banks of the mighty Colorado, and most inviolable of all, we *can* take it with us—because we do, every year. (With this trip I've completed 1,609 miles on the San Juan and Colorado Rivers, and by god, I ain't done yet!)

We dock at Lee's—nobody here to meet us but the truck and trailer, just the way we want it. For lunch we drive to Art's, which is now a bunch of ugly trailers stuck on the land he managed to wrangle above the rim, south of Wahweap Canyon. Art's not here, and the place is jumpin' with Wreck-the-nation Bureau boobies.

"Kain't understand why y'all is so upset 'bout this dam; why lookit what you'll have—a big … "

"Never mind explaining what we'll *have*, Buster," I cut him off. "It's what we *had* that your numb skull will never understand."

I remember a song Josh White taught me and sing my way out the door: "You got a head like a rock, and a heart like a marble stone!" <END JOURNAL>

Journal Note: September 12, 1957—Last We Three Trip (Day before Takeout, Navajo Bar Camp, Mile 49.5)

Our last full day on the river. We look at everything more intently, see more, smell more, and feel more. The day is hazy and clouds drift high, giving us that luminous reflected light, painting the sandstone in deep purple and blue hues, softening everything. We get up early, because here you can't do much else; the sun rises you. Snapping shutters accompany the frying bacon.

We float along slowly, not wanting to get there, really—looking for a place to wash my hair, eat lunch, and take some movies of us in line along the bank, washing dishes in the bathwater, brushing our teeth in the dishwater—the sort of thing dudes do along the river without even knowing it. Frank is throwing lunch out of the boat, and I'm catching the stuff on shore, when suddenly through the air comes the cake and plate. They separate halfway, and I get the cake in one hand, the plate in the other. It looks much different now than it did last night in the moonlight—more like a cow pie, all sunk in the middle and covered with a thin coat of sticky sugar-water. But what the hell, let 'em eat cake. Yeah, I guess that's what we're doing.

Jack Brennen (of Harris & Brennen river trips) comes by with a load of bigwigs. They have free reign to go through the dam site to Lee's. Sure, we can too, and if it were up to me, we would. There isn't anyone working down there after dark; we can easily sneak through. But Frank has to comply with their edicts if he wants to keep his reputation as a competent guide and ... uh ... have anything to do with the river's death-after-life. (My thoughts flick back to a week ago on Schock Bar— to a flaming red sunset and a sad conversation.)

Shaking the pepper can vigorously over our frying chicken, I'm wondering how Frank will manage. "Bigfeets, when will you balk? Just how far will you let these assholes push you?"

"I dunno. Probably have to go a little way with them, anyhow. I haven't told anybody yet, but it looks like I'm going to get the concession for the marina at Hall's Crossing."

"*Marina!*" I snap up from my hunker, staring at him, eyes wide, mouth open, then seeing the fact written on his face and detecting the first sign of compromise, I squeeze my eyes shut, wheeze, "Oh god!" and turn away in disgust.

His tone is defensive. "There'll be at least three, Little Wrists; at Wahweap, at Hite, and in the middle at Halls. Maybe even one at Rainbow Bridge."

I hand him the fork. "Here, turn the chicken. I think I'm going to be sick."

He swallows over a lump in his throat.

I can't look at him. I turn my back and stare at the river, talking more to the water than to him. "I feel betrayed. Homo *sapi*ens! Greedy, pathetic fools with a genetic mania to destroy all the sanctuaries that feed their souls. Well hell, I don't give a damn if we're blotted out. I don't want to be a part of the human race when I see the pimps in government and the whores who do their bidding. I'd rather be a coyote." I turn back to him, take the fork, and play with the chicken. "Next thing you know, they'll be damming the Grand Canyon."

"Yep, they probably will," he says matter-of-factly.

"Damn it! You talk like you'd *let* them." Mid-sentence my emotion trips over surprise to fall in anger. Anger at Bigfeets? Incredible!

I know my tone surprises him, too, but as always, he manages a gentle response. "It takes more than you, me and Tad, and a few River Rats to stop the Wreck-the-nation Bureau and ... "

"Right, but you *could* do something about that jerky Senator Moss of yours who wants to make aquatic parks out of National Monuments. He's probably never *seen* this river—too chickenshit to run it."

"Uh, speaking of chicken, is this one done?"

His slow, cool humor dissolves my anger. I pull the skillet from the fire, offering a feeble smile. "Poor, dear Frank. Do you know how ill-equipped you are to run a *marina* on a *reservoir* in *this* canyon?"

"It won't be easy. But the corporation—five of us, one of them Willard (his son), needs a man who knows the river. That's me. I owe my loyalty to the county commissioners, Little Wrists."

~

In the middle of the night. I hear the river say my name.

Katie! Katie, wake up ... look! But it's Tad and Frank, and when I bat my eyes open, the canyon is on fire!

Great waving sheets of light—orange, green, yellow, and blue—ripple across the sky, all rising from a red glow, north, beyond the Grand Bench. Not often have these walls been touched by such color all at once, their shapes transformed into what seem like moving beings, crouched, then standing, dancing, stumbling over each other. The light dims for a few seconds, and they fall back to their natural posture under a pale blue moon. The fan breaks open again, reaches zenith and passes it, running into the southern sky, so brilliant I can see it reflected on Frank's and E.T.'s faces—kaleidoscopes of color. Holymoses! What a spectacle!

I've never seen the northern lights before. I count it one more gift from my river to see them here, where no city's glare dilutes their brilliance and there's no haze to tarnish their glory. <END JOURNAL>

Journal Note: September 13, 1957—
Takeout, Kane Creek, Mile 40.5

Breakfast at dawn—fleeceback clouds delicately painted with sunrise colors, changing every second like the aurora borealis last night. An hour after breakfast we're at Kane Creek, (where we have to disembark now. At least I don't have to witness the shit down by the dam site, but Whitey is here with his truck, waiting for Georgie White and the Boy Sprouts. Keerist, which is worse? I thought they only went in summertime. There'd be no restraining me if she played tag with us in *this* canyon, especially with forty of the little farters in nine of her garbage scows!

Tad and I wait for our ride to come from Wahweap, but Bigfeets motors back up to Hite in the boat. With great sadness I watch him leave. This will be his last (commercial) year on the river. He's selling Mexican Hat Expeditions to Gay Staveley (Joan Nevills's husband). My eyes spill over. What a great record! Never a serious accident; thousands of river miles beneath his oars, and hundreds of people with undying memories of a place never to be equaled on earth.

But it's not over for us yet. Next year we'll make our We Three trip in Frank's new boat. It's one of the absolutes of our lives now. And when the rez starts to rise behind the coffers, I'll be able to stand it until we pass a boatload of gawkers dressed for a Sunday picnic and see my first toilet paper bush! [I didn't know at this writing that Frank would be working for the Museum of Northern Arizona supplying, guiding, and helping anthropologists document the thousands of prehistoric sites in Glen Canyon before inundation—and therefore, could not go with us.] All we've seen and done will be imprinted on our slides and in our minds, but mostly it will stay in our hearts. We are the lucky ones—we didn't just see it with our eyes. I feel its presence all the while I'm gone, an empathy with rock and river that's forever mine.

Big John Harper comes for us in the ammo truck as Frank waves goodbye and disappears around the bend upriver.

No matter how much water drowns my river's home, I'll know he's here, quietly ...

patiently ...

working his way to freedom ...

once again! <END JOURNAL>

PART FOUR

~

Fighting the
Upstream Wind

~

TWENTY-ONE

Big Dam Foolishness

During the half decade between 1957 and 1962 I rode some pretty high water. My itinerary looked like a ten-sided Rorschach test, with heavy lines down the middle where I gravitated to the river in summer and fall.

I made the New York scene—sang at the famed Blue Angel. In Chicago I took guitar lessons from my dear friend Josh White. To do it I moved from the Lincoln Park West to a rooming house. That was more than cool with me, because until then I was not aware they didn't allow "black folks" in their middle-class hotel (the fake; reality out here stinks!). Had a few dates with Marcel Marceau, spent a couple months singing in Miami at the Roney Plaza Hotel, another in New York at Julius Monk's Downstairs at the Upstairs; was on the *Jack Parr, Dave Garoway, Tonight* shows; did some Catholic Service benefits with Harry Belafonte and a couple of one-night stands (take that any way you like and you'll be right); more *Midnight Special* spots with Studs Terkel on WFMT, along with bunches of TV spots. I recorded four albums, gave interviews, did personal appearances and talk shows, put behind me thousands of highway and airway miles, driving or flying coast to coast for NBC radio and New York club dates; worked with directors, musicians, singers, actors, entrepreneurs, famous folks and not-so-famous folks; gave lectures, went through a couple of heavy love affairs, another marriage ('58–'61), and wrote a book, *Ten Thousand Goddam Cattle*. I witnessed the final depredation of my son, had dealings with lawyers, authors, editors, the press, politicians, senators, representatives, the Wreckers, even the U.S. Geological Survey. In 1961 I moved to Aspen, Colorado, kept doing gigs, gigs, gigs everywhere, and smiled all the while, all the while, all the while.

Well ... not *all* the while.

It was during this period that the river really made me take a look at what was downstream in the life of an entertainer, one who had set out to be top pussycat in her line—in other words, famous. An artist acquires, and has to keep, a kind of tunnel vision to get to the bright light at the end, but the river allowed me the time to look back down the tunnel—at myself.

I did not feel comfortable with what I saw.

My show, act, performance—whatever you call it—became progressively more complicated, required more set-up time, more wardrobe, more people to please (especially those who had no idea what folksongs were all about). People who, because they watched television (or left it on all day while they did something else), now considered themselves connoisseurs of the performing arts, unaware that the tube gave them the very tail end of mediocrity. Quite suddenly, it seemed, the types who began to frequent my workplaces were like those who wrote KILROY WAS HERE and POST NO BILLS on Glen Canyon's walls—and I noticed that some of my peers were dropping serious and artistic parts of their show for the more commercial in order to keep up with popular demand.

Was I also? Yes, I was! That was part of the tunnel.

Looking back, I can't in all honesty say that turning around was a conscious act, and certainly it wasn't all-of-a-quick-like, but somehow I knew I could never be and do what "popular demand" expected of me. My talent worked best in a quiet, intimate setting or on a concert stage, with just my acoustic, nylon-string guitar, my voice and me. Loud was not my thing and never would be. My songs were like stories—words more important than the music in most cases—songs that needed *listeners* at the other end. So, when it got to where I had to spend fifteen minutes quieting an audience with Tallulah Bankhead putdowns before I even got into my songs, I knew it was time to eddy out.

Through it all I met a world of wonderful people, six of whom I brought to the Glen—but only six. I had finally learned to keep pen from paper and my mouth shut about the place.

Too late.

My excuses were hollow nothings. Maybe I could lay the first writings at Frank's feet because I wanted to help fill the Mexican Hat passenger lists. The film/lecture and continued press releases could help more souls understand and protest the Bureau's lousy dam. But when we sent our canyon names to the Geological Survey for use on the new quad maps, that had to be some sort of ego trip I hadn't really traced to its finale. Of the six trippers, my friend Natalie Giganoux saw the overview and stuck it up my nose:

"You'll be responsible now for the influx of people—more and more people—because once a thing is *named*, it's a place to go on the map, and Katie, *you* have named a bunch of these canyons."

~

By 1960 the political drift was dense and heavy.

There was a rising river of controversy over the impending asphyxiation of Glen Canyon—plus the malignancy that the dam would surely induce in Grand Canyon—to say nothing of political-bureaucratic-engineering insanity that produced a flood of bizarre proposals to keep the reservoir from encroaching on Rainbow Bridge National Monument. They would construct a barrier dam and coffer dam (one to keep the rez *out* of Bridge Canyon, another to keep Navajo Mountain's drainage from going *into* it), with high head gates, pumping stations, a series of diversion tunnels, and multiple access roads. This worked uniquely to confuse conservationists and set them squabbling among themselves. They wanted *none* of the above, but felt pressured into accepting ... what? Meanwhile, I was performing all over the country, singing, writing, and pleading for the *practical* solution: Lower the dam. *Lower the dam*—save the Bridge. Stay out of our National Monument! LOWER THE DAM!

"The Plea" went out to Fred Seaton, Secretary of the Interior. The reply came set in dam cement (italics mine):

> When construction of Glen Canyon Dam is completed, a vast lake extending more than 180 miles up the Colorado River and the adjacent tributaries will open a much greater area of the Colorado River country for the pleasures of boatmen like *yourself* [!] to explore. The creation of this lake *will not, as you may fear, destroy the scenic beauty of this majestic wilderness.*

Holy shit!

Copies of my letter to Seaton went to David Brower, executive director of the Sierra Club; Charles Eggert, director of the Sierra Club's motion picture department; The Explorer's Club; Bruce Kilgore, editor of *National Parks Magazine;* John B. Oaks, *New York Times;* and many, many more. But it was like trying to put out a wildfire with a teacup! The Wreck-the-nation Bureau was going to *build this dam*—nothing, and no one, not even David Brower, would stop them.

1960—Utah's Senator Moss got his bill (S-333) passed, which simply *removed* the wording in the law that protected our National Monuments from encroaching reservoirs. Moss (from the *Congressional Record*):

I submit, Mr. President, that allowing the waters of the Glen Canyon Reservoir to back up under Rainbow Bridge in southern Utah will not "impair" this national monument, but will substantially enhance it. ... These [protective] provisions were written into the bill during what amounted to hysteria on the part of *extremist outdoor group*s who saw in every manmade pool in a national monument the impending destruction of the entire National Park system.

COLORADO RIVER STORAGE PROJECT ACT AMEND-MENT. S-333 (Moss) The 1956 act authorizing the Secretary of the Interior to construct, operate and maintain the Colorado River storage project and participating projects would be amended by striking out the provision that "as part of the Glen Canyon Unit the Secretary of the Interior shall take adequate protective measures to preclude impairment of the Rainbow Bridge National Monument" and the provision "It is the intention of Congress that no dam or reservoir constructed under the authorization of the Act shall be within any nation park or monument."

Immediately upon getting rid of our tiresome li'l ol' protective law, Wreck-the-nation drafted proposals for two more dams—this time in Grand Canyon—exactly as we said they would!

~

And people wrote to me. Clyde Eddy, American White Water Affiliation (March 1960):

Congratulations on being asked by Alfred Knopf to write a book on the Colorado River. I note that you will needle the Bureau of Rec ... I remember that at the time Hoover dam was built, there were people that wanted it built in Glen Canyon. The bureau said no, because the rock could not hold a dam there. Then to [sic] the evaporation reasoning they used in trying to build Echo Park dam will always be with them. ... I rather like the title that Interior Sec. McKay gave us "long hair punks." Have you read the book Big Dam Foolishness *it is about the Army Eng. system, but actually it applies to the bureau as well.*

Edwin Corle, author of *Listen, Bright Angel* (1960):

We are of one mind, I can see that. I, too, am concerned over ruining the area from Green River, Wyoming to Lake Mead. Too bad the span from Wyoming to the Gulf could not have been made a National Park strip. Dams may tame the Old Devil for a while, but not forever. He has a weapon called "silt." I agree with you, "one day he'll just rip out everything." It will be quite a sight!

Dock Marston (April 1960):

I think your proposal to lower Glen Canyon Dam is the only one that will do the job. Any dam or series of dams in Forbidding or Bridge Canyons will invade the natural scene to the point of destruction. Of course they will argue against the lowering of the dam on the basis of the engineering studies which determine the economic height of the dam. This is scientific hokum but it sounds good and impresses the legislator. ... They say there is no need to protect the Bridge. It will be wonderful to ride up to the Bridge in a motorboat. I suppose I should have gone into the business rather than selling my boats.

Bruce Kilgore, editor of *National Parks Magazine* (May 1960):

While we would prefer damsite C ... we feel the plan involving B would be preferable to doing nothing. For while we too are nostalgic about the loss of solitude in Glen and Forbidding Canyons, doing nothing and letting reservoir water rise and fall beneath the bridge will not save it from harm ... Even now it appears that the confusion among conservationists over what to do at Rainbow Bridge will permit the House and Senate Appropriations Committees to do nothing. ... We too wish we could lower the height of Glen Canyon dam and solve all our problems. But this is wishful thinking, unless you have more powerful friends than we do.

Charles Eggert (excerpt, June 1960):

Wally Stegner once said to me (after working for awhile with Marston on the latter's Colorado River History or whatever it is that Marston is trying to write) that he has observed a very peculiar phenomenon among the riders of the Colorado's rapids and that is, everyone who has seems to take on a vested-interest right in the river; a jealous attitude and an almost militant resentment of anyone else who has invaded "his" territory. I must confess that he is right and even I find myself pooh-poohing other jaunts down the river and find great exaggerations in their accounts. I honestly resent anyone else traveling the river! I note that you do too. ...

I've been down that canyon path. Lord knows what I've done in my life to gain the favor of Ta-vwoats. Maybe it was because of a little film I made, "Wilderness River Trail," which did much to arouse public support against the Echo Park project—and prevented Wrecklamation from venturing into the God's trail ... at least, in Dinosaur. Seeing the canyon path, I'm convinced the legend is true. Maybe we'll never see the wrath taking its full effect ... But one day, even if the Glen dam holds, Ta-vwoats will have the last word ... reservoirs all silted up ... the God will have his desert again, and his river will always keep his canyon path clear for the souls to enter the mythical heaven.

Dick Sprang, from notes on my river novel (October 1962):

Just don't ever give me any Sierra Club malarkey. I can't prove, but I believe they traded Glen for Echo Park—cut a deal and shoved it under the table, and then later went through the motions of pounding on that table opposing Glen Dam. A few folks agree with me, one quite bitterly—Leisa Bronson ... Democratic National Committeewoman for Arizona, and long-time member of the Sierra Club ... She and I worked with Senator Kefauver when he was a member of the Interior & Insular Affairs Committee—worked against the Glen Dam years before the Sierra Club made their protest. ... Kefauver was an old friend of Mrs. Bronson and greatly respected her viewpoints and opinions and wanted her to supply much more background on the Upper Colorado Project so that he could be informed. Having been a researcher in the Congressional Library, she got to work. Kefauver tended to oppose the dam and the Central Utah Project that the dam would bring to fruition ... because he didn't believe irrigation of new areas was worth the cost. He believed that development of marginal farmlands in the Midwest and East would be far more effective to the national good. But as a politician he knew regional pressure had to be dealt with, and he suggested our best bet would be to enlist the support of all the conservation groups of stature, and through them bring pressure against the Western politicians. ... Mrs. Bronson and I started with the Colorado Compact, went on through tons of documents including the definitive "blue back" tome ... which I possessed. We traced the whole reclamation concept of the River ... [came] up with a vast array of facts, and I boiled them down into a quite remarkable letter for Kefauver ... Reality demanded we must recognize and deal with the Upper Basin's right to its water. They would eventually get it, and thinking otherwise was merely spearing windmills. But we proposed that they could get it without the loss of Glen Canyon, could get it by means of building a series of alternate dams in less scenic canyons, dams already surveyed—one large dam in lower Cataract, some smaller ones further up that would destroy, along with the Cataract Dam, far less valuable scenic values than any dam in Glen would ... practical alternatives ... trying only to save Glen Canyon, not trying to deprive the Upper Basin of its water under the Compact.

Kefauver was impressed, but still asked that we get the conservation groups working on their theatrical rhetoric so that drama could be employed in hearings and all that necessary glunk that political dealings demand.

So Mrs. Bronson, wrote to Brower whom she'd known for years. She laid the whole deal on the line. About a month later we get a reply from Brower to the effect that yes, the S. Club had been thinking about the Glen Canyon issue, but being so heavily engaged in other matters could not now find time to evaluate it, but he would bring it to the attention of their research committee soon.

Well, Mrs. Bronson, knew a put-off when she encountered one, and she wrote back blasting Brower and enclosing our most extensive evaluation. After a while, he replied that our evaluation was faulty because we advocated dams, even though alternative ones, and Club policy would allow support of no dams.

Mrs. Bronson, a practical politician, threw up her hands. She knew that pressure, to be effective, had to be brought right then in the Senate, and not later when and if Brower got around to it.

We reported to Kefauver. We went on researching and enlisting the interest of others. Arizona was hopeless—it thought Glen Dam would benefit Arizona; of course, we knew better and finally wryly observed the uproar when Arizona, too late realized the facts, and actually issued an injunction against Glen Dam's construction. ...

... I tend to mistrust any big do-good outfit—BUR, HEW, Forest Service, Park Service, Sierra Club, State governments, mayors' committees, Jaycees, the lot. If any outfit announces it's out to do good, it's like what my Gramp told me when I was ten years old: The one thing I could learn in church—don't trust any SOB who prays out loud.

~

The Wreck-the-nation Bureau closed their diversion tunnels on January 21, 1963, turning the Eden of Glen Canyon and its River into a cattle trough.

~

The Wreck-the-nation Bureau Song

Three jeers for the Wreck-the-Nation Bureau
Freeloaders with souls so pure-o
Wiped out the good Lord's work in six short years.
They never saw the old Glen Canyon
Just dammed it up while they were standin'
At their drawing boards with cotton in their ears.

Chorus: Oh, they've gone and dammed the Frying Pan
You're next, old Roaring Fork
And when they built Glen Canyon dam
The San Juan got a cork.
No river's safe until these apes
Find something else to do,
So have your fun in Cataract
Cause after that, you're through!

Three beers for the Wreck-the-nation Bureau
For them I know there is no cure-o
All waters of the world they would impound
I'll tell ya now of their latest whimsy;
To fill Grand Canyon to the brimsy
While Rainbow Bridge comes crashing to the ground!

Chorus: Oh, they've gone and dammed the Frying Pan
The Muddy and the Blue
If we'd left it to half-Aspinall
He's got the Crystal River too!
These little hard-hats with their toys
Of dynamite and drills
Won't rest until each mighty gorge
Is choked with cement fills.

No fears have the Wreck-the-Nation Bureau
In their ignorance secure-o
What's a few more billion? ... ain't that nice!
"Bridge Canyon for the Havasupai,"
Dams and trams and tacky-poop,
I Wonder at my Canyon's slow demise!

Chorus: They've gone and dammed the Frying Pan
    The Yampa, Green and Bass
    In Steiger's book a ripplin' brook
    Was a place to drown your ass.
    He'd rather shoot a burro
    Than a rapid, anyway—
    And leave a dam down in the Grand
    To mark his cocky way!

No ears have the Wreck-the-Nation Bureau,
Blind as well, you can be sure-o
Dominy, Old Floyd, was their head *fink*.
They'd drown the wildlife of Alaska,
Build Rampart Dam, not even ask ya,
If you want the world's most useless skating rink!

Chorus: They're gone and dammed the Frying Pan
    The Gunnison and more
    For them all river's of the world
    Must be a reservoir!
    So busy with inundation
    They can't unsalt the sea,
    Cause that would mean an end
    To their pork barrel revelry!

Coda: A pox on the Wreck-the-nation Bureau
   Down with the Wreck-the-nation Bureau
   Up the Wreck-the-nation Bureau
   And their little cousins,
   Hard-hats by the dozens,
   The stupid Army Corps of Engineers!

TWENTY-TWO

At the Bedside of the River God

May 5, 1963

Slowly, like lava flowing, immured between the high canyon walls, the dead water creeps up six to eight inches a day.

But the river, born a million years ago, works assiduously, carrying the silt eroded from Earth's pockets down his contoured bed to the Sea of Cortez. With these fine cutting tools he flushes winter's deposits. Changing color, he percolates to a vigorous state of motion and power, surging, rolling, laughing in his vernal orgy, probing the rock's fissures—fecund, virile, *wild.*

Coming hard onto Trachyte Riffle, around the Dorothy Bar, scouring the bottom, shifting sand banks, grinding boulders, growling with glee, he feels a ominous pressure—as if Mother Earth had shifted again, making another pocket for him to hone and fill. With the Herculean weight of driftwood on his shoulders, he ignores it and rushes on. But there is an insidious change. Something unnatural at this corner.

Is this the time to start a new bed?

He has done it before, many times. Rivers have altered the planet, have spread, moved, re-formed, and joined. They've changed climates, fed the seas, the land, the animals—and the people. They have pointed the way, ended the search, and delivered the message.

Carry … carry … carry on … a million years toiling; an artery transporting the life blood of the Earth, the living pulse of the planet; his reward not merely getting there, but taking the burden required of him, as it has been forever.

Rivers, true gods of this earth, have been betrayed!

There is a welling up … heartbeat slowing. Suddenly the river is treading on himself ! Underwaters roil back against his forward thrust—a runner tripping over his own feet.

It must be a dream, a frustrating dream! He's unable to run or lift his limbs, is impotent against this invisible restraint. Everything is slow motion, in a stupor, tranquilized, powerless.

HE CANNOT GET AWAY!

Searching frantically for the drop in his bed, he falters. The floating cargo enmeshes his shoulders, presses him down. Imprisoned between high canyon walls, the river drops his cutting tools—the grinding boulders, the fine polishing silt.

The artery clots. His soul departs. THE RIVER DROWNS!

Letters from River Rats, Friends (May–July 1963)

Maria: We are back from the Glen [with Frank] *and I must admit that only now do I fully understand your feelings about its mutilation. It took me three days for my reaction to jell ... and then I had to compare the Glen to a handsome man whom I loved dearly and who lost his legs in an amputation ... crippled and dying a slow death. I couldn't quite understand why you wanted to go back, knowing how much it is going to hurt you. I had not realized how much exploration you had done there with Frank and Tad ... but now I know that you must go back. Katie, I understand that the loss of the Glen is a real bereavement for you because I realize that it is far more than the loss of those magnificent canyons and all the scenic wonder that will be so foolishly buried ... You really are losing the great love of your life, your own personal Paradise, the one place on earth were you could always be your true self with people who loved and understood you. This is a tragic loss and my heart bleeds for you.*

Reet: ... but you're not going to the lake, are you? Of course not. You couldn't stand it ... you'll want to remember it the way it was, so why would you torture yourself?

Frank: Why have you loved the rivers and the things associated with them so much? ... You found things and conditions that were near perfect! You relaxed and forgot the forced tempo of a night club entertainer ... I could cry too. No one, and I mean no one, could possibly know how deeply our feelings were involved on these trips. Do you really want to see Glen Canyon as it is now? ... Maria damn near made me cry ... what is going to happen when I am with you for your first sight of Glen

Canyon under a couple hundred feet of water? Today [July 14th] *the head of the lake is at Forgotten Canyon (!). Where is your boat? Do you think it will stand all the vibrations caused by an unhappy girl in her weeping activities on the first run through Glen Canyon after?*

Becky: *Well, Tinkerbell, when are you going to go have a gander at the new speedboat run—if for no other reason than to take photos of the christawful mess the Wreckers have made of the place? ... and after doing so have dumped it in the lap of the Park Service who don't even know upstream from down ... Hell, what am I saying? There isn't any UP or DOWN anymore!*

Tad (September '63): *It has been decided that you would be in misery were you to go in there now, for you would be cussing all the time at what you were not seeing ... Something new has been added ... never before have we had mosquitoes. Still, I—the indomitable Tadpole—will no doubt acquire a boat ... it seems to be the thing to do ... though I'm afraid West* [Canyon] *has had it.*

Dick Sprang: *I've been down there twice, at Halls' and Ticaboo, since they gang raped her with their flood of poison blue gisum that killed her. Glanced at her each time and turned my back and rode the hell out, hand on the horn, shook. But I never deliberately visited her grave, never sat in gloom beside her, because I honor old whores.*

~

I drove to Hall's Crossing (Frank's "concession") on a black and stormy mid-November night in 1963, slept in a sandblasted trailer that rocked all night, and shortly after sunup awoke to voices calling, gears grinding, dozers cranking, and motors revving. Stepping from the trailer, I almost laughed aloud at the absurdity of the tenement that had replaced a once wild and faraway moonwalk. I couldn't see the river canyon, so with pounding heart, I walked to where the cliff dropped to the river, across from the heron rookery ...

... and fell to my knees.

Spinach water lay in a silent trench between amputated cliffs. Wall-to-wall water, oozing into every canyon and crevice, lasciviously fingering private nooks, spreading the pink lips, licking at the sandstone, and leaving a spittle of salt against the orange cliffs. A white drawdown scar rose thirty feet above the waterline, as if someone had pulled the plug in a dirty bathtub, then stuck it in again.

Without their talus buttresses, the great walls leaned in, unsupported and menacing—all of a pink-blue-maroon hue, reflecting more of the same in the dead water. No more borders of lush green that had danced on the tawny river—everything out of balance, the harmony gone. Bigfeets (who wouldn't go with me that first time) said hundreds of animals had starved or drowned attempting to climb the slickrock. I saw the same—they would slip and fall back, only to try again. Beaver had cut every tree and sapling to stem the rising rez, but their homes were now rafts floating on dead water, the poor bewildered creatures sitting helplessly on top. It was eerily silent—like a morgue—except now and then, a rude sucking sound or the lap-lap-slurp-slurp of a dog. And what of those incomparable, evolving sunsets that each night seemed to light the river canyon from within? I waited for them. Instead, I got a sun that dropped quick and nasty behind truncated walls, like an oleo curtain on a bad act!

~

After my first look at it, the impact of the tragedy took effect slowly—a good thing, or I'd have gone raving mad. I had wanted to know every facet of the Glen, or so I thought, but after getting beyond places that had stopped us on the river, I came away certain that what had been withheld was an important part of the Glen's mystique. Those silent, sequestered, perfect places—it needed those to *be* the Glen. They had allowed me Isak Dinesen's *overview*.

Back when the canyons and river bombarded my mind and body with wave on wave of perception and stimuli, I hadn't really measured the intensity of those adrenaline rushes. Not until I found myself *embalmed* on that monotonous reservoir.

~

Screwdriver—Screwd river—a fiberglass runabout with a thirty-five horsepower Evinrude on her butt, was my waterhorse for those few times on the rez. Why I went back I could not have told you then. Now, I think it has to do with honoring Adonises and River Gods and lost loves.

Do we leave the bedside of our loved ones while they're dying?

No. Most of us watch over ... until they go.

And when they're gone, we grieve—grieve long and deep—until that grief turns to resentment and finally rage at having them taken forever from us. Witnessing the asphyxiation of Glen Canyon—slowly, inch by inch—acted like a brand on my soul, burning in my anger, my contempt for those who killed it. Anger—an emotion as powerful as love—can be used as a stimulant, exciting and creative. A force.

I would wear my anger like a crown!

Some of the first to go under were in the Wild Secret Heart of the Glen—Dungeon, Grotto, Dangling Rope, Balanced Rocks, Little Arch, Cathedral, Driftwood, Wishbone, Mystery, Music Temple and Hidden Passage—those fluted, heart-stopping, erotic sinuosities; the sequestered gracilities (anything but a slot!)—the Eros-Apollo, phallic protrusions, and all those lounging beds of tits and bums.

Getting to them was pure torture. (Yes, Reet!) Most side canyons were choked with driftwood that either lay stinking in the scum of drawdown, or was packed tight and floating. Yet, as I rocked in my own wake, I ached to be surrounded by those places I knew; a last glimpse before they were completely gone.

So I sat above the windscreen, steering with my feet, face streamed with tears, heading in their direction as fast as *Screwd river* would go, confused by all the distortion and a speed of twenty-five knots where we'd flowed with the river's pace at hardly more than two or three.

~

Hite—June 10, 1964

The White Canyon story:

Frank Barrett hears the throttle cut back on Slim's boat. The prop idles, cavitates, then churns forward, pushing its way through a thicket of half-submerged willow and eddying driftwood at the reservoir's edge. Sun on the aluminum flashes in the growth.

He walks down the road to where his cabin used to be and stands on all that remains—the front porch, now acting as a boat ramp.

He waits, arms folded, watching an open sego lily drown in the lapping tide.

Between the gunning of the motor and the banging of drift against the chine, he hears the steady punctuation of Slim's swearing. After several minutes the prow wedges through and comes to dock. Slim throws him the rope and cuts the switch.

"Did they find him yet?"

"Nope, and I don't expect they will."

They walk over the foundations of the cabin, hands in their pockets, heads down, and automatically turn up the old path to Slim's shanty.

"Water'll be up to the road in a couple more days," Barrett says. "Come up faster'n anybody reckoned—sure you don't want me to stay and help you get the rest of your stuff loaded?"

"Naw, she's all done, the heavy stuff—Jeep's at Fry already. Thanks anyway. Woody helped me load the Servel last night, all that's left is a bunch of books, maps, Indian junk, and clothes—be finished by tonight."

They reach the road and Frank stops. The moment has come that they can well do without.

"Well, old Mucker, if there's nothing I can do, Helen and me will be gettin' on." Then he allows himself one feeler. "Know where you'll be going?"

"Yup. Goin' up to my claim on the Green. I'll dig around till I find something—stay if I do; if not, probably come back and work at the Hideout."

"Mind if I come see you sometime?"

"Hell no, Frank, be glad to have you, you know that. B'sides you might need a place to hide now'n then from all the women in your family ... and anytime you want to help me work that claim, you know half of it's yours."

They shake hands, both wondering if there isn't something earthshaking they should say at this ending of an era. In lieu, Slim says: "You know the Park Service nearly lost a diver when they were looking for that guy this morning." He looks down, toeing the dirt, pondering some mystery.

"You don't say. How ... dumb luck?"

"Typical of their blunderin' ways. They're looking for him down around Ticaboo. One of them doesn't surface at the appointed time 'n' place and they know his tanks are gettin' low."

Frank removes his hat, wipes his forehead on a shirtsleeve. "Why in hell were they so far downstream? They got some imbecilic idea this is still a river?"

Slim's brows knit in puzzlement. "Funny thing, maybe it is. The diver comes up about five miles down canyon, no air left at all. Says he was caught in a current on the bottom so strong he couldn't pull out." (Storyteller's pause, hands back in pockets.) "Wha'dya make of that?"

A low whistle from Barrett and a barely audible "I'll be damned!" before he throws back his head and laughs, Adam's apple bouncing like a golf ball. "Jesus Christ! Wouldn't that be something ... if ... ah, well, does my ol' soul good to know it takes more'n a goddamn hunk of cement to kill this ol' devil."

Slim's eyes twinkle with delight. "That little bit of information could reactivate my belief in the super-unnatural."

Sharing their faith in the river's secret has made the parting easier. Barrett replaces his hat and offers, "If you need lumber for your sluices, the Bureau *stacked the boards from my shack over by the slag heap. Help yourself, it's theirs now. Woody says they're plan'in' to build a tool shed."*

Slim squints toward the water, saying with quiet emphasis, "I don't think they'll build a tool shed, Frank."

Barrett feels the anticipation and excitement of his youth feeding back to him through Slim's rippling chest muscles and the clenched fists inside his pockets. His smile makes a full crescent beneath his hawkish nose. "Good luck to you, Slim. Whatever the hell it's gonna be, I'll bet it's a gut-buster!"

"So long, Frank."

At the inside he has forty-eight hours before the reservoir reaches the road—at the outside, sixty hours. The Bureau has paid for his intact shack, and through some deal he doesn't care to fathom, will move it tomorrow, five miles upstream to the newly located Hite, for Park Service use.

From the seat of his truck he takes a .44 magnum Smith & Wesson revolver, unholsters it, and walks to his shower tank. He opens the nozzle, backs off, shoots five holes, and smiles as water squirts like cat whiskers in all directions.

"Mine tonight," he mutters. "Theirs tomorrow."

Then sets about doing the really serious work.

~

It is hard for me to believe that I made a trip a year on that rez until 1967, because the memories are so bad I've blocked most of them out. However, I shall leave you with two that will not go away.

Little Arch—May 1967

I had just passed beneath it—recognized the sluiceway it formed, or I wouldn't have had a clue. The Little Arch was but ten feet overhead. Okay, I was halfway there. When the walls began to close in on *Screwd river*, I cut the motor.

The silence rang.

No wake, no wind, no whisper of a breeze. Above the water, a brine line rose higher than my reach and was covered with blooms of dried algae. Sunlight shot almost directly down, lighting the green algae-covered slickrock underwater—I could see into the depths at least a dozen feet. I dove off the bow, down about six.

Yes, there it was! The light, perfect!

It shone through the smoke hole and against the slanting walls of the stone teepee where we had stood in the twilight bottom of that bowl of stone—the timeless womb of Mother Earth—the first *holy* place I had ever been. We felt we were the first to see it.

Certainly, I was the last.

Music Temple—1956

On our second We Three trip, we had found our way above the twisting mystery that drops into Music Temple's pool. A circuitous route of badly eroded, vertical Moki steps led us above the dome. They were terrifying, especially coming down! But what we found beyond was a place where believers in heaven would surely wish to go.

There was a constant flow of water that did not always run down into the Temple. Strange, but having been below, seen the pool empty, and on the same day played above in the running stream, I didn't question who was in authority there—just knew that the ruins, the waterfalls, and a whole other canyon with cottonwoods, redbuds, and fish swimming in the pools was a Shangri-la, and that those who'd lived there knew they were blessed, and had in turn blessed that place.

I remember well the last song I sang in Music Temple—October 15, 1962—my last trip on The Glen. It was a spiritual that Josh had taught me, *They Crucified My Lord*—only I sang it:

> They crucified my river
> And he never said a mumblin' word—
> Not a word ... Not a word ... Not a word
> They pierced him in the side
> But he never said a mumblin' word ... not a (etc.)
> And the blood came trink-lin' down,
> Still, he never said a mumblin' word ...
> He just hung his head, and he died
> But he never said a mumblin' word ...
> Now wasn't that a pity and a shame—
> The way they done my River?
> Not a word ... not a word ... not a word.

Music Temple—May 1967

Half the dome, and most of the spiral that had fed the pool, was under water. I wedged *Screwd river* in between the walls to where the chine rested on rock and I was able to climb the remaining narrows to open canyon. There'd been another drawdown, and for several hundred feet all was scaly, dead, ugly—blurring my vision for the hundredth time.

But above, out of sight and smell of the rez, the cap above Music Temple still had that aura of belonging to the past, and I ran—as fast as slickrock, pools, and stacks of rotting driftwood would let me—to the clear, untouched part of that treasured Shangri-la. I spent the whole day there, in the ruins, under waterfalls, planing around the bowls, listening to frog cantatas, watching iridescent fish in the clear spring water, and tennie-sticking the sides above potholes I couldn't get into ... or out of. A lesson learned!

I was coiling the bow rope when a shot rang out!

I yelped, but another shot covered the sound, and a ricocheting bullet hit the wall above my head.

A scream tore at my throat. "STOP IT! STOP! You goddamned idiot! There are people up here!!"

No echo—it muted out on the dead water. There was a muttering of voices from round the bend, then silence.

I was shaking so hard with anger, frustration, and the urge to get my hands around some bastard's throat, that fear didn't enter into it. I bellowed at them, "What do you morons think you're doing? It's against the law to have guns here ... "

I heard their motor cough to a start just as my own cavitated and hit the water. Backing out of those narrows was time consuming, and when I finally got to the chamber, I saw two or three men in a boat much faster than mine, heading out to open water.

Still I yelled after them ...

"You stupid fools? You're shooting in a Temple ... Music Temple! THIS IS MUSIC TEMPLE! Muu ... sic ... Teh-h-h ... "

I choked on my sobs.

Epilogue:
The River Knows The Way

When my old friend, Ed Abbey—who now lies, smiling, in his rocky desert outcrop—wrote *The Monkey Wrench Gang*, he gave those of us who knew Glen Canyon a respite from our bitterness over its demise by providing us with a vivid fantasy: the dream of a wild river flowing once again around the crumbled hulk of the most hated blob of cement and steel ever constructed.

The Glen Canyon Dam.

We laughed with him, and cried, and imagined. Wouldn't it be great if … and dreamed on … Hayduke Lives! … because it was pure fantasy.

Much of the American public, in 1975, didn't even know what such dams were for, and those who might have had an inkling didn't know where they were, or what they did. So Ed's novel, at least, put that damn chunk of cement on the map.

It also put me back onto what little remained of some of my rivers that were gone; rivers I had completely abandoned ten years before.

I have never returned to Wreck-the-nation Reservoir, nor to the truncated Grand Canyon, and I pretty much gave up on the human race after watching the bureaucrats trash a wonder of the world, then heaping further insult by naming their sump after Major Powell—a man who *did* know about sane distribution of water in the arid West.

Then I thought … Hey, I have a compact *of my very own*, made on a personal level, having nothing to do with those people, with politics, with greed or manipulation. *I* have a compact with the Colorado River and its canyons. Furthermore, I hadn't made it on any goddamned piece of paper and sent it up for approval past a row of upright, uptight, know-nothings, some of whom had never seen or heard of a place called Glen Canyon.

The compact asked that I not forget the river-that-was; that I go to canyons that drained into the once-and-future Glen and find whatever solace they might offer, thus easing the pain of the big canyon's loss. I saw how quickly wild places and rivers were being exterminated, so I packed my backpack and went searching.

What I found at least sustained me.

Now, we are nearly a quarter-century past that time, with more than twenty-five times that many rivers and secret places gone. Yet, let me urge you (no matter the odds) to seek out such a place. Why? Because you *need it*, whether you know it or not. If and when you find it, tell no one else where it is. Keep it as long as possible and, like a loved one, cherish it, being aware that love is also pain, discovery, joy unrealized and—sooner or later—loss.

~

September 1997

This morning, as I was about to experience one of my bad days—a day when my photograph of Forgotten Canyon blurred and I couldn't get beyond the old cottonwood tree to wander up that beautiful stream—the phone rang.

A young man named Richard Ingebretsen asked me if I would please come to a meeting of the Glen Canyon Institute in Salt Lake City and sing for them.

What institute? *Glen* Canyon? Why have I never heard of such an organization? Glen Canyon had been forgotten by all but a handful of souls like me. Could there be some kind of light at the end of the tunnel after forty years!

I went.

~

Never, in my wildest dreams, did I envision an auditorium of twelve hundred university students on their feet with cheers, whistles, and clapping hands after I sang a couple of my river songs! We're talking here about a fifty-year generation gap. How was that possible?

Because they wanted something back that was ripped off before they had a chance to see and enjoy it? Because we have a different political climate now? Yes. But mostly because the younger generation has something going for it that could not have happened in my Glen Canyon years. There is now a *conscious awareness* that the huge political mistakes and gross miscalculation made more than forty years ago can be corrected, and that such boondoggles that are still proposed can more often be put to rest.

Had anyone told me that I'd be sitting on a stage with even an ex-commissioner of the Bureau of Reclamation, who was urging the audience to rethink dams and what they do, I'd have called them soft in the head. Yet, Daniel P. Beard, now of the National Audubon Society, was saying:

> *The decision to build any dam isn't a scientific decision, an economic one, or a pronouncement from God. It is—pure and simple—a political decision ... The suggestion that we drain Lake Powell, and restore Glen Canyon, is breath-taking in its scope. The political and economic obstacles would be substantial, but I'm not prepared to dismiss the idea. We already spend millions of dollars each year to maintain the Grand Canyon's river ecosystem. Millions are also spent to protect and restore endangered fish and correct other environmental problems caused by the dam. Why not consider spending those millions on restoring the canyon?*
> [October 1997]

Other speakers on that stage were Dave Wegner, scientist, (another *former* employee of the Wreck-the-nation Bureau, who was basically responsible for the thirteen-year Environmental Studies Program in Grand Canyon); Richard Ingebretsen, president of the Glen Canyon Institute; and David Brower, board of trustees of the institute. Brower is putting time and effort toward righting a wrong he claims is mostly his because he didn't act quickly enough in 1956, or know enough about the Glen, to help us save it. I doubt that he could have, but it certainly got him, Martin Litton, and the Sierra Club centered against dams in Grand Canyon. The public, truthfully informed at last, stood up and said "NO!"

Yes, the climate has changed, and the public will begin to say NO! much more often.

From a workshop paper distributed by International Rivers Network, Berkeley, California:

> Some of the most extensive work on decommissioning to date has been in the U.S., growing out of successful fights such as the Edwards dam in Maine, and the Elwha River dams in Washington. Active campaigns are now under way to demolish four dams on the Snake River, and Savage Rapids Dam in Oregon, and drain the Powell Reservoir on the Colorado River to restore Glen Canyon. In 1998, demolition started on the nation's first federal project—the culmination of the Oregon Natural Resources

Council's campaign to remove the Elk Creek Dam. These campaigns have capitalized on the experience U.S. Environmental groups gained fighting destructive dam projects over the last 30 years.

Here, the word is out that rivers need to run, to keep us and our planet healthy. Tear the dam down? No. That's expensive and unnecessary. Time, and the river flowing, will take it away. Floyd Dominy wants it left there as his monument. So do I—a monument to his and the bureau's arrogance and stupidity.

The Glen Canyon Institute's mission is to provide leadership in reestablishing the free-flowing Colorado River through a *restored* Glen Canyon.

Restored.

Not by monkey wrenching, but by the best science available and the safest method of draining reservoir Powell ... and in so doing, slowly returning a sick and sorry Grand Canyon corridor to its natural state, with beaches and habitat, as it was before Glen Canyon dam.

Or, do we ...

Leave it for Mother Nature to wipe out the entire system in days, not years, with a domino effect? This she will do ... almost did, in 1983. It has been noted that she's going through menopause—hot flashes, cold sweats. That, plus being terribly pissed with human negligence, will likely put her over the edge one day soon. A few more El Niño's and that dam is GONE. As Barry Lopez, writer-poet-visionary, wrote, "You can feel the anger in water behind a dam."

There is much more than anger in reservoir Powell. It should be looked at for what it truly is—a two-hundred-mile toxic waste dump. Dangerous to your health. What lies rotting and bubbling in its bottom would boggle the mind—motors, boat hulls, batteries, bones, pesticides, toxic minerals in impacted silts—to say nothing of what lies on and near the top.

The Lake Powell National Recreational Area, part of the National Park Service, has told us that recreational boating use on Lake Powell is 466,417 boat days per year (boat day meaning one boat on the reservoir for one day). Extrapolating from those figures, we assume that 75 percent of these days are for boats and jet skis that have highly polluting two-stroke motors. The other 25 percent of the days are mostly inboard or sterndrive motor activity, and a few four-stroke outboards, all of which are fairly clean and have extremely low emissions. That means:

- 466,000 x .75 = 350,000 days per year of highly polluting two-stroke motors.
- Multiply by 5 hours or so per day of usage = 1,750,000 hours per year of total two-stroke usage.
- The average 70-hp outboard or 95-hp jetski will use 5–7 gallons per hour—discharging 25 percent (1.5 gallons) unburned, into the reservoir.
- So the unburned portion is 1.5 x 1,750,000 *hours* per year.
- This equals 2,625,000 *gallons* per year.
- The Exxon Valdez spill was about ten million gallons, so rez Powell's discharge is the equivalent (2,625,000 gallons) of an Exxon Valdez oil spill every 3.8 years. [From Russell Long of Earth Island Institute, July 3, 1997]

More …

Bacterial alerts every year are now a given. Of the millions who swim and speed across the reservoir's surface, at least 25 percent of them piss in it. Others, along with their dogs, use the sandbanks or the slickrock benches, where it washes back into the rez with rain or a rising bathtub ring; the Kleenex bushes have turned into loaded toilet paper and disposable diaper bushes. Small wonder that the place has acquired some unflattering names: Utah's Urinal. The Rotting Rez. Loch Latrine. Foul Little Fjord (thanks, Russell Martin). Dominy called Lake Powell the jewel of the Colorado. More accurately, it is: Cesspowell, the Stool of the Colorado.

~

The issue of Page, Arizona, should be addressed as well. This construction village could turn a cat's ass and be the *world renowned* Center for Free Running Rivers and the Scientific Decommissioning of Dams! Scientists, teachers, river-runners, engineers, ecologists from the world over would convene there to study, discuss, plan the restoration of ecosystems, and run a *real* river through a healthy, unsynthetic Grand Canyon. Then, Page (a place that traded more than a hundred temples, cathedrals, and shrines in the canyon for a row of tacky little churches) would gain international recognition. It shouldn't be made to go away. Seeded with a few visionaries, it could become a world-class *think tank*. And they are already prepared.

They have the golf courses. Think about it.

~

What enthralls me about Mother Earth is her disrespect for what humans consider their greatest achievements: skyscrapers, bridges, dams, etc. With a small adjustment of her girdle, they all come tumbling down, and sometimes she just wrings out her laundry.

Recently I saw a slide show of what happened in a very short time on the Escalante River—a main tributary off Glen Canyon, and identical to the Glen's geology. In 1983 the rez overfilled and flooded the Escalante way up past Coyote Gulch. During a decade of drought, it dropped as low as ninety feet. In the Escalante it left a twenty-foot bathtub ring and ten-foot mudflats—dried, cracked, and solid. In 1993 storms cut clear through the mudflats, washing the whole rotten mess back down into the rez. The ring was almost totally obliterated, springs and seeps returned, and native vegetation began to grow, with vengeance, along the original streambed. Sediment transport starts immediately upon reservoir drop.

Bill Wolverton's documentary slides spoke volumes to me.

Several years ago, hiking up a winding crevasse off White Canyon, we were stopped cold after five miles at an impassable pourover, an enlarged area with hollowed dome—maybe half the size of Cathedral in the Desert—the drop into a pool through corkscrewed sandstone, perhaps twenty feet. It was one of those places where you backtrack, find a route up, out, around, and finally back into the streambed. A few years later, one of our party returned to that canyon, rappelled in about a mile *above* the place we were stopped, and hiked it all the way to White Canyon with no rope, encountering no large pouroffs or drops. The hollow had been filled with sand and gravel (from Woodenshoe Mountain) by a slow, three-day spring rain. By now, it has probably been flushed out again with heavy storms. Such is the nature of the Colorado Plateau … and of Glen Canyon.

A drained reservoir will make Future Glen Canyon temporarily ugly, that's true, but not for as long as you may think; and with a flowing river there will be more and cleaner water for use, because the reservoir evaporates and seeps far more than it saves.

Our Grand Canyon river corridor is also in a sorry, unnatural state. Icy cold, clear water released from beneath the dam has killed most of the native fish, and the once-upon-a-time-mile-long, sandy beaches ringed with driftwood, no longer exist. They all lie immersed behind the dam, gathering toxins. Once those sands and silts were full of nutrients gathered from the lush flora and fauna in the Glen; a rolling river carried them down the Grand, where they nourished both aquatic and streamside life all through the canyon.

The return of a free-flowing Colorado River is not a matter of IF ... only WHEN.

I would give the Future Glen a new identity ... a new status, as yet unnamed. It was unlike any other place on earth and should be treated as such—as a haven, a refuge, an ivory tower, a sanctuary—the heart of the Colorado Plateau should be allowed to beat again. Glen Canyon should have *commercial and political* asylum; it should be a place where no engines or motors whine, where only the sounds of the canyon, the river, and the dipping of oars are heard. And when it arrives once again to the light of day, you fighters out there ... you activists ... apply constant vigilance. Respect the bones of ages past. Honor the River God. Don't let anyone or anything trash the magic of that very special place.

~

Wherever I am at day's end ... watching a sunset ... at peace ... hearing the canyon wren's goodnight—I thank no man-invented god for my great good fortune. I thank the Earth Mother for allowing me aboard her space ship—and for the River of Life that takes me through. And I claim full responsibility for the rapids I've run, or not; the eddies I've used, or not; the River God's advice I've taken, or not; and whatever strength I've had, to get around the boulders, over the sandbars and through the narrows, in that Great River. No fault but mine, if the current, ever present, did not bring me through.

The River knows the way.

The Giants Once Among Us
There's a canyon in the desert
There's a river in the canyon
There's a spirit on the river
And her song is my companion ... when I'm free
She's the eagle with her children
She's the feather of the eagle
She's the stream that floats the feather
On incredible and regal ... mystery!

Chorus:
> Come with me ... come with me
> Where the water's gone or going

> Where the children do not know
> Of the giants once among us
> I am singing soft and low
> *Listen to me!*

Once the river was a warrior
Dressed in golden spume and tearing
At the granite round the Temples
Where the water God were daring ... destiny
Came a breed of men, undaunted
By these rapids of the ages
Now their burning eyes are haunted
Mystic journeys are for sages ... Majesty!

Chorus:

> Follow me ... follow me
> *(same as above)*

Now the river lies in drowned arena
Coiled and waiting for the spilling
Mighty serpent of the legends
Stream of Life beneath the filling ... Treachery!
And the Giants, unforgiving
Jealous lovers of the Spirit
Be they lost, or drowned, or living
Know my song and when they hear it ... Liberty!

Chorus:

> Liberty! ... Liberty!
> Where the water's gone and going
> Where the children do not know
> Of the Giants still among us
> I am singing, not so low
> *Listen to me ... !*
> > *Set him free ... !*
> > > *Set him free ... !*
> > > > *Set him free ... !*

Annotated Bibliography

Obscure Antics, Mixed with Dates and
Semantics and Flavored to Taste

Ed only saw the Glen once or twice—no matter—his writing is unsurpassed. Two of his books have interesting things to say, and *do*, about it. **Edward Abbey:** *Desert Solitaire: A Season in the Wilderness*. (New York: McGraw-Hill, 1968). *The Monkey Wrench Gang*. (Philadelphia: Lippincott, 1975).

~

I took Bruce on his only Glen Canyon trip and my last, 1962. His journal sparkles with wit and clarity. **Bruce Berger:** *There Was A River* (Tucson: University of Arizona Press, 1994. Original pub. Mountain Gazette, No. 31. Aspen). Amid the hilarity of his most recent book *Almost an Island* (University of Arizona Press, Tucson, 1998), is the story of our forays into Baja, California, after the river was gone.

~

Often I have lamented not meeting Mr. Crampton—but I managed to speak with him on the phone, and corresponded with this greatly respected historian/anthropologist, whose heart led him way beyond the canyon's dry statistics. **C. Gregory Crampton:** *Ghosts of Glen Canyon— History Beneath Lake Powell*. (Salt Lake City: Rev. Cricket Productions, 1994). *Standing Up Country*. (New York: Knopf, 1964). *Outline History of the Glen Canyon Region 1776–1922*. Anthropological Papers, Number 42. (Salt Lake City: University of Utah Press, 1959). *Historic Glen Canyon*. (Utah Historical Quarterly, July 1960). *The Hoskininni Papers—Mining in Glen Canyon 1897–1902*. Edited with Dwight L.

Smith. Anthropological Papers, Number 54. (Salt Lake City: University of Utah Press, 1961).

~

If ever a man knew the country, rock by rock, bush by bush, spring after spring, it's Kent—boatman, trail blazer, and with his wife Fern, Jeep-masters of Southeastern Utah. Read him. **Kent Frost:** *My Canyonlands.* (New York: Abelard-Schuman, 1971).

~

Steven went to a lot of trouble to disguise this beautifully designed "how to" book; what's more the Wreckthenation Bureau *helped* him! **Steven Hannon:** *Glen Canyon*, a novel. (Denver: Kokopelli Books, 1997).

~

A loving relationship between **Phillip Hyde** and the canyon he pho-tographed exudes from the pages of *A Glen Canyon Portfolio.* In black and white, he captured more of the Glen's intense beauty than Eliot Porter did with all that color. The accompanying text is a second print-ing (rev.) of Berger's journal, "There Was A River." (Flagstaff: Northland Press, 1979).

~

Eleanore put this amazing collection together after searching for and viewing over 6000 slides and photographs; then spent many more hours finding historic quotes to fit the pictures. I'm very proud to have nine-teen of mine included; they should have been Tad's, but my dear old buddy procrastinated too long. **Eleanor Inskip, ed:** *Glen Canyon Before Lake Powell*, Historic Photo Journal 1872 To 1964. (Moab: Inskip Ink., 1995).

~

Betty Leavengood has a work-in-progress about *Grand Canyon Women.* These biographical sketches are about main events in the lives of women who have hiked, rafted, and worked in and about the River Corridor, Glen included. (Pruett: Boulder, November 1998).

~

Uh-h-hh, and then there's MeMeMe—if you haven't had enough by now—earlier stuff: *Folk Songs of the Colorado.* (*Arizona Highways:* May

1954). *Traveling the Canyon's White Water Highway.* (*Arizona Highways:* June 1960). *Glen Canyon Diary, 1956* (Journal of Arizona History 17, Spring 1975). *Katie Lee, An Interview.* Everett L. Cooley Oral History Project. Tape No. U-118, April 14, 1984. (Salt Lake City: Marriott Library, University of Utah). And later; *Boatman's Quarterly Review.* Vol.10 No.1. Winter 1996–1997. Oral History Project. Eds., Lew Steiger & Brad Dimock. (Grand Canyon River Guides: Flagstaff). After I join the River God, my journals, photos, etc., will go to the Cline Library, Special Collections (Flagstaff: Northern Arizona University). Disclaimer: I was never, am not now and will never be (my line ends with my childless son) any relation, whatsoever, to the Many Multitudinous Mormon Lees.

~

Really the best and only place to go for the information gathering of **Otis "Dock" Marston** is to the Huntington Library, Marston Collection. (Berkeley: University of California).

~

For the title of **Russell Martin's** book they should have used his name for the Rez—A Foul Little Fjord—instead of *A Story That Stands Like A Dam: Glen Canyon and the Struggle for the Soul of the West.* (New York: Henry Holt, 1989). But behind the clumsy name you'll find easy reading and stimulating research—a Dam good work.

~

If you care to know more about weakening and eventually breaking the steel-cable-tunnel-vision politics of dam building, read **Patrick McCully.** *Silenced Rivers: The Ecology and Politics of Large Dams.* (New York: Zen Books, 1996).

~

Nancy Nelson, from her river running, became fascinated by stories about Norm; enough to start digging for the dirt and booking it. She interviewed his friends, his not-friends and the whole famdamily, turning out an excellent character study of this controversial riverman. *Any Time Any Place Any River: The Nevills of Mexican Hat.* (Flagstaff: Red Lake Books, 1991).

~

My dear old friend, **E. Tad Nichols**, actually moved his skinny buns enough to get *Glen Canyon as It Was: A Photographic Record*, in The Journal of Arizona History 17, Spring 1976. Now, it looks like after 23 years of everyone begging, urging, cajoling and threatening him, he'll produce ('scuse—have others produce for him) the photos he took in the Glen during our We Three explorations—with, believe it or not, some of his tear-jerking stereos! *Glen Canyon Through My Eyes*. A photo essay, work in progress, publication, 1999. This will be treasure worth waiting for!

~

Strange as it may seem, the prose of **Eliot Porter** explains Glen Canyon far better than his photographs. He wrote passionately about the chameleon light and color he captured there in *The Place No One Knew*. (Foreword and Edited by David Brower—Sierra Club Books, Exhibit Format. San Francisco, 1963). Make every effort to find a copy of the original because in a later edition (Peregrine Smith. Salt Lake City, 1988) the color is atrocious, and for some incoherent reason the text has been rearranged! Mr. Porter would not be pleased.

~

P. T. Reilly. *Lost World of Glen Canyon*. (Utah Historical Quarterly, Spring, 1995) In Grand Canyon we would see the red paint from Pat's chine on rocks several feet above our heads; his run being a week before ours on higher water. He was a serious historian, and sadly for us, has recently gone to join the River God.

~

Marc Reisner's *Cadillac Desert: The American West and its Disappearing Water* (New York: Viking, 1986) is a classic of the twentieth century. What a writer! What a sense of history of the short-term solutions and the blind progress that drives us to sop up our life-giving water. The 1997 four-part PBS series, made from his book, should win every documentary award going!

~

Barry Scholl. *Double Identity: The Two Lives of Dick Sprang* (*Salt Lake City Magazine:* May-June 1996) is an excellent piece on my friend Dick who has always been kind of a recluse; he doesn't give a lot of interviews, but he has always been helpful to those who love his canyon country. Gary Topping's book is also dedicated to him.

~

I can safely say that you're not quite with it, canyonwise, unless you've read **Vaughn Short**, or had him read or recited to you. Most camp guides and boatmen know this and have his books on board. Vaughn is far more than a poet—he's a philosopher, guide, photographer, humorist, a gentleman and sympathetic human; he makes you laugh and cry. *Raging River-Lonely Trail—Tales Told By the Campfire's Glow*, 1978. *Two Worlds—Recollections Of a River Runner*, 1994. Both are illustrated by Joanna Coleman. (Tucson: Two Horses Press).

~

The best way to read about Major Powell, other than his own journals, is through **Wallace Stegner**. *Beyond the Hundredth Meridian: John Wesley Powell and the Second Opening of the American West*. (Boston: Houghton Mifflin, 1954).

~

Gary Topping camped year after year with Dick Sprang when he'd take his month long journey to the Halls Creek area. Sharing the country's secrets, Dick told him stories about the places, cattlemen, rivermen, and miners he had known. In return Gary wrote a history that ranks with the very best: *Glen Canyon and the San Juan Country*. (Moscow: University of Idaho Press, 1997).

~

Christy G. Turner is the anthropologist from Arizona State University that Frank Wright worked with and supplied from 1958 to 1963. Once or twice I found them deep in the dust at sites along the river. *Petroglyphs of the Glen Canyon Region: Styles, chronology, distribution and relationships from Basketmaker to Navajo*. (Flagstaff: Northern Arizona Society of Science and Art, 1963. Museum of Northern Arizona Bulletin No. 38).

~

There is someone else who knows about the sensuousness, the palladium, the eroticism, the nurturing in sandstone; one who has felt the passion in moving water, the anger in that behind a dam. She is **Terry Tempest Williams** and she writes what I call "Wonder Books"—*An Unspoken Hunger*. (New York: Vintage Books, 1994). *Desert Quartet—An Erotic Landscape*. Illus. Mary Frank. (New York: Pantheon, 1995).

~

Periodicals and Hideholes for Glen Canyon Material

Canyon Country Zephyr. Bimonthly. Ed. POB 327, Moab, UT 84532.
Colorado Plateau River Guides. POB 344, Moab, UT 84532.
Boatman's Quarterly Review. Journal of Grand Canyon River Guides, Inc., POB 1934, Flagstaff, AZ 86002.
High Country News. Biweekly. POB 1090, Paonia, CO 81428.
Waiting List: Quarterly (More of Less) of the Grand Canyon Private Boaters Association. POB 2133, Flagstaff, AZ 86003-2133.
Cline Library Special Collections. Northern Arizona University, Flagstaff.
Marriott Library Special Collections. University of Utah, Salt Lake City.
The Marston Collection. Huntington Library. University of California. Berkeley.

Whoa! Enough! Awready!
No need to say this list is incomplete—
It's complete enough for me.

Acknowledgments

Gracias ... Thank You ... Bless You all

In April of 1964, lying on the beach beside Rock Creek and the booming Pacific Ocean in Big Sur, California, I wrote the first paragraph of what I intended to be the Glen Canyon story. Writing may be a lonely task, but it's not done in a vacuum. Along the way, and in manner multifarious, these people have helped me pull it all together. Of course, after thirty-four years, I'm bound to skip a few. Please forgive me. Some are gone, some far away, but as I write and think about you—regardless of where you came from, or where you are now—we are sitting around a campfire ... beside the talking river ... in Glen Canyon.

Those who sit, slightly removed, in half-tones, yet just as vital, I remember well

Jim Rigg, Art Greene, Frank Barrett, Woody Edgell, Arth Chaffin, Leo Walter, Rusty Mussleman, Beth Nielsen, Mary (Becky) Beckwith, Rosalind (Ros) Johnson, Paul & Helen Wright, Otis (Dock) Marston, Buck Buchan, Hugh Cutler, Maria de Strokosch, Josh White, Willie Taylor, Bill Belknap and Martin (Marty) Koehler ... who shared hours, letters, songs, photos and canyon stories that I could never have gotten elsewhere. And Ed ... in 1971 Ed Abbey read the novel. *"Rewrite the book as a straight-forward autobiography. Why? Because the truth in this case is more interesting than your fictional version."* It was 1995 when I began this version, taken mostly from my river journals. How right you were, old man, but now your Buzzard will be reading it!

Writers, artists, musicians, riverfolks and cowpokes

Bruce Berger—companero, fellow camper and hiker; award winning author, poet, musician, punster and critical reader through all the various versions ... sometimes I even took his advice. **Su Lum**—our mutual friend—an author and journalist with a brilliant mind and a magic eye. As with my last book, she cut the flack and took the lead out. **"Army" Armstrong**—also went through every version, is tired of the whole thing and glad it's over. He has an eye for every blooper on the page. Beware, the published version! **Susie Henderson**—ranch lady, fountainhead of knowledge about western literature, and generous friend, proofread; rode my split infinitives like a bucking horse, even managing to corral some of the meaner ones. **Dick Sprang**—once sent me a fifty-four page essay-analysis-critique after he read, reread and read some more. No way could I thank him for such dedication ... unless he would write his *own* Glen Canyon story. **Chuck Bowden**—fantastic author, agreed with Ed without reading half of it; after that I began to think about what all these smarter-than-me writers had to say. **Peter Bowen**—the Montana factor; loner, backcountry man, detester of phonies, touri and eco-freaks, is the author of many novels; the kind that have me doubled over with laughter. Peter's phone calls sparked my days and drove me on. **Douglas and Mable Anderson**—two who have shared whatever they had, and have often given shelter, as well as gentle encouragement to continue the quest. **Marc Reisner**—honored me by reading one of the novel versions; said it would "make a good movie" ... I think he meant "would have, before the deluge." **Terry Tempest Williams**—a most beautiful and rare woman, truly understands the spirit of the canyonlands and takes my breath away when she writes, or speaks, for it. To have her introduce my story is a blessing beyond words. **Douglas Snow**—longtime friend, superb artist-teacher-intellectual-wit, is a man of gentle persuasion, whose dramatic canvasses prove he too has hungry eyes for rock and walls and skies like those once seen in Glen. **Serena Supplee**—boatlady-artist-"sister," paints the very soul of water, rock and canyon, even in moonlight. I'm so happy to have her creations on the cover of my book, my CD's and cassettes ... as well as several more in my home. **Merlin Wheeler**—river crony, hiking mate and explorer, has run many free-flowing wild rivers and was just the person I needed to get me through that network of canyons far away from Cesspowell. Merl's a hydrologist, teaches kayaking and climbing, and writes nice poetry. **Ken Sleight**—was in Glen before and during my time. Had I known him then, together we might have found a way to push Floyd Dominy off a cliff. Ken's been writing "his book" as long as I have; so get on with it compadre/cowboy/riverman/dude rancher/seldom seen-in-church/dam-hater/defender-of-the-indigene and husband-to-Jane, best chef in the state. **Slim Williams**—the man from Missouri, took me to hidden ruins and little known trails, saved my ass in the Glen and let me bathe in his sink; plus he's a damn good cook. We're both Scorpios but from different ends ... since he's so funny, I must be the tail. **Richard Martin and Lew Steiger**—boatguys; one private, one commercial—friends of mine, of each other, and of the river. Richard showers me with praise when I most need it; has named his neoprene *Naked Katie*. I feel honored. Lew serves us all, not just me; is a fine writer himself. He produces the Grand Canyon Oral History Program. With brother **Gail**, he's making my new cassette/CD, *A Glen Canyon Journey*. I think it's time to flip the process and record Lew's history. **Diane & Kenton Grua**—Diane, of Special Collections at the Cline Library at NAU, is a whirling dervish of energy and laughter ... knows everything, where to find it and how to use it; without her, I'd still be writing. Kenton, her loving husband and master Grand Canyon boatman, is also a lover of live, undammed rivers. **Jack Treece**, who pulled his first oar on my San Juan 1954 run, writes a poem for me now and then, making me feel that all has not been in vain. **Rita (Reet) Plahetka**, one of the last of the old River Rat gang, does the same with her letters of love and support. **Susan Kouyamjian**—my intuitive friend, is a theatrical director and a cowboy therapist (but they don't know it). We met at a poetry gathering where she insisted, "You could teach them a thing or two." No, Susan, it was you who could, and did. **Tim Henderson**—a man too bright for his own good (and ohhh, what a poet/songwriter) has helped me in so many ways there's no telling; his humor and smile alone have kept me afloat. **Travis Edmonson**—best folksinger/guitarist of them all, wrote the first verse of "The Giants" and gifted it to me as a poem—after that the music and my own verses came easy. **Tom and Ann Gale**—open-armed and caring companions: this architect/decorator duo have yet to refuse my wildest last-minute request. They should have some sort of rosy wreath for all their generosity. **Mary and Mack Shroyer**—owners of Marina de La Paz, Baja California Sur, have been friends since the early '70s and have given me and mine a hidey-hole whenever needed, to write, fish, swim and reeee-lax in the beautiful land of manana. **Durrett and B.J. Wagner**—"Hell, all my rivers are gone," I once said to Durrett. "Hey, that's the name of your book," he said. And his wife, B.J., teacher of writing teachers, offered more helpful suggestions than I can count; as well as home and bed to lay on. **Wyn Bundy**—(bless her buns) of Singing Wind Bookshop at her ranch in Benson, AZ, is a true believer in my first book, *Ten Thousand Goddam Cattle*, and continues to believe in this one throughout its many stages. **Carl Brandt**—since the mid-sixties has been a wise friend and informal agent; 'tiz he who sent me to **Stephen Topping**, my gentle editor, and the wonderful crew at **Johnson Books**—couldn't have been a more fruitful choice. Stephen's lovely wife, **Debra Topping**, most artfully designed the cover of the book. **Allan Sutton**—copy editor; without this man's expertise, you readers would have had one helluva time! He smoothed the roughest water so y'all didn't find yourselves rowing through more bubbles (ellipses) than even a river can make. **Richard Ingebretsen** and the dedicated mob at **Glen Canyon Institute**—have, at last, put the fire under those institutions, bureaucracies and politicians who turned their middle fingers up to all our proposals in the '50s. With their help and direction the River God will rise from his forced slumber, thus ending my life cycle in pure bliss!

Category indefinable

I know for certain that I would not be in this happy place in life with what little (yet pleasing) success I've had, were it not for The River ... and **Diane Rapaport**—this little chunk of Greek dynamite—*magna cum laude* Cornell graduate, owner of Headlands Press, lecturer, teacher, author—has five revised editions of her own book, *How To Make and Sell Your Own Recording*, to her credit. All the above is secondary to the fact that she is my closest friend and confidant. Because she is younger and her brain is so big, she flows with the winds of change much easier than I, still, she drags me, kicking and screaming, toward the light. Without Diane's council on recording, marketing, contracts, copyrights, PR, brochures (even affairs of the heart), all that jazz ... I'd be up Shit Creek without a paddle. She is fast, sometimes sloppy, not always right, but in the end, she wins. I can teach her only two things: *where* to hike and *how* to drive. There's not a word of this book she hasn't gone over twenty times, yet, her most precious gift is to insist that I be me and not some reputation that follows in my wake. I hope you have a friend like this.

And then there's Joey, mi inamorato, the Aussiefied Dutchman. **Jo van Leeuwen**—birdman, appleseedman, handyman, ladysman, artisan and wonderman, but above all, gentleman, with everything that word really means. Joey is the much needed oil on the roiling water of my Irish temperament—took me nearly sixty years to learn how to pick 'em.

About the Author

Katie Lee was a prominent singer, songwriter, Western historian, river runner, actress, environmentalist, filmmaker, explorer, and author. She was born in Aledo, Illinois on October 23, 1919. However, she referred to herself as a native of Arizona as her family moved to Tucson before she was a year old. Lee worked her way through the University of Arizona by singing at a local hotel, foreshadowing her future singing career. After earning her Bachelor of Fine Arts in drama from the University of Arizona, she embarked upon a Hollywood career working in films, television, and on the radio, while also singing in lounges.

After a decade in Hollywood, making films and signing, Katie Lee returned to Arizona, where she began establishing herself as a folk and Western singer, working with many top artists like Josh White, Ramblin' Jack Elliot, and Harry Belafonte during her long career.

Perhaps the most significant chapter in Lee's life began in 1953 when she first ran the Colorado River in the Grand Canyon. Later that year, she took her first trip through Glen Canyon, falling deeply in love with the Glen Canyon area. Over the following years, Lee and two companions, Frank Wright and Tad Nichols, made 15 more trips through the canyon. We Three, as they referred to themselves, named 25 of Glen Canyon's side canyons during their trips. Lee fought long and hard against the damming of the Colorado River to create Lake Powell, joining other prominent figures and friends like David Brower, Martin Litton, and Edward Abbey in standing against the Glen Canyon Dam. Lee was a prominent member of the Glen Canyon Institute, which today (2020) continues the movement to restore Glen Canyon. She settled in Jerome, Arizona in 1971, where she ran Katydid Books and Music, her publishing company.

Katie Lee had a distinguished publication and recording list. She recorded nine albums during her career, including *Folk Songs and Poems of the Colorado River* (1964), *Songs of Couch and Consultation* (1958), *Life is Just a Bed of Neuroses* (1960), *Saucy Songs for Cool Knights* (1960), *Ten Thousand Goddam Cattle* (to accompany her book, 1976), *Fenced!* (1983), *Colorado River Songs* (1988), *The Best of Katie Lee* (1990s) and *His Knibbs and the Badger* (with Ed Stabler, 1992). She wrote articles about cowboy poetry for *Arizona Highways* and the *Journal of Arizona History*. Her documentary, The Last Wagon, won the 1972 CINE Golden Eagle Award. Interviews with cowboys Gail Gardner and Billy Simon were preserved in her short film *The Last Wagon* which won the Golden Eagle Award in 1972. *Ten Thousand Goddam Cattle* was published by Northland Press in 1976, and *All My Rivers Are Gone: A Journey of Discovery Through Glen Canyon* (1998) and *Sandstone Seduction: River and Lovers, Canyon and Friends* (2004) were originally published by Johnson Books and republished by Bower House (2023).

Lee died peacefully in her home in Jerome, Arizona on November 1, 2017, shortly after her 98th birthday.